Odyssey of the Heart

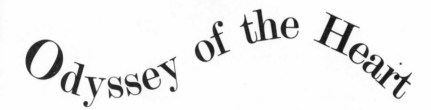

Odyssey of the Heart

THE SEARCH
FOR CLOSENESS,
INTIMACY,
AND LOVE

JOHN H. HARVEY

W. H. Freeman and Company
New York

Library of Congress Cataloging-in-Publication Data

Harvey, John H., 1943–
    Odyssey of the heart : the search for closeness, intimacy, and
love / John H. Harvey.
        p.   cm.
    Includes bibliographical references and index.
    ISBN 0-7167-2599-1.   —   ISBN 0-7167-2589-4 (soft)
    1. Intimacy (Psychology) 2. Love. 3. Interpersonal
relations. I. Title.
    BF575.I5H37   1994
    158'.2—dc20   94-30159
                                                        CIP
ISBN 0-7167-2599-1
      0-7167-2589-4 (pbk.)

Printed in the United States of America

1 2 3 4 5 6 7 8 9 0 VB 9 9 8 7 6 5 4

This book is dedicated to all of my loves, in the broadest sense of that term. They have educated me in what I know about closeness, intimacy, and love to depths of understanding that research and books could not possibly achieve.

CONTENTS

ACKNOWLEDGMENTS

I am indebted to my colleague and close personal friend, Dr. Ann Weber, of the University of North Carolina at Ashville for her review of an early draft of the book. My references to "Weber (1993)" reflect the special treatment she gave this manuscript. I am also grateful to her for sharing her considerable wisdom garnered from years of teaching, investigating, and writing about close relationships. Similarly, Susan Finnemore Brennan, Senior Editor at W. H. Freeman and Company, provided more detailed, constructive input to every aspect of the manuscript than any other editor I have encountered. She saw the potential in a book on close relationships for a general audience of people who desire to think broadly and carefully about the nuances of their relationships. Diane Cimino Maass, the book's Project Editor, adroitly edited the manuscript and, in so doing, greatly improved its intelligibility and incisiveness.

Early on in the writing of this book I was privileged to get feedback from Sheila Mulligan-Webb. Her helpful comments and encouragement were invaluable. She also did a wonderful job in helping with permissions and reference work. I would not have been able to complete the first draft of the manuscript of this book were it not for the friendship and nurturance provided by Christina Davidson. I am very grateful for her care and for that of her daughter, Ashley Smith.

Another important contribution to his book was made by my colleague, Dr. Terri Orbuch of the University of Michigan. Not only did she make helpful comments on the manuscript, but I have also benefitted from several years of working with her and being the recipient of her splendid wisdom about relationships.

I only hope that you will find that the material in this book is both useful and intellectually stimulating. During the last year, students in my classes would often come to visit and would indicate that they, a friend, or a member of their family was having some difficulty with a relationship. Invariably, I would hand them a relevant chapter from the available manuscript to read or pass on to the person experiencing the problem. Thus, in addition to my students, a final set of persons to thank are the friends and family members of students who have read and commented on portions of the manuscript over the past year. They have let me know how close the book's discussion is to the real issues in their lives. A dictum, attributed to Kurt Lewin, the foremost pioneer in social psychology, is as follows: "There is nothing as practical as a good theory." I have amended Lewin's contention somewhat to say ". . . as a good idea." For at is most basic level, this book is about the ideas that form the conceptual bridges to the hundreds of relationship events, raw feelings, and dilemmas that delight, depress, and descend upon most of us in our personal lives.

John H. Harvey
September, 1994

FOR THE READER:
AN INTRODUCTION

First you must have the images, then come the words.

—Robert James Waller,
The Bridges of Madison County

What were the images that contributed to the development of this book? First, they were of the readers, whom I hoped will span a considerable range and continuum of age, education, and experience in close relationships. Then there were the neglected topics and perspectives that demanded inclusion in a new volume on close relationships, including: how self-empowerment and self-identity are overarching determinants of the patterns of closeness people pursue; how our close relationships show passages and developmental eras in the same way that our individual lives reveal these characteristics; how darkness, cruelty, and grief are as much a part of the contemporary scene of close relationships as are joy, love, and hope.

Foremost among the images is my own passion about the study of close relationships. I have long believed that the close relationship is the cauldron (or boiling pot) from which all major life experiences must emanate. I found it intriguing that an early meeting between the publisher's representatives and myself about this book digressed at times into consideration of each of our real, intimate lives. For example, one person was in the middle of a divorce and had recently met someone who appeared to be very special. We discussed our own interpersonal dramas, even as we discussed how this book attempts to probe such dramas in general.

Close relationships are associated with the greatest highs and greatest lows we as humans ever experience. They are at the heart of many of the decisions we make about ourselves, our careers, and our hopes for the future. If we are lucky, over a lifetime we will experience several periods of deep intimacy and closeness. However, each of us also must also experience loss in our relationships, including the painful endings of relationships because of death or dissolution. Thus, given the inherent importance of this topic in human life, I hope that you the reader also are, or will become, passionate in your study of close relationships.

This book has its contemporary lens the decade of the 1990s. The 1990s represent a dynamic period in close relationships. We have reached a time at which the nature of closeness is analyzed regularly in books, the media, college courses, and even in our daily conversations. Surely, no previous era has been more obsessed with "relationship talk" and "relationship think" as is the present one. We all face many relationship-oriented dilemmas in our personal lives. We are confronted with questions about our behavior and values emerging from the intense female-male dialogue. We struggle regarding how to balance family, work, and self-growth needs. We grapple with how sexuality is related to intimacy and closeness.

The word "odyssey," used in the title of this book, derives from an epic poem attributed to Homer that described Odysseus's adventures in his 10-year journey home after the Trojan War. The path of close relationships often resembles an odyssey of the heart, a long, wandering course marked by the peaks and valleys of our experiences. Each of us is searching for our own state of perfect closeness, intimacy, and love. But unfortunately, we do not usually find perfection, nor are we readily satisfied with what we do find. Rather, we wander until we find peace with ourselves and our partner. Our wanderings will be more fruitful, however, if we allow ourselves to be guided by the extensive research and theories now available on closeness, intimacy, and love.

Why are we compelled to follow an odyssey of the heart? The heart is a metaphor for our most intense and influential emotions. In close relationships, we follow our hearts—often in deference to our minds or our best judgment. The odyssey that I will describe leads to a two-part goal: for one heart to link up with another heart, and for one mind to link up with another mind. While I will suggest ways that we can better use our minds to guide our relationships, I in no way propose that closeness is found without the significant involvement and struggle of what we humans know as the heart.

Relationship is

a pervading and changing

mystery . . . brutal or lovely,

the mystery waits for people

wherever they go, whatever

extreme they run to.

—Eudora Welty in *The Quotable*

Woman, 1991, p. 44

1

CLOSE

RELATIONSHIPS

Our culture is fascinated by the various states of distress or heavenly bliss found in our close relationships. As David Myers (1992) wrote in *The Pursuit of Happiness,* people say they are happiest when they feel satisfied with their love life, or their close relationships in general. Myers also noted that people who enjoy their close relationships cope better with various stresses, including bereavement, job loss, and illness. In *Meanings of Life,* Roy Baumeister (1991) presents evidence that people often feel that their lives are the most meaningful and fulfilling when they are involved in satisfying close relationships.

When we are young, we are often drawn toward certain individuals as if they were magnets, often saying it was "chemistry." We usually learn much later that this magnetism or chemistry was merely illusory. Many of us have become disillusioned by our experiences with romance. While there may be a lot of positives in experiencing these passionate feelings, they often exist without a clear enough understanding of the nature of the relationship. We project our feelings of romance and passion onto our beloved (who may not necessarily feel the same way) and neglect the warnings being sent out from our more logical minds and intuition. We are being human. That is fine. But lest we regularly repeat our mistakes, we need to learn from the pain encountered in being human.

The Origins of Romantic Love

Has an emphasis on romantic or passionate love contributed to our disillusionment with our closest relationships? Part of the answer lies in the origins of romantic love. As discussed by Anthony Walsh (1991) in *The Science of Love,* this form of relating appears to have surfaced as early as the Middle Ages as a sort of chivalric parlor game for aristocratic troubadours, who sang soulful ballads about their desperate love for persons they could not have. You see the troubadours played the game of courtly love with persons to whom they were not married—that is, they pursued extramarital affairs. Their pursuit of such relationships sprang partially from the inadequacies of their own arranged marriages. The romantic love ideal for the troubadour involved deep idealization of and yearning for the loved one, coupled with physical restraint (at least an attempt at such restraint!). These purveyors of romantic love considered themselves to be noble and deeply spiritual—they believed they were showing the same level of devotion to their loved one as they showed to God. Such a heritage is of small comfort to anyone who wishes to believe that romantic love is the sole requirement for a successful relationship.

Another part of the answer to why we experience disillusionment may be found in the very nature of how these forms of love are defined. Romantic or passionate love is a type of love usually defined as including: very strong emotional attachment to another; feelings that one cannot live without one's partner; the desire to be with one's partner most of the time; feelings of oneness with one's partner; feelings that one would do anything (however much at odds with one's own values?) to help one's partner; and excessive jealousy concerning the partner's time and attention (Walster & Walster, 1978).

Today this experience may be referred to as infatuation, i.e., not even a type of love. If it is love, it usually is not a "thoughtful" kind of love; it's more driven by primitive emotions—including lust. In its extreme, romantic love can represent an illusion that likely will be hazardous, such as when it appears as an addiction, defined as such by Stanton Peele in 1975. Even in a less extreme form, certain commonly held principles of romantic love can hinder the emotional growth of the individual or the couple. Romantic love, alone, cannot produce the kind of sound, close relationship that can weather conflict and lead to long-term happiness. When romantic love is premised too much on passion, desire, and unchallenged feelings and hopes, it makes the lover vulnerable to dashed expectations and dreams.

Growth cannot occur in a close relationship *if romance is not leavened with a considerable dose of reality,* which involves both challenge and debate regarding what is valuable and true in oneself, one's partner, and the relationship. Without growth in the lovers, the love will surely die.

We do not always have to be with our significant other. In fact, to best relate to our other, we must do without them to the extent that will allow us to develop ourself. Before we can make a strong contribution to our partner, we need to work diligently on who *we* are and what *we* want to achieve in life. We need those achievements, including the establishment of our own identity and career, regardless of what our romantic partner is doing along these lines or what he or she wants us to do first. For example, a man may say, "In my idea of how to start a family, my wife stays home and makes sure that the kids get all the care and attention they need during their formative years; then she can think about having a career." Such a proposal, however, may be at odds with the woman's personal and professional developments, growth that, in fact, might make her a better mother as well as one who is more comfortable with the timing of her own involvement in the raising of kids. Relationships based *principally on unchallenged romantic love* are too inflexibly conceived. They do not tolerate consideration of alternative positions, the likelihood of change in the participants over time, and the possibility that the romantic way will not be sustainable over the long-term. Welwood (1990) suggests that each partner should be willing to take on the hard work of relating: each responding with patience, compassion, and courage to the other's endless demands, contingencies, and expectations.

In sum, this analysis has focused on some of the negatives of romantic or passionate love in the context of our quest for satisfying, durable close relationships. On the positive side, romantic love involves hope, which is a crucial element in relating. Romantic love represents an experience that we all cherish and one that we can celebrate in close relationships. We also, however, have to be aware of our penchant to make it a touchstone for happiness in our close relationships. The following lines by Adrienne Rich are eloquent in representing my own perspective on love:

> An honorable human relationship—that is, one in which two people have the right to use the word "love"—is a process, delicate, violent, often terrifying to both persons involved, process of refining the truths they can tell each other.

Building a close relationship is not like building a house or developing a career. It does not involve a linear, logical, step-by-step process. Rather, it often is a "seat of the pants" bumbling along until a right answer or seemingly tranquil path is found. It involves initiating and responding to changes in our environment, in those we are closest to, and most importantly, in ourselves.

The Nature of Close Relationships

This chapter is about change. As we will see, there is some truth in the line used by Annie (played by Diane Keaton) in the movie "Annie Hall" when she had decided to broach the topic of a break-up to her partner Alvie (played by Woody Allen): "You know a relationship is like a shark. It has to keep moving forward, or else it dies." Close relationships always are, by their very nature, in flux. They may move from ecstasy to other lesser states, such as contentment, or even boredom, but they do move—often before we realize that anything is happening. Contrary to what we may wish to believe, close relationships are fragile and can easily disintegrate. Further, there is change afoot always in the world surrounding and affecting close relationships. Today, the sheer volume of this change and diversity affects how our relationships are carried out. For example, the variety of configurations of families in the Western World and in the various ways couples (both heterosexual and same sex varieties) discharge their agreed upon roles in domestic life adds complexity to our lives. Even the terms appear to change by the day—"domestic partner" has replaced "significant other" as, perhaps, a more politically-correct term.

"Close relationships" or "closeness" covers more territory more objectively than "intimacy," which often suggests the involvement of sexuality, or "love," which often has a great amount of "connotative baggage." In general, it is quite significant if you say you are "close" to someone. You may or may not be in love; you may or may not be having sex; you may or may not be married or headed toward marriage. But, clearly, there is a specialness to your relationship. Conversely, it is possible to have sex with another person, or experience some degree of love for this person, *and yet not be close to this person.*

Given the range of possibilities in our relationships, it is important that we define close relationships before we examine the social context in which they take place. In one of the first textbooks to emphasize a scientific orientation to the study of close relationships, a team of psychologists led by Harold Kelley (Kelley et al., 1983) defined a close relationship as "one of strong, frequent, and diverse interdependence [between two people] that lasts over a considerable period of time" (p. 38). Kelley et al. conceived *interdependence* as the extent to which two people's lives are highly intertwined, both in terms of their behavior toward one another and in their thoughts and feelings about one another. An essential element of this definition is that the partners in the relationship do a lot of thinking, feeling, and behaving with respect to each other. Usually, we devote more energy to our primary close relationship than to any other relationship. (It is important to note that this energy is not necessarily positive; sometimes it can be quite negative or destructive.)

There has been one compelling scientific investigation of this definition. Research by Ellen Berscheid, Mark Snyder, and Allen Omoto (1989) showed that a relationship-closeness inventory that measured aspects of interdependence—diversity, frequency, strength, and duration of interconnected activities—predicted whether or not couples would break up better than did a subjective index of how close the couple felt and length of time the couple had been together.

Psychotherapist John Welwood (1990) said a close relationship, "rather than being just a form of togetherness, is a ceaseless flowing back and forth between joining and separating" (p. 117). "Joining and separating" refers to the partners' attempts to balance their need to be united against their individual needs to achieve autonomy.

For the purposes of this book, a close relationship will refer to a relationship that has extended over some period of time and involves *a mutual understanding* of closeness and *mutual behavior* that is seen by the couple as indicative of closeness. Further, while a couple may use the term "love" or some other term for "closeness," the key in my definition is that they *each believe* it exists to some degree between them and that each engages in acts that are consistent with that sentiment. This kind of relationship is distinguished from a familial relationship because it involves voluntary commitment between the individuals to engage in a relationship that may involve degrees of emotional and/or sexual intimacy and love over an extended period of time.

Variability and Ambivalence in Close Relationships

Over time, most couples usually show some variability in their feelings and behavior toward each other. Mutuality in feeling and behavior may ebb and flow over a long relationship such that at some points, one or both parties may be essentially acting as if no close relationship exists. This is a common occurrence. Whether or not they come back together is determined by many factors. For instance, if one partner has an affair that is discovered by the other, the perceived betrayal might force the end of the relationship.

But what if the nature of the relationship is one of erratic on-again-off-again character? Is it still a close relationship? Often one party will vacillate greatly between feelings and expressions of closeness and ones that paint a picture of ambivalence ("I love you, but I don't know if I want you in my life"); while the other party generally is consistent in his or her feelings and behaviors, which suggest closeness. While some degree of ambivalence exists in most close relationships, if a high degree of ambivalence continues, one or both parties will likely choose to "undeclare" closeness. However, couples experiencing a high degree of ambivalence may find therapy helpful, especially if the party bringing the greatest degree of ambivalent behavior into the union honestly wants to work toward restoring the relationship.

Personal Responsibility for Change We change whether or not we want to; it's a fact of life. I believe that we can intentionally change for the better in our relationship orientations. We must. But positive change does not come about through magic or genetic wiring. It comes from hard work, effort, and the will to make it happen. Indeed, it is the hallmark of sound therapy or counseling for relationship problems. We can affect major change in ourselves, in our minds and ways of behaving. However much we may desire to change some major aspect of another, such as influencing them toward some desired goal or feeling toward us, the power to change another's principal behavioral tendencies or ways of thinking will come mainly from their decisions and actions—not ours. Life presents couples with a host of areas for negotiation or discussion: their "rules" for the relationship can involve agreements about trust or openness; outsiders, including in-laws; friends, and potential romantic partners. The negotiations each couple engages in as they customize their relationship may seem overwhelming at times. It is easier to have a cognitive understanding of how to do something than it is to actually do it. This is, in part, because others are involved.

Love in a Complex World

> In a real sense, all life is inter-related. All men are caught in an inescapable network of mutuality, tied in a single garment of destiny. Whatever affects one directly affects all indirectly. . . .
> I can never be what I ought to be until you are what you ought to be, and you can never be what you ought to be until I am what I ought to be. This is the inter-related structure of reality. —Martin Luther King, Jr.

There is great power to be found in recognizing this complex world of change, power, and responsibility. It also is important to recognize the brevity of our time to make positive changes and contributions with our lives.

Peter Berger's (1963) *Invitation to Sociology* persuasively introduced the importance of regular scrutiny of our values. Berger provided a compelling argument for our need to challenge established truths in human affairs and to accept ownership of our choices and their consequences. He borrowed philosopher Jean-Paul Sartre's term "bad faith" and applied it to our tendency to try to avoid making a decision. According to Berger's use of the term, "bad faith" means pretending that something is necessary, when it is in fact voluntary—"Bad faith is thus a flight from freedom, a dishonest evasion of the agony of choice." (1963, p. 143)

In close relationships, it is especially important to avoid making decisions based on bad faith reasoning. We sometimes have to make difficult choices, such as how best to leave someone with whom we have had a longstanding relationship. Leaving them may be the kindest action for all concerned, if the relationship is only continuing in "bad faith." For example, if one partner in a long-term marriage is an alcoholic, that person's drinking and its effects will have a highly destructive effect on the marriage and on family life in general. The decision-maker may diligently try to encourage the alcoholic partner to get help for his or her problem, each time making it clear that the relationship is "on the line." Yet these efforts may be unsuccessful. In each instance, however, the decision-maker's "agony of choice" must be confronted in order for the relationship to function in an atmosphere of "good faith."

Context and Relativity Every event pertaining to a close relationship can be referenced back to a particular point in time, place, values, and the special influences that shaped understanding of the event. To understand a relationship, we need to understand the context of that relationship. Context provides the framework for our thoughts, feelings, and behavior. A person's first sexual, romantic relationship likely will have different qualities than that person's later relationships. The surrounding culture represents another contextual aspect of relationships. Well into this century, our culture implicitly supported men's tendencies to have had more sexual partners before marriage than women had experienced. However, beginning in the 1960s, that trend changed as our culture began to implicitly endorse increased equality in premarital sexual experience between men and women.

Contextualism provides critical information of how something is embedded within a large universe. Relativism helps us understand that, as humans, we are constantly making comparisons in our judgments. We may proclaim to the highest that our present love is our one and only love and that we were meant to be together. But our propensity to make comparisons may cast some doubt on such conclusions; it may cause us to challenge the specialness of this love versus others who may have been in our life or yet may come into it.

An example from the late fiction writer Raymond Carver may help us understand the idea of relativism. Carver had a great capacity to see into the deepest recesses of human thought and feeling about relationships. In the course of one of his most well-known short stories, "What we Talk about when we Talk about Love" (Carver, 1986), Mel, a middle-aged man, is sitting at the kitchen table visiting with his wife, Terri, and their friends, Laura and the unnamed narrator. During their conversation, Mel begins to philosophize about past loves and to ponder what any of us really knows about love.

> "There was a time when I thought I loved my first wife more than life itself. But now I hate her guts. I do. How do you explain that? What happened to that love? What happened to it, is what I'd like to know. I wish someone could tell me. Then there's Ed [Terri's ex-husband]. Okay, we're back to Ed. He loves Terri so much he tries to kill her and he winds up killing himself." Mel stopped talking and swallowed from his glass. "You guys have been together eighteen months and you love each other. It shows all over you. You glow with it. But you both loved other people before you met each other. You've both been married before, just like us. And you probably loved other people before that too, even. Terri and I have been together five years, been married for four. And the terrible thing, the terrible thing is, but the good thing too, the saving grace, you might say, is that if something happened to one of us—excuse me for saying this—but if something happened to one of us tomorrow, I think the other one, the other person, would grieve for a while, you know, but then the surviving party would go out and love again, have someone else soon enough. All this, all of this love we're talking about, it would be just a memory." (p. 133)

This fragment of Carver's story is but one example of how people cope with the transience of their feelings of love. It is important to note, however, that many of us do not easily get over the images and feelings associated with our past loves. They are back there ready to jump out and grab us at a moment's notice—or as is often true, in the still of the night. While most of us do move on with our lives, no amount of forward movement and change can completely erase our deep memory of the past. This recognition of our mind's and heart's ability to be influenced by our memories and feelings from past relationships drives home the need to develop an understanding of the nature of close relationships.

Stories and Accounts

The universe is made of stories, not of atoms.—Muriel Rukeyser

The story by Raymond Carver illustrates the human capacity to develop and tell stories and thereby create meaning. As Victor Frankl (1959) cogently argued, humans cannot survive if they cannot find meaning in what they do and think.

In this book, I will embrace the importance of our ability to cope with change as it is formulated in and affected by the stories or accounts that all of us develop as we pursue close relationships. Our stories are one of the most effective ways we have of conveying meaning. They invite us to step into someone else's life for a while, and to witness, perhaps in a gripping way, a set of images of acts, thoughts, and feelings that had meaning to the story-teller. This experience allows us to better understand the story-teller and how that person perceived the events represented in the story, and by our reactions to the story, to better understand ourselves.

We all have at least as many stories as we have close relationships, and they interlock in what we might call master stories, or one large master-account of our life. Our stories are by their very nature incomplete. As we gain insights from private reflection and confiding in others, we frequently add to, or subtract from, the elements in our major relationship stories. After we have worked on them for a while, and probably told parts of them to others, our stories usually lie dormant until we encounter cues in our ongoing life that trigger memories of them, prodding us to pursue further work on them.

Weber, Orbuch, and I (1990) have argued that people develop and often tell their stories to others for a variety of reasons: to clarify events in their minds; to gain emotional support from others; to learn more about who they are or are becoming; to better present themselves to their intended audience as someone with whom that person could have a relationship; and to gain strength, hope, and the will to go on with their lives.

Over the course of this book, you will notice a deliberate emphasis on story-telling and narratives. The use of narratives is now widely accepted across different fields of scholarship and has been embraced by both humanists and scientists. Finding oneself, or coming of age emotionally, is often marked by the ability to see one's life as part of a larger narrative. Robert Coles' (1989) *The Call of Stories* suggested that a respect for narrative is everyone's rock-bottom capacity—a universal gift to be shared with others. In *Acts of Meaning,* Jerome Bruner (1990) suggested that the lives and selves we construct are the outcomes of the process of meaning construction that is embedded in particular sets of cultural and historical circumstances. Bruner argues that a modern psychology will be far richer in its understanding of human life to the extent that it views people as meaning-making and meaning-using.

The Changing Social Context

Close relationships don't occur in a vacuum. They are greatly influenced by the social world surrounding them. The late twentieth century sees a social world in flux, presenting innumerable challenges to such relationships.

Demographics   Philip Blumstein and Pepper Schwartz (1983), sociologists studying different types of close relationships, summarized much of their evidence from a large-scale study of American couples conducted in the late 1970s with this prophetic statement:

> Families are in a significant state of flux, and the uncertainty reverberates throughout society. One consequence is that people are apprehensive about the future—the future of personal relationships in general, and the future of the specific relationships that nourish them. They do not know how to design what they want or protect what they have. They are unsure about the future of marriage. (pp. 35-36)

Our brief examination of demographic statistics will suggest that these conclusions continue to ring true as we approach the beginning of the twenty-first century. For some time now there has been a crisis in trust in marriage. Even though we are a prolific marrying culture, we have less trust in marriage's permanence or its sacrosanctity than ever before. For many, the late 1980s and the 1990s have been a time of faded dreams of finding permanent happiness when they find romance. Fewer people than ever believe in the permanence of the traditional family. Today, many new configurations of relationships and people form the "modern family."

The most publicized catalyst for these changes in the traditional family structure is the divorce rate. In the last decade, there were one million separations per year in the United States; close to one in two recent marriages ended in divorce. In the last century, there has been a 700 percent increase in divorce in the United States. In a review of divorce data, Andrew Cherlin (1992) reported that in 1930, 9 percent of all brides had been divorced, but in 1987, 32 percent of all brides had been divorced. Divorce has replaced death as the most likely cause of marital dissolution. The high incidence of divorce cuts across socio-economic, ethnic, and racial lines and can be found for marriages of various durations. The rate of divorce is increasing among people married more than 15, 25, or even 40 years. We may never again have a segment of the population in the United States, as we do now, in which there are a substantial number of golden anniversaries. Even long-term marriages of the present and future may last only 20 to 30 years, simply because they are the second or third marriage for one or both of the partners.

The number of persons in this country who live in blended families (families begun after the divorce of one or more of the parents and often involving different configurations of stepchildren and biological children) is estimated to approach tens of millions, making the blended family the most typical American family in the '90s. Current data indicate that one of every five children under age 18 is a step-child, and that by the year 2000, half of all Americans will either be members of a stepfamily—or will have been part of a stepfamily at one time. A final statistic about stepfamilies that is noteworthy is that each day 1,300 new stepfamilies are formed.

Attitudes about the acceptability of divorce have changed remarkably in this country since the 1970s, and divorce is now frequently treated as "no big deal" (as in our daily conversations, countless afternoon television soap opera dramas, and situation comedies), unless of course it happens to you or people close to you. The stigma of divorce has become much less pronounced during the last two decades. No longer are most couples contemplating divorce deciding to stick out their marriage until their kids get out of college. In a typical large college class, half of the students will have divorced parents.

The number of single-parent families in the United States is in the millions and rising at a steady rate each year. Census Bureau data for 1992 show that the proportion of African-American children living with one parent (usually the mother, as is the case across socioeconomic, racial, and ethnic lines) rose from about 32 percent in 1970 to about 58 percent in 1991. In 1993, it has been estimated that more than 3.2 million youngsters are being raised by at least one grandparent—a 40 percent increase since 1980—because the custodial parent works or has abandoned the child. A child's chances of living in poverty in a single-parent household are six times as high as they would be in a two-parent family.

Seven million children live with an alcoholic parent, and almost 1.2 million children run away from home each year. Not surprisingly, in this context of changing structure and meaning, suicide is the leading cause of death among American teenagers. A large-scale, multinational, collaborative study published in the *Journal of the American Medical Association* (1993, 268, 3098–3105) revealed a significant increase in the rate of depression among people age 25 and younger in the United States. The investigators speculated that the increased vulnerability of younger persons may be due in part to the rising divorce rate and the accompanying stress experienced in American families.

The quality of marriages that remain intact over time is also of interest to marriage and family analysts. At the 1992 meeting of the American Association for Marriage and Family Therapy, it was reported by Don-David Lusterman, a marital therapist in New York, that 10 percent to 12 percent of married people have had an affair lasting at least one month. He estimated that 50 percent of spouses who suddenly find out about such a protracted infidelity show some symptoms of post-traumatic stress disorders, including recurrent thoughts, images, and dreams of the event (e.g., it has been reported often by men that they had trouble avoiding imagery of their partner in sexual embrace with the outside person); difficulty concentrating; trouble sleeping; obsessive ruminations; and outbursts of anger.

Lusterman suggested that this reaction is a "disease" caused by being ripped apart by the deceit of the involved partner's lying and loss of trust in him or her.

Because of a number of factors, including the high divorce rate, many people are delaying marriage beyond their 20s. Recent Census Bureau data indicate that in the United States, there were 41 million never-married adults in 1991 (twice the number that existed in 1971). According to Census Bureau figures, the number of men and women 30 to 44 who have never married more than doubled during the last 20 years. By 1991, the median age for first marriage had risen four years since the 1970s to about 24 years of age for women and 26 for men. Other reasons for this delaying or foregoing of marriage is women's greater financial independence, the growing acceptance of alternative life-style choices (including staying single, homosexuality, and cohabitation without marriage), and the downturn in the economy in the late 1990s which provides less incentive to get married. A 40-year-old female insurance claims assistant discussing why she has not married:

> I have my friends—both male and female. . . . And when I'm
> not with someone else, I'm really content by myself.

A 38-year-old female lawyer quoted in the same article offers these reasons:

> It's not going to make me any happier; I'm happy already. . . .
> There are people who would say I'm not being honest with my-
> self. The traditional notion is that if you are by yourself you
> can't have a good time. But that's really passé. It seems the
> longer I stay single, the less I'm inclined to give up that life-
> style. (*Los Angeles Daily News,* September 26, 1992)

The latter woman noted that having children is not precluded for women who choose to remain single longer. She said, "As each day goes by, I'm always hearing about women at 45 and older having children." She went on to mention that she someday may adopt a child or possibly have a biological birth while still single. While the prevalence and acceptance of this lifestyle have increased in recent years, there still is prejudice against people—especially in mid-life—who choose not to marry. Some people think that "there must be something wrong with them," or that they must be unhappy because they are single. But as our understanding of close relationships increases, it appears that the most unhappy situation for someone to experience is to feel trapped in a miserable marriage. Such a situation eats away at the very integrity and honor of the individuals involved, including children and relatives who are close to them.

David Popenoe (1988, 1993) has reviewed census data suggesting that the traditional nuclear family, composed of mother, father, and children, is on the decline. Not only are people delaying marriage, many are choosing not to marry. For some, choosing not to marry does not mean ruling out having children. For others, choosing to marry doesn't necessarily mean choosing to have children. Homosexual unions may or may not include children. Some couples are choosing to live together without marrying. And some are married but not living together most of the time because of one partner's need to commute a long distance to work.

The decline of the traditional nuclear family has generated considerable debate among politicians, scholars, and religious leaders in the 1990s. I believe that we have naturally evolved toward this eclectic array of living arrangements and that such arrangements in no clear way portend the downfall of our culture or bad outcomes for children who grow up in nontraditional family situations.

Values Values, specifically "family values," are at the core of most dialogue involving the decline of the traditional family. Never before have we had so many non-traditional families, and their numbers beg the question: Are alternative family arrangements (e.g., involving single parents or same-sex parents) conducive to positive socialization experiences for children and enriched atmospheres for living and learning? Other related issues include the question of abortion, the role of religious training in positive socialization experiences, and the value of sex education and relationship-type course work in public elementary and high schools.

Before the presidential elections in 1992, Vice President Dan Quayle criticized the television show *Murphy Brown,* for an episode in which the lead character gave birth to a child while she was single. He argued that this did not represent a good family model to show on television. His criticism inspired a wealth of commentary, much of which argued that "good" and "bad" families can be found in all types of living arrangements. In *Brave New Families,* Judith Stacy (1990) argues that, for the children involved, single-parent families are often improvements over two-parent families in which there is an extended period of marital conflict or strife. People who scapegoat unconventional families should note that President Bill Clinton was raised by a single parent, as was George Washington.

Beyond *Murphy Brown,* there has been increased debate in the '90s among politicians and various kinds of family theorists about whether public policies should be used to shape family welfare. For example, should states make it more difficult for parents to get divorced? Or should schools hand out free condoms? The Clinton administration has been focusing new attention on what it calls the "responsibility agenda" and the importance of stable families. One step in that direction was the signing of a Family and Medical Leave Act that makes it easier for employees to take leaves for a period of time, without loss of seniority, and then return to their jobs after they have addressed certain parenting or medical needs.

Stephanie Coontz's compelling analysis in her 1992 book *The Way We Never Were: American Families and the Nostalgia Trap* provided a fuller commentary on the family values debate. The much-ballyhooed traditional, self-sufficient family usually includes a father who works outside the home, homemaker mother, at least two children, and a house in the suburbs. According to Coontz, that kind of family is a figment of our nostalgic imagination. It did not even exist in such a pure form in the 1950s, when, for example, we had the dichotomy of government programs that provided subsidies for most suburban families, alongside an all-time high for babies born out of wedlock.

Why are we so often nostalgic about the way it was in the family or other areas of intimate personal life? We may assume things were easier four decades ago. And we fear the different and unknown family structures that are emerging in the 1990s. Today's families and close relationships involve less structure and often are forged to accommodate the particular desires and needs of the individuals involved. It is difficult, therefore, to easily characterize them. It also is difficult to predict their success over the long term. These new arrangements fly in the face of the mores of yesteryear so much that they may threaten people who have lived their lives according to certain well-structured guidelines for behavior.

Thus, when we grow tired of the myriad problems in relationships in the 1990s, we need to remember that people in earlier decades had their own troubles. And in those times, they were less open in discussing them. Problems such as wife battering, for instance, were much less scrutinized for their impact on the woman and other members of the family than they are today.

There have been several broad analyses that have strong relevance for discussions about family life and values in the 1990s. In 1985, sociologist Robert Bellah and colleagues published *Habits of the Heart,* a provocative book that reported on results from a limited sample of 200 white, middle-class Americans concerning their views on such topics as the family and community. These authors used such data to suggest that Americans needed to come back to a spirit of love and commitment to the family and community that had prevailed earlier in this century but had disappeared as a result of fierce individualism, greed, mobility, and suburbanism. They also blamed romantic love for part of the aura of individualism in this country. They said, "Romantic love is a quintessential form of expressive individualism. When it becomes not only the basis for the choice of a life partner but the condition for the continuation of a marriage, it tends to make marriage itself a lifestyle enclave" (pp. 73-74).

Later, they continued:

> Love, then, creates a dilemma for Americans. In some ways, love is the quintessential expression of individuality and freedom. At the same time, it offers intimacy, mutuality, and sharing. In the ideal love relationship, these two aspects of love are perfectly joined—love is both absolutely free and completely shared. Such moments of perfect harmony among free individuals are rare, however. The sharing and commitment in a love relationship can seem, for some, to swallow up the individual, making her (more often than him) lose sight of her own interests, opinions, and desires. Paradoxically, since love is supposed to be a spontaneous choice by free individuals, someone who has "lost" herself cannot really love, or cannot contribute to a real love relationship. Losing a sense of one's self may also lead to being exploited, or even abandoned, by the person one loves. (p. 93)

Bellah et al. contrasted the family of the present with that of a previous era, emphasizing extended groupings of family members who collectively attended to one another's welfare. They said:

> To summarize the changes in the American family since the early nineteenth century, the network of kinship has narrowed and the sphere of individual decision has grown. This is even

truer today among the middle class than among the upper and lower reaches of our population. The nuclear family is not "isolated," as some over-zealous interpreters of that metaphor have implied, but contact with relatives outside the nuclear family depends not only on geographical proximity—not to be taken for granted in our mobile society—but also on personal preference. Even relations between parents and children are matters of individual negotiation once the children have left home. (p. 89)

I believe that there is some value in Bellah et al.'s arguments. In their decrying of this culture's movement away from certain cherished values of the past, they represent an increasingly vocal faction of commentators on family life. The honoring of commitment and obligation is essential to the success of a close relationship (and to live a good and morally tenable life in general). These writers, however, were painting an extreme picture of the dilemma between individualism and commitment. Why is it not possible for couples to create a context in which both partners can be fulfilled, but at the same time raise a family? Sure, it is not easy, but that is not the question. The question is, can and should it be done? Furthermore, the greater emphasis upon expression of feelings is one of the major accomplishments of the last decade in close relationships. Being expressive and committed are not mutually exclusive.

Another element that might make this time difficult for lovers and the family has been proposed by Kenneth Gergen (1991) in *The Saturated Self: Dilemmas of Identity in Contemporary Life.* Gergen argued that our personal lives are changing in profound ways. He suggested that our lives are saturated by others. Relentless, inescapable encounters with disparate people change our deeply held beliefs about truth, character, coherence, and commitment. The diversity of modern self-conceptions and life-styles, he argued, erodes our commitments and stability. Various others offer us options for self-definition (e.g., "good

husband and father," "boring teacher," "dedicated community ser-
vant"), and evaluate particular identities we assume. This atmosphere
makes it difficult to feel secure about who we are, about our "core
identity."

Gergen went on to argue that too often, our relationships are
played out through impersonal technologies, such as faxes or computer bulletin boards, that allow us to reach across the world without
looking into the eyes of those we "relate" to daily. Sometimes these
stressful inputs can be too much, resulting in confusion over what's
important, how to be sincere, and whom to believe. He said that
many of us are stretched out all over the place, "panting from a race
that never seems to be over." Unlike Bellah et al., Gergen did not
blame romantic love for anything. Rather, he seemed nostalgic for the
return of a period in this country (soon after the turn of the century
and the so-called Victorian era) when romantic beliefs as grounds for
closeness were beginning to take hold. It was a period that emphasized inner joy, moral feeling, and loyalty.

What Gergen seems to be suggesting is that for many of us, the
impersonal "rat race" of modern life is impeding our ability to be
intimate and committed. While that may be true, it does not have to
be. As I elaborate in the following chapter, people have the ability and
right to structure their lives so that the outside world's impact on
their peace, joy, accomplishments, and fulfilling close relationships is
minimized.

Economics We all know that part of the burden on contemporary families is the frequent necessity that all adult family members
hold jobs just to make ends meet. This burden may be particularly
daunting for the one-parent family, since single parents have to make
a living, care for and nurture the children, and try to take care of
themselves. All of these activities simply do not fit into the average
week, and the parent is totally exhausted before the week is done. In

two-parent families in which both parents work, they often come home well after children arrive home from school. Or various day-care options—that too commonly offer marginal care—are pursued while the parents work long days. Blended families face special stresses. There is often a competition for resources. For example, a stepfather may be working two jobs to support both his original family and a new, blended family. Wrangling with ex-spouses regarding visitation rights and holiday vacation plans for kids also is a problem of gigantic proportions for many blended families. In this context, the couple's own close relationship often begins to suffer because of the stresses of trying to juggle arrangements and responsibilities.

Predictions about economic change in the future suggest that many people face a continuing struggle to make ends meet. Major companies increasingly have engaged in a massive elimination of both blue-collar and white-collar jobs since the beginning of the 1990s. We are all too familiar with the stories of college graduates being unable to find decent employment and of menial jobs being staffed by overeducated individuals. Such sad realities indirectly affect relationships through the loss of self-esteem, job-related depression, and anger and embitteredness caused by a person having little control over their career opportunities and income.

Writing Your Own Story

For each of us, the most important story of change is our own story. It is a story that is incomplete and that never will be complete, but that we must strive diligently to examine. Such examination will motivate us to want to understand ourselves and our pasts more fully and to develop well-conceived future lines of action. Many of the pieces of our personal story can be put together. Our minds are powerful, penetrating entities that can problem-solve toward achieving our goals. A major initial step in successful relating is to take charge of your own life—to fully recognize your power to write your own story.

The only way to be fully engaged in the process of loving and caring for another is to first love and care for self, such that what self offers to another and life in general is of substantial merit. Merle Shain (1989) in her insightful book *Courage My Love* . . . offered the following sage advice on personal responsibility in relating:

"There isn't a perfect person somewhere, only a more perfect person we might become, and there isn't a paradise someone can lead us to unless it's the world we make for ourselves when we stop expecting it to be delivered by someone else. . . .

"And as long as we think we need love to make us something more than we are alone . . . it isn't love, the one who doesn't [receive] love is yourself. . . .

"And as long as we think we have to have somebody to adore us to be somebody, we are stuck in a holding pattern, whining and waiting, impotent and injured, blaming those who have failed us, not knowing we are complicitous in keeping ourselves from becoming the persons we are meant to be." (p. 15)

Close relationships relate to practically all that we are and all that we do. They can bring forth our most cherished states of activity and being. This chapter has been about the centrality of close relationships to our identity as human beings and to the meaning we ascribe to our lives. In this chapter, I have outlined the changing terrain of relationships and the family in the 1990s. To be empowered in our relationships, we need to understand these recent changes and their implications for our lives.

THERE CAN BE NO HAPPINESS

IF THE THINGS WE BELIEVE IN

ARE DIFFERENT FROM

THE THINGS WE DO.

—Albert Camus

Chapter

2

SELF-EMPOWERMENT
IN CLOSE
RELATIONSHIPS
AND
BEYOND

Everything we do follows our own uniquely personal system of meaning and logic. This system is composed of our priorities, attitudes, and values and is expressed to others by our behavior. Self-empowerment is about learning how to recognize and reinforce our personal belief systems, so that we can act on a daily basis in a way that is, indeed, consistent with our values. By giving ourselves power, we are less likely to be blown about by the winds of change that regularly blow through our lives.

Self-empowerment is not magic; more than anything, it is common sense. It is based on principles derived from a variety of sources, including Merle Shain (1989) and John Welwood (1990). Self-empowerment will, by its very nature, change your life. However, it is not a cure-all. It will not help you make the "perfect" decision regarding a life-long close relationship. Nor will it give you a sixth sense, enabling you to discern the sincerity of others. It won't prevent the breakup of a close relationship or mend a broken heart.

So, what *will* self-empowerment do? It will reinforce the importance of working on your closest relationship—your relationship with yourself. It will help you like yourself. The principles behind self-empowerment apply equally to times of great stress as well as those of tranquility. They are just as valuable for success in one's work as they are in one's close relationships.

In this chapter, I will outline the basic principles that are the foundation for self-empowerment, which in turn is a necessary condition for developing strong, positive close relationships. In later chapters, I will elaborate on how self-empowerment enhances, or facilitates our transition through, various stages of our close relationships.

Principles To Relate and Live By

1. *Try to achieve balance in your daily life.*
    Balance in one's views and behavior is crucial to finding tranquil-

ity in life. Balance is an in-between position: one is neither too daring nor too cautious. In relationships, some people take untenable risks all the time—everything from falling head over heels for someone the first time they meet to having unprotected sex with anyone before having an AIDS test. It is even risky to agree to marry someone with whom one has major differences in attitude and values—expecting a change in major values and attitudes is highly unlikely. Therefore, marrying them in the hope that their attitudes will change is taking an untenable risk.

On the other hand, certain risks are worth taking. Let's say that you have a chance meeting with a stranger. If he or she shows some qualities that are appealing, and you are looking for a partner, why not take a chance and try to find out more about this person and in so doing risk revealing more about yourself. If you are searching for a partner, you need to be alert to such opportunities for risk taking and having scripts in mind as to how to show interest (asking the person how he or she feels about meeting new people in public settings). Being open to new experiences, whether or not it involves a new close relationship, is one of the chief ways we grow psychologically, learn about the world, and create new vistas of opportunities for ourselves.

For each of us, there is a "golden mean," our own perfect balance between caution and risk taking. Clichés like "nothing ventured, nothing gained" may seem to make sense, but you have to decide if the timing is right for you. For every maxim, there is usually an equally persuasive counter-maxim. That is part of the thesis of *Ideological Dilemmas,* a fine, scholarly work by Michael Billing and several other authors (1988). They argue that contradictory strands of logic abound within both ideology and common sense. Such dilemmas, the authors imply, challenge us to develop our own sense of what is right and wrong. That is, they challenge us to find our own "golden mean."

We should strive for balance in other areas as well—for instance, it is important to weigh the need and obligation to take care of oneself against the need and obligation to reach out to others. If we are to err on one side or the other, I would favor the communal approach that Bellah et al. (1985) also seemed to espouse. Uriel and Edna Foa's (1974) book *Societal Structures of the Mind* suggested an important direction along this line: when you give love to others, the process of giving actually returns love to you as well—and in even greater proportions.

2. *Try to achieve empathy and breadth in your dealings with others.*

Our most important moments occur when we interact closely with others. To be empathic—to take the time to see the world from another mind's eye and feel what they feel in dealing with their dilemmas—takes practice. Practice being a discerning listener; practice asking thoughtful questions about others' lives and the topics they want to discuss; and practice being careful when giving advice— taking questions under consideration if they require more thought.

To develop a breadth of experience in dealing with others, travel as much as you can. The interaction with various individuals and cultures stretches us and is invaluable to the development of empathy. Try to take time to learn about people whom you would not encounter in your daily walks. Their stories and experiences teach us much about others, as well as ourselves.

3. *Develop and nurture a network of close friends.*

Having close friends makes one happier to be alive and provides a bulwark against life's difficulties. All available research on the support value of friendship emphasizes the role of friends as companions and confidants who are there for you in times of stress (Sherrod, 1989). People often tell me that their "friends" let them down in times of adversity. That is not unusual because the people we call friends may be acquaintances who are untested in such circumstances. It takes time and experience to know the people on whom you can depend for faithful, long-term friendship and support. But to earn such support, *you* must also be highly dependable.

A network of close friends takes a lot of time—and testing—to develop. I believe that the best way to maintain such a network is regular, meaningful communication—taking the time to write a long, descriptive letter periodically or calling and spending some time sharing the details of your lives with each other. Try to be there, too, when a friend is very ill or experiencing a crisis. You should be able to expect the same from your best friends in return.

I realize that this line of reasoning is axiomatic. But it appears more self-evident to women than it does to men (see Chapter 4). Men often look to women as the key confidants in their lives; and then they may rely on one person for that role. Especially when they become romantically involved, men sometimes drop their good female friends. That is psychologically fatal! You will always need them. They can nourish you in ways that your partner cannot. Do not put all of the responsibility for confiding and psychological sustenance on your partner, and be open to your partner sharing confidences with others.

4. *Nourish the mind and work the body.*

Read widely and devoutly to nourish your understanding of others and the issues in the world. In so doing, you will learn about yourself. I personally like to read from diverse sources, such as major newspapers, novels, and poetry and keep files of especially valuable pieces. Many large newspapers now have Sunday or daily sections that contain useful material on close relationships. Fiction writers, such as Raymond Carver and Laurie Colwin, have provided profound insights about humans and close relationships in their writing. In all of this reading, however, it is important to ask questions, such as: Do their ideas represent different sides of an issue? Or for newspaper pieces, is the writing based on research?

Exercise regularly. Working the body hard and regularly gives us self-confidence and endurance—we often can persevere much better in the face of stress or personal crises. When we come up against difficult hurdles in our work or personal lives, a solid history of physical fitness activities may immunize us against caving in to pressure. Everyone encounters stress, sometimes of even life-threatening magnitude and duration. Regular, intense exercise is widely recognized as a form of stress management. (Yoga and meditation, though less vigorous, also fight stress.) It burns up energy that otherwise might have been ineffectively spent worrying about how to deal with one's problems. Also, I believe that hard exercise gives a person a feeling that he or she can rise to the occasion in dealing with many of life's crises. The person may say, "If I can run these 26 miles, I can take on whatever other challenges life has to offer." A fascinating new college course offered at Northern Iowa University entitled "Fitness and Mental Health" involves training all kinds of students, many of whom are not very athletic at all, to run a marathon before the end of the course (reported in the *Chronicle of Higher Education,* August 25, 1993). Note that the course is about mental health!

Regular exercise may give us a sense of control, even when, objectively speaking, we have little. This sense of control is conducive to health (Rodin & Langer, 1977). It also improves our appearance—which is why people often begin to work out after separation or divorce, when they will be meeting and dating again.

If at all possible, don't stop exercising when problems or heavy work/school schedules intrude, or when the weather is poor. It is of such nourishing value that it should almost always take precedence over other activities. Friends and family may say that you owe them your time first, but you will be a better friend and relate more effectively to them if you take care of your own needs.

5. *Keep a diary or daily record book.*

Be bullish about your diary or record keeping. It's easier than it seems. Buy an inexpensive calendar or notebook and mark down your physical workouts and other easy-to-record accomplishments. This activity is a powerful tool for pushing yourself. It's a permanent reminder of what you have accomplished thus far, and it will provide you with the strength to strive for similar goals in the future.

Once you are accustomed to daily record keeping, try keeping more extensive notes, or a diary, about the major aspects of your life, such as your loves, hopes, fears, successes, and failures. Remember, this diary is for your eyes only; no one else will see it. It is important to be as honest with yourself as you can. Do not allow yourself to be influenced by how you think you *should* frame events. Therefore, it is important to remove all outside distractions when you write—ignore the door bell, turn on the answering machine, and generally do whatever you can to avoid being interrupted.

Over time you will find that writing down your thoughts and feelings will give you a clearer perspective on your life, and may give you insight into how to change your behavior in the future. In fact, as we will see in the chapters on dissolution and grieving, diary keeping may be one of the most effective ways of coming to grips with loss. It gives you a safe outlet for your most private thoughts. It allows you to vent your feelings. It gives back to you not only a record, but also evidence about who you were at critical points in your life.

6. *Take responsibility for your life.*

Treat problems in life as the challenges they are, not as impossible obstacles. Everyone has major dilemmas in their lives. For some, they occur regularly. Some of us face up to our dilemmas better than others. They deal with their problems as best they can, and then move on in a timely fashion. This ability to *do what you can* and *then let go* is a critical life skill. Moaning, whining, and complaining about the powers that be, the system, your parents, lover or spouse, your job, your looks or abilities is not useful. Why waste your energy?

It is important to remember that some problems cannot be effectively addressed, no matter how much thought and action we direct at them. For example, say a good friend of yours regularly chooses people for close relationships who will clearly be hurtful to him or her, and despite your best efforts to work with your friend on this problem, he or she persists in this pattern. You may be frustrated with your friend's behavior, but you should move on to other problems for which your actions can be effective.

Some problems can be solved only with much effort by two people. The British psychiatrist R. D. Laing wrote penetrating books about problems in close relationships. One of his books, *Knots* (1970), used riddles and short verse to depict some of these. Here's one verse:

Jack can't tell Jill what he
  wants Jill to tell him.
Jill can't tell him either
because although Jill knows X
Jill does not know
  That Jack does not know X. . . .

 Jill
  can see that he does not understand her
and can see that he can't see that he doesn't: and she can see
and she can see
  that he can't see that he can't see
   she sees he can't see he doesn't
Why does she still feel confused?
She cannot understand why he can't see that
she sees that he can't see that he does not understand. (pp. 74-75)

What is going on in these lines? One can imagine Laing saw some interesting knotted relationships among his patients, and possibly in some of his own personal relationships. The first stanza might be construed to mean that Jack wants Jill to tell him she loves and needs him. Yet she does not know that he does not know this; hence, she defers telling him—thinking he will ask her directly if he loves and needs her.

The second stanza is even more cryptic, but also very realistic. What might it refer to? Assume that the understanding pertains to Jill's desire and need for more in-depth discussion about the intimate core of their relationship. The poem says that Jill knows:

1. Jack does not understand this need on her part.

2. He does not know that he does not understand her.

3. He does not know that she knows that he does not understand her.

Finally, it says that Jill remains confused because of Jack's ignorance about a matter so critical to her. Even if my interpretation is incorrect, any interpretation will likely focus on the divergence in their understandings.

Why don't Jack and Jill simply talk to one another and thereby resolve their misperceptions? They probably do talk but not effectively or enough. And their problems, or "knots," grow more imposing with every failed effort to reach an understanding. Misunderstanding is a huge obstacle to closeness. It is common in all relationships and takes a lot of work to overcome. At the minimum, the couple has to be motivated to desire bridging the gap in understanding each other. They then need to figure out *how* to do so, and to take the required actions. None of these steps is easy.

The problem can be solved only through honest efforts on the part of both parties. Both need to try to understand and appreciate their partner's position and also to openly express their own position. They are wasting precious time and "relationship resources" by not recognizing the necessity of these steps. The couple, in this instance, may have to seek a counselor to help them build this communication bridge. If their "knots" are too convoluted or if they are unable to articulate their needs and concerns, the conflict likely will continue and erode the relationship more, as well as deaden each person's morale, until somehow someone has the guts to end it.

7. *Learn to endure and help others endure.*

We all are subject to pain such as that found in knotted relationships. This vulnerability does not mean that we had an impoverished family background or that we have personalities that make close relationships impossible. When such difficulties arise, however, we likely will benefit from taking a good, long look at our lives and how well we are pursuing our own system of meaning and logic. Such a look may humble us.

Since my own divorce, I have believed that divorce is one of the most humbling—and thereby valuable—experiences in living. For me at least, divorce after a marriage of more than nine years took the wind out of my sails in all areas of life, including work. My divorce helped me recognize that I could not take anything that mattered for granted. Also, before my divorce, I had considered the literature, ideas, and evidence concerning divorce as rather abstract. They made sense, but I did not have enough first-hand experience to say, "That proposition is correct. I have been there." Getting such experience was not fun. But you have to endure it sometimes in order to grow, and perhaps you can give something back to others that derives from your learning.

Divorce turns our world on end. Ronnie Janoff-Bulman's (1992) influential book *Shattered Assumptions* discusses how people often experience major losses—divorce, death, a serious accident, major business failure—that shatter their taken-for-granted assumptions regarding the "goodness," "fairness," and "justice" of life. Life becomes grubbier after these experiences. But if we survive the early period of feeling that we have little control left over our lives, these events often leave us very humble beings—and that is empowering. Why? *Humility is a state of mind that is in close contact with reality.* A humble person has a broader perspective and less intense self-interest. He or she may endeavor to facilitate others' self-empowerment as well.

Telling people to learn to endure may sound a bit cynical. It is, however, the type of advice that derives from the "wisdom of the ages" in human experience. Listen to what Scott Skiles, a starting guard on the Orlando Magic basketball team, has to say about how he has overcome having only a modicum of natural ability as an athlete to rise high in the world of competitive sports (from Sam Smith's article, "Scrappy Skiles Scorns Sceptics' Scrutiny, *Chicago Tribune,* March 21, 1993, Section 3, p. 3):

> "I'm not particularly gifted . . ." says Skiles, often noted for
> what he's lacking—speed, size, jumping ability, and defense.
> "My main gift is my ability to persevere."
>
> "When I was in junior high school, they said I was too small
> for high school," said Skiles, who went on to lead his Plymouth,
> Ind., school to a Hoosiers'-like upset . . . to win the Indiana
> state championship.
>
> "When I was in high school, they said I was too fragile, not
> durable enough, too slow for college ball," said Skiles, who be-
> came a first-team All-American and an NBA first-round pick
> from Michigan State.
>
> "And it has been the same when I came in this league. . . ."
>
> "The guys who are in the front in battle, when they're charg-
> ing, are they courageous or stupid? I'm not sure what I am. But
> it gets me by."

"I'm not a sprinter. . . . But I'm the guy who can run the marathon. And that means I can do more than people realize. I've run the whole gamut in this league, from not playing to playing when we need a three to playing all the time. I've been in every situation and come through it. I didn't have everything handed to me."

All of us encounter situations in which we are up against the odds, or in which others do not think that we can excel. But when we have learned how to persist against the odds and to let adversity motivate us, we can accomplish deeds that we might otherwise have seen as well beyond our means.

8. *There is always enough time to do what you want to do.*

People in the '90s often feel that there never is enough time to do what they must do with regard to their partner, children, and friends, not to mention their work and themselves. Albert Camus summed up our obligation to use time in a way that reflects our values when he said, "I shall tell you a great secret, my friend. Do not wait for the last judgment. It takes place every day."

The problem of dealing with demands on your time is best addressed by taking an organized approach to living that involves deciding what your priorities are and giving them the highest quality of attention and care. Give them the best moments of your day, and do not permit undue intrusions. Whether it is loving behavior and sexual relations, helping others solve problems, or visiting with a dear friend, find a way to fit the activity in among others because it is that important to you.

Also, some activities presumed to take a long time take less time if you learn efficiency techniques and note that time can also be "created" by wedging into the seams of mundane activities, such as standing in line, more sublime activities, such as planning your next book.

I realize that these approaches might seem unrealistic to the woman who has a part-time job, two kids at home who require full-time care, and a spouse upset that they never have sex anymore because she is too tired at the end of the day. I cannot be sensitive enough, or do enough justice, to such legitimate and common pressures on the individual and family. While only those who have had to cope with such situations have the right to preach, I can suggest that the individual's system of meaning and organization of behavior may have to be reevaluated. The primary relationship needs nourishing or it will crumble, causing other relationships to suffer as well. One solution to consider in demanding family situations is trading services, such as child care and shopping, with close friends.

9. *After you have developed your goals, principles, and behavioral approaches to living, trust thyself.*

In his essay "Self-Reliance," Ralph Waldo Emerson said, "Nothing is at last sacred but the integrity of your own mind . . . Trust thyself; every heart vibrates to that iron string." He also said, "It is easy to live for others. Everybody does. I call on you to live for yourselves."

These words speak volumes, especially in the context of a person's work to develop himself or herself. Frequently, people will challenge our logic and the way we do business. You and your ways may be the target of harsh criticism, even from those whom you care about deeply. A lover may complain regularly, for example, about your perceived inadequacies. While it probably is always useful to hear out such criticism, and changes may be warranted, if you have worked hard to order your life, you should trust yourself most in how you conduct it.

To the extent that we know ourselves, we can trust ourselves. Unfortunately, in our early development and socialization many of us are not encouraged by parents and other key individuals to develop ourselves fully, and hence to learn to know ourselves. Let's consider the words of Jean Baer, who has written self-help books about women and relationships for more than two decades.

> I was always the responsible one in my family. My mother, Helen Roth Baer, got sick [with cancer] when I was 13 and because I was the oldest of the three children I had to take charge. I stayed to live with my father after my mother died, even though I could have moved to New York and had an apartment of my own. I went on being the responsible one in my adult life, always assuming every responsibility. . . .
>
> Because of my need for approval, I've attached myself to a lot of users. I was brought up to invite people for dinner, be the good girl, take a seat in the back of the bus. I hope I'm a little tougher now. I think people get so used to being what they are in childhood, such as the scapegoat or the star, that somehow they go on playing that role forever, even when it isn't called for.
>
> I can think of countless ways I've changed myself. . . . I always had let other people direct me, preferably mother types. . . . Today, what has changed about me is a sense that I can do more. . . . It's up to you to make your own life, to reach out. It's not a question of "I'd like to do this," but "I'm going to do this." You've got to take advantage of opportunities that come your way. An awful lot of people don't. I think there have been hundreds I passed up. At *Seventeen* magazine I had constant offers for other jobs, but I couldn't leave "mother," my female boss. I stayed because I wanted "mother's" love. ("Tempo Woman" Section, *Chicago Tribune,* September 11, 1988, p. 3).

Baer speaks cogently to the importance of listening to your own intuitive voice of self-understanding and being willing to act on it. The idea is not to derogate "mother" figures but to use your own wisdom to decide if their—or anyone else's—advice is sound.

10. *Don't make excuses.*

That is what Bob Wieland, former strength coach of the Green Bay Packers football team, suggested in 1986 when he completed a "walk for hunger" from Los Angeles to Washington, D.C., to raise money for disabled veterans. Wieland had lost his legs—totally—in 1969 when he stepped on a booby-trapped 82mm shell in Vietnam. He made the walk on his hands, wearing rubber pads on both hands and a leather strap under his torso. He is the only double amputee to compete in the Ironman Triathlon in Hawaii. He bench-pressed 507 pounds in 1977, breaking the world record in his weight class. Wieland wrote a book about his experience entitled *One Step at a Time*. His message was simple: You're alive, so use your life to the fullest.

My premise in including this chapter on self-empowerment, or general principles of living, in a book on close relationships is that self-empowerment is essential if we wish to experience satisfying close relationships with others. Self-empowerment comes about through self-knowledge, self-dedication, self-discipline, and self-growth. It is also necessary if we wish to lead a satisfying personal life. Indeed, developing these areas not only serves to enrich our lives, it allows us to make meaningful contributions to the world at large, which, in turn, enhances our ability to experience greater empathy with, and appreciation of, one's partner.

"What lies behind us and what lies before us are tiny matters compared to what lies within us."—Ralph Waldo Emerson

I LOVE YOU.

I'VE LOVED YOU SINCE THE

FIRST MOMENT I SAW YOU. I

GUESS MAYBE I EVEN LOVED

YOU EVEN BEFORE I SAW

YOU.

— Montgomery Cliff to

Elizabeth Taylor

in the movie *A Place in*

the Sun

3

DATING

AND

MEETING

OTHERS

FOR

CLOSENESS

FROM THE MOMENT DIANE SAT DOWN NEXT TO ME
THERE WERE CERTAIN SILENT MESSAGES BETWEEN US. . . .
THERE WAS AN ELECTRICITY BETWEEN US, A PHYSICAL
ENTICEMENT THAT WAS NEW, EXCITING
AND VERY STIMULATING.

—Former Chicago superintendent of police
Richard Brzeczek describing how an affair
started with a plane ride as
he was seated next to an off-duty
flight attendant.

These quotes point out two key features of meeting significant others: people often believe that they can sense almost immediately who will be the "right person" for them; and the mechanism for meeting others is often chance or serendipity.

In the 1990s, singles are more cautious in searching for a partner than they were 10 or 20 years ago. People have been made wary by the divorce rate, which they believe to be a consequence of not being choosy about the qualities of one's partner. The drive to find a partner must be weighed against the possibility of becoming involved with a person who has the AIDS virus or a history of violence in relationships.

Another fact of modern life that keeps people from connecting is the abundance of choice. Single persons, especially those in their 20s and 30s, both desire and are accustomed to a huge array of choices—from the many channels on TV to the variety of flavors of ice cream to the different kinds of music on the radio. This desire extends to the world of dating and mating. Some singles may be overwhelmed with too much choice. They have so much that they are excessively finicky about who they will date; they may reject possibilities at the least sign of imperfection.

Why People Get Close

People usually say they want to meet others in order to "fall in love." More specifically, there are three basic reasons for wanting to meet others for closeness:

1. for the fullest kind of relationship, including satisfying sexual activity and the having and raising of children

2. for friendship and companionship and to share confidences

3. mainly for sex and erotic companionship.

The latter two kinds of relationship may be a prelude to the fullest form of relating. People sometimes develop good friends with whom they later become lovers and develop full close relationships. Likewise, people sometimes enter relationships mainly for sexual pleasure, but the relationship then turns into a full-blown close relationship.

Are people aware of what motivates their behavior when they meet potential partners? I do not believe that we have good research data on this question. An argument has been presented in social psychology that people often are unaware of their cognitive processes (Nisbett & Wilson, 1977), which perhaps would include their reactions to others and attempts to become close to them. I think that when people meet strangers on the spur of the moment—as in shopping areas—their awareness of what they are thinking and feeling may be dampened or distracted.

However, there is a great body of popular writing regarding tactics that people can use to advance their cases with others—for example, how to flirt. During social occasions when people anticipate meeting potential partners (e.g., at singles dances, nightclubs, or bars), they often are quite strategic in how they conduct themselves. They put on fronts (Goffman, 1959), suggesting how important or desirable they are. In these settings, people also try to make determinations about good prospects for them. As people become more experienced in these types of encounters, they may become highly aware of their thoughts and motives, and they are likely to be pretty good judges of others' thoughts and motives as well.

Chemistry A compelling idea among most people is that there is some hard-to-define quality that sometimes emerges in the interaction between people and that it is like a chemical reaction. Consider these observations by a Chicago pastor regarding how some forms of "chemistry" may make relationships work better.

I think chemistry, that immediate sense of warmth that is somehow inexplicable, is very important. But you have to distinguish
between physical attraction and a "personality chemistry." It's
the ability to communicate and the way two personalities com-
plement one another that are key to a successful relationship.
(Kathleen Furore, *Chicago Tribune,* April 28, 1991.)

This article went on to suggest that chemistry can both unite and
divide people. A sampling of experts interviewed believed that chemistry based only on physical attraction or sexual interest can be problematic because it can lead to impulsive behavior, such as two people
jumping into bed the instant they meet. The article also asserted that
true chemistry never dies, and that when it is a part of marriage, helps
cement the union.

As he contemplates beginning an affair with a woman associate,
Rusty, the main character in Scott Turow's (1987) acclaimed novel
Presumed Innocent, provides an illustration of the sexually charged form
of chemistry.

While I stood there, in that pose, she returned.
  "Rusty," she said brightly. A chipper greeting. She pushed
past me. I watched her bend to pull a file from her drawer.
A parched arrow of sensation ran through me, at the way her
tweed skirt pulled across her bottom, the smoothness of her
calves flexing in her hose. . . .
  "I'd like to see you again," I said. (p. 138)

Another example shows that chemistry may be experienced very
quickly in quite unusual circumstances:

Romance blossomed for Doris and Nick when they were stuck
in a traffic jam on Manhattan's West Side Highway—in separate

cars. "We rode next to each other for a while, then he waved and motioned for me to pull off," Doris recalls. "I figured, what the heck, it was broad daylight and he was cute. So I did."

Giving Nick only her first name, Doris agreed to meet him for a drink in a bar later that evening. The chemistry was right, and they began seeing each other intermittently, then regularly, then permanently. The couple, now married and parents of two children, apparently still have a happy relationship. (Carolyn Rushefsky, "A Smile, First Words Open Up the Path to New Romance," Newhouse News Service, December 22, 1987.)

Ellen Berscheid and Elaine Walster (1978) argued that a "magnetic pull" occurs when an individual is physiologically aroused in the presence of another person and has a strong sense of attraction to this person (they called this state "passionate love"). Matches get made when two parties react this way to each other. Such a magnetic pull may occur at first meetings; it also may develop over time in a relationship.

In this culture, we value chemistry in our relationships to a very high degree. We sometimes think that we should not go on with a relationship unless we feel strongly some "electrical spark." This value was displayed in a recent letter to "Dear Abby." A woman in her 40s was engaged to a man who in many ways was perfect. He was successful, handsome, had a great personality, was kind and supportive of her and her career, and was a wonderful companion. The only problem was that she felt no chemistry in their relationship, especially in comparison to an old lover with whom she had felt great chemistry—but who abused her. Should she dump "Mr. Almost Perfect" because she felt no big spark?

Abby said no, that the intensity that this woman desired is not enough over the long run in a relationship—it will fade or come and go. She contended that it was much better to be with a person who had fine credentials but who elicited little chemistry than to be with a more exciting person whose behavior is destructive. Abby suggested that the woman's fiancé sounded like a "first-class catch" and that she would be a fool to leave him and try to find something better. I agree. Angry or violent behavior should not be a necessary condition for achieving chemistry. The type of chemistry involving regular stormy fights and name calling and culminating in wild lovemaking will not nurture a relationship very long. The relationship will surely die if more stability and rationality are not achieved.

Romantic Love Romantic love usually is a powerful magnet for early desire to be with someone and to be physically and emotionally close. It is said to come quickly into the hearts of potential lovers, as illustrated by these lines from Sappho:

> Without warning,
> As a whirlwind swoops upon an oak
> Love shakes my heart.

Romantic love also is said to transform us. When we fall in love, a new world opens up. The senses are more finely honed than usual. Immersion in this experience colors all that we see and do in our daily life—at least for a time—and usually brings with it a torrent of hopes and fears. It sends people down totally different paths in life. As Elizabeth Barret Browning said,

> The face of all the world is changed, I think,
> Since first I heard the footsteps of thy soul
> Move still, oh still, beside me, as they stole
> Betwixt me and the dreadful outer brink
> Of obvious death, where I, who thought to sink,
> Was caught up into love, and taught the whole

Of a new rhythm. (*Oxford Dictionary of Quotations,* 1953, 2nd ed. p. 88, London: Oxford University Press)

Advertisements use romance to sell products. Popular songs speak of love lost and love found. Movies and TV shows glorify romantic love. It is so pervasive in the media that it may become a part of our defining condition. Either we have it and are happy, or do not and are unhappy. Mental and physical health depend on being in love.

People often have stories to tell about when they first knew they were in love. The following was sent to Cheryl Lavin's "Tales from the Front" column in the *Chicago Tribune* to complete the statement "I knew it was love when I . . ."

> In the midst of an argument, he said, "I know how you think." The rest of his statement confirmed that he did. I was out of town at the time and I was so charmed that I took an early flight home so we could wake up together the next morning. (December 16, 1992, "Tempo" section, p. 2)

Falling in love presumably can happen at any moment. Many people believe that they can have a close relationship only with a person for whom they feel strong romantic love (see Averill and Boothroyd, 1977, for a study of college students of that time period and their subscription to romantic love ideals as necessary for close relationships). Many people also believe that this love can go away as quickly as it came, though they usually suggest that the demise of their love is quite remote.

Romantic love has the stature in our moral system of providing a mitigating excuse for unacceptable behavior. People sometimes explain why they strayed from their partner simply by asserting that they started to fall in love with someone else. Professors, doctors, and attorneys have justified dating their students, patients, or clients on this basis. People have even tried to justify plotting murder of their erstwhile partners on the grounds that love for someone else "made them do it."

Some are skeptical about romantic love happening so quickly or about its merit as a basis for a close relationship. Many people have believed lines such as "I love you, and I always will" only to discover that "always" was a pretty short time. A person who has experienced such disillusion will usually place less value on words and immediate impressions about another possible partner. When he or she does begin to believe in a partner and make a commitment to closeness, it likely will have been tested and will have some durability to it. The psychologist John Welwood (1990) suggested that only when people experience heartbreak and shed their idealized images of how a relationship should be are they able to achieve a state of vulnerability that allows them to understand themselves and their partner (or ex-partner) in a much deeper and more compassionate way.

Love and Limerence, a book on romantic love by Dorothy Tennov (1979), suggested that there are people who cannot experience romantic love; thus, they will not meet others for closeness in that way. She also suggested that there is another group of people who are "limerent": that is, they can experience romantic love. Her observations were based on people she interviewed and questionnaires she sent out to diverse groups regarding their romantic love experiences. For example, Tennov said that she met a woman on a flight from Paris to New York who epitomized the nonlimerent type. This woman had experienced many lovers and apparently had had many men fall in love with her. But she was not buying the haste and intensity of their loving gestures: "I simply don't understand how anyone could feel like that, how anyone could be so important to another person." (p. 14)

Although this woman had received some counseling concerning the "neurotic" nature of her skepticism, Tennov did not believe such an attitude to be pathological, just different.

Tennov passed on the following account from a man whom she defined as limerent:

> I think I noticed Sue and felt physically attracted the minute I entered the room that evening. When I saw her dance, I was also impressed with her extraordinary talent. At that point I was ripe, and when she gave me that look, I succumbed totally. We danced together several times, and I was in seventh heaven. At the time, I wasn't thinking, I'm in love with Sue. I was just thoroughly enjoying the situation. I was also noticing everything about her. And everything was beautiful, especially the fact that she seemed to be having the same experience. (p. 18)

This account is similar to the ones we discussed in which people feel an immediate chemistry for one another, but it is less singularly focused on a sexual experience. In fact, sexual passion may not be particularly important for some limerent couples, according to Tennov. On this point she cites the ethological writer Desmond Morris:

> . . . if two young people are in love today, they will laugh at the desperate athleticism of the copulating nonlovers. For them, as for true lovers at all points in history, a fleeting touch on the cheek from the one they adore will be worth more than six hours in thirty-seven positions with someone they do not. (p. 79 in *Love and Limerence*)

Tennov admitted that there are some disadvantages to limerence. For instance, some limerent people become fixated on someone who does not reciprocate their love. As one respondent told Tennov:

> How can I say that my seemingly interminable passion for Eric, a 15-year obsession, was reasonable? Consider the 30,000 hours—I actually calculated my estimation—I spent going over every word he said, every gesture, every letter he wrote, when I

might have . . . been enjoying the company of others. Instead, I was caught in a merry-go-round of wondering how he felt, wishing he would call, anticipating our next time together, or endlessly searching in my recollections of his behavior and my convoluted reconstruction of the possible reasons for his actions for the shreds of hope on which my madness fed.

Long after he no longer bothered to hide from me certain signs of the loss of interest and his vulnerability to the enticements of other women, I could still *see* love in his eyes, even in his ill-treatment of me. (p. 105)

Tennov does not provide a clear, tight definition of limerence, other than a person's degree of susceptibility to romantic love. Nonetheless, her work shows how much value many people place on the feeling of romantic love in deciding whether to try to develop closeness with others.

Readiness To Meet Others

Several factors determine when we are ready for love. Let us consider some of them.

Grieving The process of heeling varies greatly across people and as a function of the type of loss they have experienced. A 60-year-old person suffering the sudden death of their spouse, for example, may grieve for years before feeling ready to try to meet other possible romantic partners again. On the other hand, someone who went through an emotional divorce (see Chapter 8 for discussion of this concept) may move quickly into another close relationship. In his book *Opening Up,* James Pennebaker (1990) suggests that a typical recovery period following divorce or the breakup of a long-term close relationship is eighteen months. But some will take much longer than others. A dating relationship may require less time for healing, but, again, it depends on the individuals involved.

Loneliness In the United States, 9 million men and 14 million women live alone, according to 1990 Bureau of Statistics figures. They are single, divorced, widowed, separated. But living alone does not necessarily produce loneliness, nor does living with others provide a guarantee against it. Indeed, we are all subject to some degree of loneliness. Loneliness reflects mainly a lack of intimacy. It often is a state of mind that involves some unfulfilled goal, such as to have and be with a lover (who may have spurned the lonely person). There is much truth in the saying that a person can be in a room full of people and still feel very lonely.

Louise Bernikow, author of *Alone in America* (1987), argued that women are more willing to admit their loneliness than are men. Women may be more in touch with their feelings, or they simply may be more verbal and articulate about their feelings than are men. Based on her interviews with people across the nation, Bernikow suggested that men often reacted to the loneliness of divorce or dissolution of a close relationship by moving quickly into new romantic liaisons. Women, on the other hand, took longer to reengage.

One of the major findings in Bernikow's study concerned men's reactions when women left them. She said:

> The question of attachment or support or intimacy or connection had risen up like a dragon, quite suddenly and almost always precipitated by a crisis. Women tended to pay more attention to these issues, to worry or care almost constantly about their relationships with other people. Men took it for granted that there would be "someone there." It was as though, for many of them, they felt that if they did what was expected of them—

namely, got good jobs and made decent livings—the rest would somehow fall into place. . . . I had the impression, particularly with men who had been left by women, that those women had been background noise, like the television set turned on. They had been "someone there" at the end of the day. (p. 61, *Alone in America*)

Bernikow's evidence resonates with the view that women not only are more articulate about relationship issues, but are also more adroit at buffering themselves against loss and consequent loneliness by using their skill at nurturing networks of friends. Bernikow's respondents indicated that loneliness may come upon us quickly, at unexpected moments. You may look at your marriage partner across the breakfast table and wonder what is wrong. You are not supposed to feel detached in the company of the person you love. But you do. As the mother's advice to the new bride of another time went, "Now, you'll learn what loneliness is all about." This sensation is frequently the start of a slow erosion in one partner's love for and commitment to another.

When people are lonely, they frequently reach out to others for comfort. When this is done before they have had time to work on and heal from a past relationship, it is untimely for the individual. If it is perceived as an act of desperation rather than a quest for an equal relationship, others likely will be less supportive. When a relationship is begun because of the needs of a person who is "on the rebound," it has a major handicap at the outset. Such situations are not conducive to healthy, stable close relationships. Often one partner is too needy while the other feels too used. Nevertheless, many relationships start this way, and some—probably not a lot—survive. In others, the new partner may be merely a good distractor for the needy person and help that person get back on his or her feet and begin to heal.

Social Anxiety As Mary Leary (1983) has documented, some people have chronic feelings of social discomfort and are awkward in interacting with others—especially others with whom they wish to be close. All of us probably have acute feelings of social anxiety in various social settings or in our interactions with certain other people. But when we have those feelings all the time, we very probably will not be able to meet our needs for closeness.

Intimacy Motivation This term was coined by Dan McAdams (e.g., see his 1988 book *Intimacy: The Need to Be Close*), whose work over more than a decade makes a strong case for the existence of a personality factor in which some people have a strong need for close, warm, intimate relationships. These people appear to emphasize depth and quality of interaction with a few others to whom they can dedicate a lot of time and focus. Theoretically, they are not interested in controlling others and are more trusting, experience greater subjective well-being, and are driven to want to make contributions to others based on their experience and resources.

Criteria People Use in Deciding Whom To Date

Social psychologists have invested 20-plus years in establishing a number of factors that contribute to why people *like* others and sometimes become close to others. I will briefly review some of these factors. (Brehm [1992] provides a relatively full treatment of theories of interpersonal attraction.)

Similarity of Attitudes, Beliefs, and Values Starting with Byrne's classic (1971) research, a large body of work has pointed toward the power of attitudinal, belief, and value similarity as posi-

Drawing by Ziegler; ©1991 The New Yorker Magazine, Inc.

tively affecting the liking of another person at all stages of relating. Presumably, people similar to ourselves validate our own opinions and also lead us to anticipate positive interactions with them. Usually, attitudes, beliefs, and values are socialized into us in a certain cultural context—loosely forming "our background." Although people tend to like and develop relationships with persons of similar backgrounds, there is now considerable dating across ethnic, racial, and socioeconomic lines. Perhaps the socioeconomic barrier is the greatest barrier of them all, because people who differ in this dimension often have quite different attitudes and beliefs.

Theodore Newcomb (1961) addressed the question of whether a given person A likes person B because A *thinks* that B is similar to A, or because B *actually is* similar to A. In an ingenious study at the University of Michigan, he collected information on the attitudes, personality, and various demographic factors of male undergraduates living in a rooming house. Then, he randomly assigned them to roommates. At the start of their acquaintance, men who thought they held similar opinions on important issues liked each other more than did those who thought they did not hold similar opinions. When students started going to classes and actually spending time with their roommates, actual attitudinal similarity became a better predictor of who liked whom. Men who indeed had similar opinions were more likely to become friends than were men who actually had less similar opinions. This effect has been supported in further research and suggests that actual interaction may offset initial expectations about another's similarity and have the greater impact on liking.

Physical Attraction

My looks grease the palm of life, but I resent that they're so important in our society. I resent that people are excluded. . . . But I'm certainly not talking about myself, because it's clear I've gotten the long end of the stick. (Candice Bergen interviewed in *The Kansas City Times,* April 14, 1984, p. C-2)

Candice Bergen's point about her looks reflects a potent truth for early relating and dating. Physical attraction is a factor that determines people's choices, and on which people tend to match themselves when they settle into dating relationships. Physical attraction appears to be a critical early ingredient that is necessary for the relationship to go forward. As a couple becomes deeply involved, however, physical attraction may become mixed with "psychological attraction." Research evidence suggests that physical attraction probably will not hold the relationship together over time; it is not as good a "glue" for a relationship as the similarity factor (Berscheid & Walster, 1978).

To a high degree, beauty is culturally determined and in the eye of the beholder. Nonetheless, our perceptions of beauty matter a lot in how we treat others. Actress Kim Basinger told *Allure* magazine in September 1993 that being physically beautiful has its drawbacks. She said that many men seemed to want to "jump your bones," and that was something her husband, actor Alec Baldwin, has had to learn to deal with.

Those not blessed with what our culture deems to be good looks have a different experience, as seen in the following column by Cheryl Lavin ("Tales from the Front," *Chicago Tribune*, June 9, 1991, Tempo Section, p. 3).

Your mother told you: "Beauty is only skin deep. Pretty is as pretty does. You can't tell a book by its cover."

Was your mother wrong? Was she lying?

Do you have to be good-looking just to get a date?

Do you have to be attractive to have a relationship? . . .

Diane is 35. She has a good job, plenty of friends. But she hasn't had a date in 11 years.

Why?

"The bottom line is that guys don't like me because I'm not pretty. I'm not so ugly that people cross the street to avoid me. But I also would not make a man feel proud to have me on his arm."

The last relationship Diane had was when she was in her early 20s. She was engaged to Dale, who used to tell her how lucky he was to have found her. . . .

It seems that the reason Dale felt so lucky to have found Diane was because he was tired of dating pretty girls. Pretty girls always cheated on him. So he took some personal advice from that old Calypso song, "If you want to be happy for the rest of your life, never make a pretty woman your wife."

He had made up his mind to find a girl that no other guy would want.

"And that was me," says Diane. "The first time he told me that I cried."

Dale felt bad and apologized. . . .

"He asked me if I thought I was pretty. I said, 'No.'

"He said, 'Well, then, what's the problem?'"

Since then, Diane has only had one real date [she did not continue with Dale]. In the middle of the evening, the gentleman told her they wouldn't be going out anymore because his friends wouldn't understand if they saw them together. He had a reputation to maintain! . . .

The most traditional way to meet men is probably through friends, and Diane has a lot of them. But they don't fix her up. In fact, she has been fixed up only once in life.

"I'll never forget the guy's face when I opened the door. He looked at our mutual friend who was standing there and said, 'Thanks a lot. I owe you." And it wasn't in a pleasant tone of voice. . . ."

As revealed in Elaine Hatfield and Susan Sprecher's (1986) provocative book on physical beauty, *Mirror, Mirror,* physical attractiveness appears to have a broad impact on our minds. If we are not careful, we form halo-type, global impressions that attractive people are necessarily intelligent, socially skilled, wise, virtuous, and so on. In point of fact, they may be deficient in many of these areas. On the other hand, our feelings about physical attractiveness also affect us when we believe that we are interacting with a less attractive other.

Looks can even affect an interaction between two strangers talking on the telephone. In a classic study, Snyder, Tanke, and Bersceid and colleagues (1977) led college men to believe that they would be having a phone conversation with a woman whose picture showed her to be either very attractive or very unattractive. It did not bear the image of the actual woman to whom they would talk on the phone. During the call, the men who thought that they were talking to an attractive woman were more friendly and sociable than were the men who thought that they were talking to an unattractive woman. The woman on the other end of the phone line—also a college student participating in the study—showed in-kind behavior. If the man was friendly, she was friendly. If he was abrupt, so was she. Thus, the men's expectations about the woman's looks had channeled the phone conversation to make it one of positive or negative interaction.

A Complex Set of Qualities One final story will end this discussion of how beauty and other elements blend together in relationships—even as people age. In 1992, Senator Edward (Ted) Kennedy, age 60, of Massachusetts married Victoria Reggie, a 38-year-old Washington, D.C., attorney whose family had been close to the Kennedy family for many years. While each had been divorced, their love story is vintage Americana. An older wealthy, educated, powerful, legendary, historically important man marries a younger well-educated professional woman who happens to be quite attractive. Interestingly though, this relationship, which appears to be going along well, is one that involved a merger of some dissimilarity. His background is New England, wealthy, public service oriented, and liberal. Hers is Louisiana, Southern, business oriented, wealthy, and more conservative. Apparently though, as revealed in a *Boston Globe,* October 7, 1992, interview by Jack Thomas, the dissimilarities are dissipating in light of the worldview commonalities being established in the relationship. In this interview, Vicki held his hand—which the interviewer reported trembled slightly, presumably because of Ted's long-term drinking problem—and even jumped into the conversation to defend the Senator against people who had attacked him. She said: "My sense is that those are people who don't know you. They're people who don't know us together, and I think it's gratifying that people who, when they get to know Ted, all that falls away and they get to know the real person."

Later in the same interview, Vicki again intervenes in a question-answer exchange by, as the interviewer says, "refusing to join in conversation that diminishes him." Such a loving scene, carried out in the Senator's Cape Cod summer home, portends well for this relationship. Possibly Ted and Vicki each has found a partner who meets well the complex set of criteria they have for closeness at this point in their lives. The moral of this story is that criteria cannot be readily analyzed apart from the web of circumstances each of us has around our life and the needs manifest in our particular passage at the time we look for closeness.

The "Marriage Crunch"

There has been great media attention given to the differential availability rates of males and females for marriage. In 1986 Yale sociologists Neil Bennet and Patricia Craig and Harvard economist David Bloom disclosed data indicating that for white, college-educated women born in the mid-1950s who are still single at 30, there is only a 20 percent chance that they will ever marry; by the age of 35 the odds drop to 5 percent, and by age 40, the odds of marriage are 2.6 percent. Within days of this disclosure, a dialogue of awesome proportions began about the merit of such data and what they meant for single, career women near or in their 30s.

While they raise important questions, Bennet and colleagues' data are subject to serious qualification. For instance, they were based on a limited sample and have not been replicated since the mid-1980s.

And unfortunately, the authors overlooked several important aspects of women's approach to marriage. For one thing, failure to marry does not necessarily mean failure to be close to someone. And unmarried close relationships have certain advantages. As one single woman put it,

> The difference between being unhappily single and unhappily married is that, in the first case, one phone call can turn it around. The other takes a lot more work. I enjoy having control over my environment. (*Newsweek,* June 2, 1986)

Other reasons why some women have not married by age 30 include the following: (1) They may have been pursuing their career, as many men do during this period; (2) in the pursuit of their career, these women may have moved often, making the formation of a close relationship difficult; and (3) they may plan to get married after dating widely and establishing their career—feeling that such preconditions are conducive to better marriages.

The thesis of the 1986 study had been discussed before. In 1978 Sociologist Jessie Bernard postulated that educated, career-oriented, 30-ish women had a bad lot in the numbers game because the majority of men available for these women had much less impressive qualifications in terms of education, sophistication, and ability to express feelings.

My observation is that the "marriage crunch" is a real issue for many women approaching mid-life, especially for those who want to find similarly educated men, get married, and have children. If a woman does not want that whole package—for example, if a similar level of education is not important, or if the woman does not want to have biological children (and thus could more readily sample from men who are older and already have had children)—she will have an easier time finding someone.

More imposing for women is the lack of available men age 65 and older, mainly because men die at an average of seven years earlier than do women. A 67-year-old widow in the Boston area made the following statement regarding the availability of males for women in her age group:

> I went to a party last week, and there were 49 women and 11 men there. . . . And when you go on any kind of trip with older people, there are never any men. . . . I'll tell you the truth . . . We're all looking for a man. Maybe not for a marriage, but for companionship—to go out to dinner, to a movie, to a concert. And to take us home afterwards. I wish there were more men around. You find you don't know how to converse with a man after you lose your husband. It's very, very lonely. And how can we—at our age—find a man? (told to Nathan Cobb in a *Dallas Morning News* article entitled "Lack of men plagues events for elderly," April 3, 1983, p. 10F)

As this woman implies, women in this age range may not care if they remarry. Mostly, they just want companionship. The same article made a couple of other important points about closeness in the person's later years. One, men who are in demand in retirement settings often extend themselves in intimacy the same way they would in marriage, but may not want to go to the trouble of getting married. One man said, "I'm just better off this way. . . . There's nothing hanging over my head. If I want to help her out with things, I do. If I don't, I don't." Too, as age increases into the 80s, when men are really in short supply, women tend to compete less for men and to bond more with one another. As one said, "The longer you live alone, the less you care about living with a man. . . . You find that you can go out when you want and come in when you want."

What about people in their twenties? According to the Census Bureau, there are 121 to 128 single men for every 100 single women in the 20 to 29 age range. So rejoice if you are a woman born after about 1965. However, these women may divorce after a lengthy marriage and then not be able to readily find a new husband. The pools of men who are well qualified for marriage appears to get smaller each decade as a woman ages.

There are others ways that the pool of available partners becomes expanded. For example, a common practice in this culture is for older men to date younger women (with the age discrepancy sometimes as much as 20 or 30 years). Presumably, such a practice relates to the lure of the women's youth and attractiveness and the men's resources such as wealth and maturity (Kenrick & Trost, 1989). Increasingly in recent years, however, older women and younger men also have formed relationships, perhaps because the women desire the men's youth and attractiveness, while the men value the women's resources.

Women seeking male partners are not the only ones facing a potentially tough challenge. What about men seeking women, or women or men seeking members of the same sex as partners? Not as much has been written about these questions. But from visiting support groups for widowed, divorced, or separated people, I can tell you that there are many men at all ages who feel that they cannot readily find the "right person" for closeness. They may have options, but they often speak of the practical problems involved in trying to meet single women in the same age range who have strong qualities for relating and are ready for a close relationship. They too complain of not knowing the new rules for dating, after having been "out of circulation" for many years. They too indicate disappointment that some women want them "just for sex," rather than for fuller closeness and intimacy. In short, there likely are as many men who periodically are miserable in their quest to find closeness as there are women who feel this way.

Homosexuals usually have more restricted sampling pools. That is particularly true in areas of the world where there are relatively few of them, where acknowledging one's homosexuality could put one in danger. In addition to the obstacles they face in their search for available partners, they have to deal with the stigma associated with their behavior. Most large cities now have gay and lesbian bars where meeting potential partners is common.

How People Meet

Opening Lines All meeting situations require us to say something to a stranger. Knapp (1984) posits a set of stages of interaction from the very beginning to the end of a relationship and typical lines that go with these stages. These lines, presented on the facing page, show that after *initiating* a conversation, a person may *experiment* with a different line to see if the other person seems interested. Then the stages progress through *intensifying, integrating,* and *bonding* the relationship. A few interim steps could be added between experimentation and intensification, which might include determining if the other person wants to go out on a date, regularly go out together (and possibly terminate other ongoing relationships), and have sexual relations. Each of these interim steps also has its own set of typical lines. The ending of a bond is shown by the stages Knapp refers to as *differentiating, circumscribing, stagnating, avoiding,* and finally *terminating* the relationship.

For practically every social occasion and motivation, there are lines and scripts. As we become experienced in the meeting and dating game, we learn these—sometimes so well that we become cynical about their use. Nonetheless, there are not many other ways strangers can begin the process of meeting others than via such conventions.

Social Penetration Theory The process in which strangers size up one another, go into greater and greater depths of self-

Stages of Interaction and Possible Interaction Lines

Process	Stage	Representative Lines
Coming Together	*Initiating*	"Hi, how ya doin'?" "Fine. You?"
	Experimenting	"Oh, so you like to ski . . so do I." "You do? Great. Where do you go?"
	Intensifying	"I . . . I think I love you." "I love you too."
	Integrating	"I feel so much a part of you." "Yes, we are like one person. . ."
	Bonding	"I want to be with you always." "Let's get married."
Coming Apart	*Differentiating*	"I just don't like big social gatherings." "Sometimes I don't understand you. . ." "I'm certainly not like you at all."
	Circumscribing	"Did you have a good time on your trip?" "What time will dinner by ready?"
	Stagnating	"What's there to talk about?" "Right. We each know what the other will say."
	Avoiding	"I'm so busy. I just don't know when I'll be able to see you." "If I'm not around when you try, you'll understand."
	Terminating	"I'm leaving you . . . don't bother contacting me. . ." "Don't worry."

Source: Adapted from Knapp, M.L. (1984). *Interpersonal Communication and Human Relationships.* Newton, MA: Allyn & Bacon, p. 33.

disclosure, and finally become intimate has been studied by social psychologists. Irwin Altman and Dalmus Taylor's (1973) provocative social penetration theory focused on the early aspects of close relationship formation. They proposed that this process is analogous to peeling back the skin of an onion, as people first get to know others superficially and then dig deeper into feelings and important attitudes and beliefs.

Often in early relating, one partner moves more quickly than does the other in "peeling back his or her onion skin," and this person may feel vulnerable. This problem can be corrected by each partner working toward a more equal level of self-disclosure. A reasonable deduction from research and therapy work on this issue is that such equality is essential if a relationship is to prosper (Kelley et al., 1983).

Flirting   Flirting has not received sufficient attention in the close relationship literature. Sociologist Georg Simmel in 1950 described flirting as a nonserious, playful activity between persons possibly interested in one another that is participated in simply for the pleasure of the actors involved. More recently, communications scholar Barbara Montgomery (1986) conducted some of the most systematic work on the purposes and nature of flirting. Montgomery found that people indicated they had a variety of motives when they flirted, from simple friendliness to a desire to attract another for sexual relations. Sometimes, of course, respondents indicated that they were not aware of their motives when they flirted; they may not even have been aware of their flirting behavior or the flirting behavior of someone interested in them.

Montgomery emphasized the nonverbal cues that people send to one another when they flirt. One of the most powerful of these is how one dresses. For example, in this culture, miniskirts and leather skirts are often considered trademarks of sexiness when worn on bodies that carry them well.

There are major sex differences involved in flirting. In an experiment conducted by Antonia Abbey (1982), male and female college students engaged in a short group discussion and then answered questions about the event. The males rated the females' behavior as indicating more sexual interest in the males than did the females in explaining their own behavior; in fact, the females believed they were just being friendly. Thus, the sexes likely interpret differently signals emitted in mixed company. Apparently, college-age men (and probably men of all ages) tend to look for clues telling them women are interested in having sexual relations with them. Montgomery's research also supported this conclusion. In her work, women mainly emphasized the fun and friendly nature of flirting. Date rape may be one consequence of this difference between the sexes.

Instructors in the art of flirting emphasize limited self-disclosure (one should not reveal too much about oneself too soon or discuss delicate topics, but should open up a bit in order to move the other person in the same direction), careful listening and observing skills, and focus on feelings. But the rules of flirting are neither fixed, well known, nor clear cut. What is acceptable at one time and in one social climate may not be at another. And those who flirt also might misunderstand one another's intentions.

Flirting is a particularly hazardous endeavor. When flirting occurs in work or educational contexts and among persons of different levels of power in the institution, it may be construed as sexual harassment.

Popular Advice about Meeting People

Magazines, newspapers, therapists, match-making services, and commentators of all stripes join in providing advice on meeting that special person. It is a huge industry that has developed parallel to the development of a high divorce rate and the mobility in jobs and where we spend our lives.

The Singles Almanac by Jeffrey Ullman provides all kinds of advice on dating and what to beware of on the singles scene. For example, Ullman suggested that singles should: keep a sense of humor; listen well when on a date (people often talk too much and mostly about themselves in first encounters); do not expect perfection; do not bash the opposite sex, regardless of how many times you feel you have been "burned" by its members; and do not drink too much.

Dallas therapist Bill Entzminger conducts a class called How to Marry Someone Stable. He tells people to look for signs of instability in a person's life such as financial chaos, drug and alcohol use, and mental disturbance. He also suggests that people recognize that time is their best friend in relationships. He advocates at least one-year waits between engagements and marriage. More subtle pieces of advice were offered in a November 1992 *Chicago Tribune* "Tales from the Front" column by readers such as: Never date a man who does not smile when he sees kids doing cute things. Never date a man who tells off-color jokes and giggles. Never date a man who takes money from his parents after age 30, or who flirts with your girlfriends. Never date a man who does not like any kind of animal. Never date a woman who still keeps all her stuffed animals on her bed. Never date a woman who cannot keep a secret, or who reapplies her lipstick after every course at the restaurant and looks at herself in every shiny surface.

In the August 1989 issue of *Cosmopolitan,* an article entitled "Hunting the Buried Treasure: A Good Man," by Patricia Bernstein, advised women as follows: to avoid the recently divorced man; to go for a man with a sense of humor and with whom you can be your "true, unvarnished self"; to not be swayed by a man with a lot of money—who will be spoiled; and to consider friendship as a better basis for lasting relationships than passion.

Where People Meet Others

Bars and the Pickup Scene As they have been throughout the last two centuries in the United States, bars and nightclubs are places where people seek partners for closeness. Bars, in particular, have a poor reputation, even among their most devoted clientele. People contend that potential partners found in bars often have alcohol problems, AIDS or other sexually transmitted diseases, or histories of violence in relationships. (One might note though that a good percentage of potential partners in any setting may have some of these same qualities.) As one searching physician, age 33, said about the Dallas, Texas, bar scene: "I think the bar scene is horrible. A lot of people who go there go there to hunt rather than to strike up a friendship—or, as the song goes, they want to be abused or to abuse" (article on "The Dallas Singles Scene," *Dallas Magazine,* June 2, 1985).

Bars are known for the deception practiced by people "on the make." They are seen as "meat markets." Consider this story told by a woman age 21 and single:

> The funniest thing happened to me in a country-western bar. This guy asked me to dance. He handed me his card, and said, "I would really like to call you." So I gave him my telephone number—which I really shouldn't have; I really wasn't interested, but it just blurted out. So I had this card, and I filled it over, and on the back side it said "Deanna" and a telephone number.
>
> So the next day, he called me and said, "Let's get together and do something." So I was perfectly honest. I said, "Thank you for teaching me to two-step, but I don't really want to go out." And I said, "But would you like Deanna's number?" There was this long pause on the telephone, and he goes, "Well, yeah."

So I gave him the number and he goes, "This is the weirdest conversation I've ever had."

Personal Ads Despite some lingering embarrassment, personal ads are increasingly becoming an accepted way to meet others. Consider the following ad appearing in the *New York Law Journal* in 1989: "Striking, blond, blue-eyed, female attorney (Italian), 27, enjoys film, theater, country weekends, zoos, travel, museums, seeks male counterpart for lasting relationship.

This ad is aimed toward a specific audience, namely other lawyers, and like most ads, it paints a quite favorable picture of the person placing it (whether or not that picture is deserved). As reflected in this item, many people who take out personal ads today are highly professional and well educated.

Some people prefer to meet others via personal introductions made by friends, in the belief that the people met this way will be more similar to them than those met through an ad. But friends' lists of eligible persons are only so long. The college setting provides a ready meeting place, but most people are not in college and may not encounter many singles in their work environments either. Ads therefore can be a logical way to increase the number of people you meet. The provide anonymity, unless you wish to disclose your identity. And they can be targeted quite specifically (e.g., to a specific religious orientation). They also offer a variety of formats. In addition to the standard one, in which respondents send letters to an ad-placer's box number, there now are several nationwide personal ad companies using 900 numbers. They purchase space in newspapers and invite people to place free personal ads there. Respondents who see an ad they like can call an extension and hear a greeting from the ad-placer; then they can leave their own message. The price of the call can reach $7 per minute, or more.

Other Meeting Grounds The workplace traditionally has been a good meeting ground for singles. That fact remains true, especially in work environs in which there are many singles representing a range of ages. In this setting, one gets to know someone fairly well, and chemistry can develop quickly or over a period of time. In her book *Love, Power, & Sex in the Workplace,* management professor Lisa Mainiero (1989) discussed meeting in this setting. She argued that people should: (1) stay away from extramarital affairs; (2) not meet behind closed doors for passionate embraces or more; (3) not call each other by cute nicknames; (4) not touch each other in the office; (5) make sure they do their jobs well; and (6) beware of the company's policies about romances between two people in the same office.

In many large cities, museums, supermarkets, laundromats, and a variety of organizations have "singles nights" that invite people to mingle—with the idea that just maybe they will meet someone special. Health spas also have been a popular meeting ground for singles. Many large churches and synagogues now have singles activities. And secular singles organizations that plan social events and dances now exist in practically every sizable city in the United States. Of course, there are more exotic ways to meet: For instance, members of the Sunbelt Singles Auto Club in Atlanta, Georgia, stick a numbered decal on their car windows, hoping to meet a partner as they drive along the area's freeways and streets. When drivers spot someone who appeals to them, they can send a note to the club, which forwards the message, unopened.

Mail-Order Partners This method of meeting has become somewhat popular among males looking for younger, old-fashioned wives and among women outside the United States who wish to marry an American in order to enhance their material quality of life. It also has traditionally been used by males whose life-styles do not allow them to meet many women (e.g., farmers, and ranchers in relatively isolated locales). An article in the *Dallas Morning News* by Maryln Schwartz (July 29, 1982, Section C) reported that mail-order introduction services in the late '70s and early '80s had sparked more than 7,000 marriages between American men and women from such countries as the Philippines and Australia. One correspondence organization called American-Asian Worldwide Services provides information on hundreds of men and women who desire to meet potential marriage partners in these different countries. A 46-year-old man who had used these services revealed in an interview that "I had a long talk with myself about why I wanted to do this. . . . I asked myself if it was an ego trip, a way to get such a young, pretty wife. But no, I know this is the right woman."

This man went on to say that he had tried everything—singles organizations, being "fixed up" by friends, personal ads, etc.—but that he had not found the right mate. He said, "I wanted an old-fashioned woman. I wanted someone who catered to me."

Such remarks at one time were not unusual among men using the mail-order method of finding a wife. They often claimed that American women have become too independent and are not good homemakers anymore. However, recent work by sociologist Davor Japlicka (reported in the *Dallas Morning News,* October 1, 1989, page 4F, article by Paula Fombi) has indicated that the stereotype of a dominating Western male and a subordinate Asian female is no longer tenable. He argued, based on a sample of 2000 couples, that these types of marriages were just as egalitarian as were marriages fashioned in other ways.

Alternatives to "Traditional" Close Relationships

We now can celebrate a diversity of close relationship life-styles in this culture. Each can work and be psychologically beneficial for the individual. People may have gay or lesbian relationships, may remain single and date different people, or may be alone and not date at all. Although prejudices are fading somewhat, and terms like "old maid" have just about died out in the last couple of decades, people who remain unmarried or engage in alternative relationship arrangements continue to endure stigma. As one single man in his 30s said in reference to how he is perceived by married associates, "Some men are jealous of my lifestyle, and others see me as a poor, unfortunate soul looking for love. The truth is probably somewhere in between" (Peter King, "Singles say they're content with what life alone has to offer," *Dallas Morning News,* December 15, 1985, page 4F).

Many singles view their lives in a positive light. A middle-aged single male discussing his life situation in the King article said, "It provides a tremendous opportunity for personal growth . . . to direct my life in a way that I'm most comfortable with. . . . You make your own decisions." A 31-year-old single woman interviewed for the article indicated that independence was the main advantage of singles life for her. As for drawbacks, she said, "The biggest downside is when I'm ill. I haven't trained my cat how to make toast."

Many people have come to the conclusion that because of their looks, their physical condition, their age, or some other reason, they never will have a marital partner, or even a romantic close relationship. They may or may not grieve this condition and feel very lonely. Any human being can make her or his life valuable, however, regardless of whether that life has been blessed (or cursed) with the presence of lovers.

THE WOMEN ARE NOT SOLITAIRES.

THEIR STRENGTH LIES IN THEIR

CAPACITY FOR ASSIMILATING

PERSONAL RELATIONSHIPS,

IN LIVING FOR THE PRIMACY

OF FAMILY . . .

—Author's note for

class discussion, 1988

4

MALE-FEMALE
DIALOGUE

LUST FOR FREEDOM, LUST FOR INTIMACY; THE INVETERATE

YIN AND YANG OF THE MALE PSYCHE

—Anonymous

In this chapter we will consider the ongoing and often fervent dialogue about the differences in how females and males engage in close relationships, including such issues as how such relationships have changed over time, language differences between men and women, and gender stereotyping. But first we will look at a subject often overlooked in the "war of the sexes"—what men and women have in common.

Fundamental Commonalities Between Women and Men

Analyses of gender differences abound in the study of how males and females approach close relationships. At a deeper level, however, men and women share many of the same motives, hopes, fears, and strategies for living. As the psychologist Harry Stack Sullivan (1953) once commented, "We are all much more simply human than otherwise." Both sexes want to find meaning and make their lives more stimulating and satisfying. Women and men strive for personal control and the power to achieve their desired ends. They each seek opportunity, accomplishment, and the resources necessary to meet personal goals. They want to be accorded the esteem of their family and colleagues and to be duly recognized for their contributions to society. Members of each sex hurt and experience mental anguish when close relationships end. Both can be very loving or very hurtful. These are human attributes that cut across all kinds of groupings such as gender, ethnicity, race, or nationality. They are universals and reflect a tremendous foundation of commonality.

In *The Lenses of Gender: Transforming the Debate on Sexual Inequality* (1993), Sandra Bem offered an argument that is congenial to this emphasis on commonalities. She took issue with what she viewed as this culture's imposition of a strict male/female dichotomy on virtually every aspect of human experience. She further argued that this "gender polarization" is one reason why America is so uncomfortable with gender nonconformity, particularly homosexuality.

Too often, gender-stereotyping is a knee-jerk behavior in this culture. And it is a problem. Where differences clearly exist in how females and males behave and relate, it may be that neither sex's approach is less effective or represents a morally incorrect position. We like to find scapegoats for what is wrong with us or our world. We often look for easy answers by blaming the other sex and by claiming that there are major differences between "us" and "them," implying that "we" are the more evolved representative of the human species. This scapegoating tendency coupled with the gender polarization Bem discussed contribute much to what has been referred to as a virtual "war of the sexes" in this culture.

Traditional Relationships

Beth Bailey's (1988) *From Front Porch to Back Seat* urged that in the decades preceding the late 1960s, there were relatively clearcut rules for how men and women courted and later performed the roles of husband and wife in marriage. The rules of courtship (e.g., who picked up whom on a date and who paid for the date) and marriage (e.g., the different responsibilities of the husband and wife) were prescribed by what people learned from those around them. Most of the time, these rules were not challenged. The 1960s, however, began a time of serious challenge to prescribed marital and gender roles and to the prevailing conception of the family.

In the traditional relationships that dominated before the mid-1970s, the husband focuses on career and out-of-home activities, while the wife focuses on supporting the husband's career, raising the children, and in general taking care of the domestic side of life. Implicit in this scheme is the second-place status of the wife and her work; she does not develop her career potential as the husband does and, accordingly, does not rate the same priority in major decision-making situations.

By the mid-1970s, more egalitarian close relationships began to appear. In the purest form of this arrangement, the two partners recognize and communicate about one another's desires regarding career and family decision making. They cooperate in the responsibilities of daily living, equally sharing child rearing and domestic responsibilities. In principle, control and manipulative strategies of influence are less likely to occur in egalitarian relationships. Based on my own research and discussions with many couples, I believe that egalitarian relationships now strongly rival traditional ones.

Women's motivations to reject traditional relationships and seek more egalitarian forms are well illustrated in the following quotes.

I come from the wrong generation, and I hope that there'll never be another one like us. We were taught—no, we weren't taught, we were brainwashed into believing that his work was the most important thing. I hated taking care of the kids by myself all the time. I wanted him to be involved. But I didn't even dare ask for it because I thought there was something the matter with me. (quoted by respondent in work reported by Rubin, 1983)

Over the last 30 years, I have grown and moved on to become a much broader person. I have finished my college education, developed a profession, new friends, and a strong sense of self-confidence. My husband has not grown. He has not changed or moved forward in our relationship. He continues to live in the past. He was short to condemn me for going forward, telling me

I was not totally committed to our relationship. He lived in jealousy, mistrust, denial, and wanted to be central in all that I did and thought about. The relationship was strained for the last 20 years and had begun to drain my energy. (Harvey, in progress)

Without denouncing traditional approaches to relationships per se, I do take issue with the lock-step processes of decision making that sometimes characterize these approaches. There should be no presumed givens about whose needs come first in a relationship. Each partner should have a voice in determining matters such as whose career is given priority and when the conception of a child (or children) will occur. There also should be choice in how a couple decides to conduct their relationship. They should not feel compelled to do things the way their parents did. Further, each partner deserves an opportunity for self-fulfillment. Relationship contributions and personal needs have to be balanced to accommodate long-term personal and relationship growth. Finally, couples should regularly and explicitly discuss their arrangement, its possible long-term implications, and what is fair to all parties concerned. They should avoid resorting to the tactics of control and manipulation that plague some traditional relationships.

Two Disparate Marriages In her 1982 book *The Future of Marriage*, Jessie Bernard argued that men and women had such disparate experiences of traditional marriages that there really were two marriages, "his" and "hers."

She believed that traditional marriage—with its domestic, child-raising, and emotional caretaker obligations falling mostly on the female—constitutes an emotional health hazard for the female. Bernard said, "Until yesterday, and for most women even today, every wife becomes a *house*wife" (1982, p. 43). Bernard asserted that in this context, marriage made the woman sick, both figuratively and literally. Bernard argued that women who were exclusively housewives were more subject to depression, low self-esteem, sleeping and eating disorders, and other maladies than were women who were out in the work world. Bernard also discussed how marriage even led to a lower status for women because when they married, they lost certain legal rights. In commenting on evidence that married women tend to say they are happier than do unmarried women, Bernard said:

> . . . to be happy in a relationship which imposes so many impediments on her, as traditional marriage does, a woman must be slightly ill mentally. Women accustomed to expressing themselves freely could not be happy in such a relationship; it would be too confining and too punitive. We therefore "deform" the minds of girls, as traditional Chinese used to deform their feet, in order to shape them into happiness in marriage. It may therefore be that married women say they are happy because they are sick rather than sick because they are married. (p. 50)

Bernard went on to say that because "yesterday's wife" has put so many eggs into one basket, to the exclusion of almost every other pursuit, she has more at stake in making a go of it. When marriage fails, the woman has more to lose—everything, in too many instances—and nothing to fall back on (such as a good career that was uninterrupted by marriage). The high divorce rate in recent years has made it clear that there was much truth to Bernard's assertions. Many women who put their careers on hold to raise families indeed had little to fall back on when divorce occurred. That reality has become clear to the daughters of many of these women. The daughters have learned that they must be careful not to give up their independence, which is premised in large measure on having a career. While many of these younger women have been the primary caretakers in their families, they also have managed to keep their careers going.

Bernard's position, which is generally consistent with much current feminist theory on relationships, probably contributed to the evolution of women's rights and equitable close relationships with men. However, it and similar ones have stimulated counterarguments, frequently from women. For example, there are different types of "traditional" close relationships. They vary in degree of mutuality, explicitness in decision making, and the extent to which the couple rigidly adheres to one set of role prescriptions. Not all of the women in these relationships are (or were) deluded in thinking that the traditional orientation was best for them. Bernard's linkage of traditional marriage and a wife's poor mental health may be unfair to women who have not been deluded, did have options, and yet have elected some form of traditional marriage.

Bernard (1982) contended that, unequivocally, traditional marriage is good for men. She said:

> There are few findings more consistent, less equivocal, more
> convincing than the sometimes spectacular and always impres-
> sive superiority on almost every index—demographic, psycho-
> logical, or social—of married over never-married men. Despite
> all the jokes about marriage in which men indulge, all the
> complaints they lodge against it, it is one of the greatest boons
> of their sex. Employers, bankers, and insurance companies have
> long since known this. And when they know it or not, men need
> marriage more than women do. As Samuel Johnson said,
> marriage is, indeed, "the best state for man in general, and
> every man is a worse man in proportion as he is unfit for the
> married state." (pp. 16-17)

She also argued that "At the present time, at least, if not in the future, there is no better guarantor of long life, health, and happiness for men than a wife well socialized to perform the 'duties of a wife,' willing to devote her life to taking care of him, providing, even enforcing, the regularity and security of a well-ordered home" (pp. 24-25)—and connected this to the fact that men typically remarry much more quickly than do women—usually within three years of divorce.

Bernard's evidence notwithstanding, how convincing is her case for the value of marriage for men at the present time?

It seems that to the extent that couples share economic and domestic contributions to their relationship, no great advantage accrues to either partner. Also, there certainly are men who feel that they are trapped in marriages that are not good for them. They may feel that they are staying in the marriage mainly because of their obligations to their children. They are not happy men.

If women in the past were often deluded in accepting traditional roles, what did that make men who left this arrangement undisturbed? Were they not also deluded: Of course, it could be argued that men recognized but did not take steps to change the inequities in their marriages because the inequities were in their interest; that is, their career progress was enhanced because they had someone at home taking care of them, their children, and domestic responsibilities. But it seems that men could have prospered even more, psychologically at least, if they had bought into an egalitarian form of marriage. As Margaret Mead said, "Every time we liberate a woman, we liberate a man" (in *The Quotable Woman,* 1991, p. 109). Unfortunately, Bernard did not address the possibility that men, too, were deluded in thinking that traditional marraiges were ideal.

Nor did she give men credit for the many instances in which they mentored women in their careers so that they could begin to achieve equity. Many women were involved in traditional marriages for years before starting careers that were stimulated by male mentors who wanted them to succeed and in general have more diverse lives. Some of these men were their husbands while others were teachers in the business or educational communities.

Overall, though, I think that Bernard has provided a useful view of men and what marriage meant to them before the mid-1970s. If Bernard's arguments were rhetorically extreme, perhaps they needed to be, in some cases, in order to challenge and motivate her readers and listeners. She began her work well before the 1970s, when there were few commentators challenging the status quo in how people conducted their marriages.

The Loss of Intimacy

The Loss of Intimacy Lillian Rubin (*Intimate Strangers,* 1983) provided a view of sex differences in close relationships that is complementary to Bernard's treatment. Based on her research conducted via clinical-type interviews, she argued that men and women in traditional close relationships were "intimate" but paradoxically "strangers" in that they were unaware of their partner's unfulfilled emotional needs, hopes, and fears. In Rubin's analysis, genuine intimacy involves putting aside one's public persona and believing "we can be loved for who we really are, that we can show our shadow side without fear, that our vulnerabilities will not be counted against us" (p. 68).

Rubin's position was that the traditional marriage involved a clearly defined, highly specific set of roles and responsibilities for men and women in relationships to fulfill. It was not, however, an arrangement that adapted well to changing times; so the arrangement was not satisfactory for many couples. Women became depressed. Men withdrew emotionally and sometimes physically as well. Both men and women became angry and increasingly felt helpless in these relationships.

Rubin poignantly described her own first marriage as falling victim to this historical moment:

Married at nineteen to an up-and-coming professional man, I spent years trying to fit myself to the model of the times: happy suburban housewife, charming hostess, helpmate to a husband's burgeoning career. I knew, of course, that I awoke most mornings wishing I could stay in bed. But I told myself I was just tired. I knew there was an uneasiness that lived inside me—nothing intense, nothing dramatic, just a low-level malaise. But I told myself I was just a chronic malcontent as I tried to brush it away. (pp. 20-21)

In Rubin's view, the different roles assumed by husband and wife in a traditional marriage contribute greatly to the devastation of intimacy. Another intimacy destroyer is the different "logics" used by men and women who have been traditionally socialized. Men learn to repress emotions. They live by the logic of the mind, not the heart. Women, on the other hand, more readily move among emotional, cognitive, and intuitive states, but principally live by the logic of the heart. Women are usually the ones who try to draw out the men regarding their feelings. For men, silence is more common, and it is a silence that isolates.

According to Rubin, while men have more obvious intimacy problems, women experience them as well.

. . . when we look below the surface, a reality emerges that's more complex than we have heretofore understood. Then we find that women have their own problems in dealing with intimacy and build their own defenses against it—that, like their men, women also experience internal conflict about closeness which creates anxiety and ambivalence, if not outright fear. In relating to men, however, women rarely have to face the conflict inside themselves squarely, precisely because men take care of the problem for them by their own unmistakable difficulties with closeness and connection. (pp. 96-97)

Like Bernard, Rubin was a trail-blazer in analyzing traditional close relationships and suggesting that their inflexible character was harmful to women's self-esteem and fulfillment. Her work helped pave the way for a dialogue that led to more egalitarian forms of relating. She also exhibited sensitivity to the possibility that in an earlier era many males may have felt an oppressive responsibility to financially support a family. Rubin noted that earlier in her life, at a point when she had taken on the role of supporting her family, she had said to her husband, "I think you men are crazy to live your whole life this way. If I were a man, I wouldn't have waited for women to call for a liberation movement: I'd have led it" (p. 24).

Language Differences Between Men and Women

Linguist Deborah Tannen (1990) has presented a very influential argument that may help us understand some of the difficulties men and women encounter in trying to achieve intimacy. She argued that intimacy is critical in a world of connection "where individuals negotiate complex networks of friendship, minimize differences, try to reach consensus, and avoid the appearance of superiority, which would highlight differences" (p. 24). Tannen suggested that women are better at intimacy than are men, and men value independence more than intimacy. Men value independence because it is a primary means of establishing status in the world. Tannen's thesis is that men use talk to preserve independence and negotiate and maintain status in some type of social order. On the other hand, she believes that women use talk to connect with others and express intimacy.

According to Tannen, boys and girls grow up in psycholinguistically different worlds, where people talk to them differently and they, in turn, learn how to have conversations in ways that mirror their gender. Girls learn intimacy both from their mother (and to a lesser degree their fathers) and from their best friends. Boys, on the other hand, play in groups, compete, boast, and learn to get attention through their competitive and often aggressive behavior. Boys also learn at an early age to "talk over" and interrupt girls, behavior that is presumably a mark of status seeking.

Tannen made a persuasive case that gender differences in conversational style begin early in life. Unfortunately, she failed to clarify why boys learn to be more aggressive in their interaction and conversational styles than do girls, and why boys learn their more aggressive style of behavior outside of the home in interaction with other boys, while the girls learn their style in the home in interaction with their mother.

Tannen made a strong point about the importance of the listener's attributions to the intentions of the talker. A significant school of thought in social psychology contends that we perceive the world in terms of our own experience, needs, desires, motivations, and prejudices (e.g., Jones, 1990). Tannen said:

Much—even most—meaning in conversation does not reside in the words spoken at all, but is filled in by the person listening. Each of us decides whether we think others are speaking in the spirit of differing status or symmetrical connection. The likelihood that individuals will tend to interpret someone else's words as one or the other depends more on the hearer's own focus, concerns, and habits than on the spirit in which the words were spoken. (p. 37)

The implication of this reasoning for the close relationship is that, if we cannot step outside the narrow bounds of our understanding of reality and try to understand the perspective of our partner, we can never really connect with our partner.

Tannen suggested that adult women are often unhappy with the reactions they get in daily interaction with men with whom they are close. Misunderstandings and the resulting discontent are especially likely to occur when the women try to start what Tannen calls "troubles talk," which refers to conversation aimed at working out interpersonal and other kinds of problems. Men do not readily engage in this kind of talk, at least in the form that women do. Tannen pointed out that in these situations, men also are often unhappy because they are accused of responding in the wrong way when they are trying to be responsive. They may be trying to fix the problem, when women simply want to air their concerns.

Another kind of misunderstanding that Tannen spotlighted involves the typical scenario in which a husband arrives home from work and immediately turns on the television and begins reading the newspaper, while his wife tries to begin a conversation. The wife wants to talk not only about troubles, but also as a form of rapport building. The husband feels tired and does not have anything to say, except a few grunts. He wonders why the wife cannot respect his desire to relax and do what he usually does when relaxing—which is not talk to her! She, in turn, may nag or become angry about his silence. Repeated instances of such miscommunication lay a foundation for deep division in the relationship.

Tannen noted that, regarding talking strategies, men and women have different ways of coping with the breakup of a close relationship. While men try to get moral support from members of the opposite sex, women seek comfort from their friends of the same sex. Because men usually talk only about topics such as sports, business, politics, or perhaps women whom they would like to get to know, whereas women are much more likely to discuss relationships, and in effect to be seen as relationship experts, women are the comforters of choice.

Tannen argued that men typically are oriented toward facts in their talk, while women are oriented toward talk as a means of connection. An example might be:

"She said, 'Don't the stars look particularly bright tonight?'"
"He said, 'You're looking at Venus. It's not a star, it's a planet.'"

Tannen suggested that such a trivial dissonance between two people's statements may signal a larger reality. It is that men and women in close relationships do not understand one another in some subtle but vital areas of relating. The man seems to be insensitive to the woman's desire to view the sky in a spontaneous, energizing way as a means to relate romantically. But is that a fault of the man, who may reasonably suggest that his knowledge compelled him to correct the woman? We really do not know since we do not know enough about the context of the discussion. Were they in a setting in which romance might have been plausible, or perhaps driving along on an automobile trip when staring off into the sky might have been dangerous for the driver?

Tannen's example suggests that the man in this discussion values information, while the woman values intimacy with the man. He corrects her technically incorrect statement because of his orientation, just as she made the statement because of her orientation. Tannen contended that neither person was wrong but that both sexes must be more aware of and address the almost inherent differences in the way they usually communicate. They (particularly men) must become better listeners. If they do not, these differences can lead to the dissolution of their relationships.

> If you understand gender differences in what I call conversational style, you may not be able to prevent disagreements from arising, but you stand a better chance of preventing them from spiraling out of control. When sincere attempts to communicate end in stalemate, and a beloved partner seems irrational and obstinate, the different languages men and women speak can shake the foundation of our lives. Understanding the other's ways of talking is a giant leap across the communication gap between women and men, and a giant step toward opening lines of communication. (p. 298)

Unfortunately, Tannen failed to recognize the common observation that a significant percentage of men, many raised by single mothers, have learned to be sensitive to others in their communication styles and to appreciate how intimacy and communication go together. She also neglects to address whether the differences in communication styles that she observed are based on roles prescribed in current work, social, and family situations or are due to gender differences rooted in early socialization and/or biology.

Some evidence supports the former idea. It has been observed that when women become executives, their communication style and behavior often approximates those typically shown by men in such positions. These women embrace control-oriented, dominant communication patterns in their interactions with subordinates at work (Risman & Schwartz, 1989).

Gender Stereotypes

In the book *The Longest War,* Tavris and Wade (1984) discussed instances in which women have been viewed as the "second sex" or the "weaker sex." Too often, every society has distinguished between "men's work" and "women's work." Too often, literature has viewed the woman as not only weaker than the man, but also as a manipulator or sexual seducer (e.g., Adam had to beware of succumbing to Eve's wiles in the Garden of Eden). This tendency has been complemented by the double standard that labels promiscuous men "studs" and promiscuous women "sluts."

Gender stereotypes are still everywhere in our society. We may be more sensitive to them now, but it takes only a quick tour of the local magazine rack to discover the frequency with which females and males are portrayed in rigid, stereotypical ways.

A March 1990 article in *Cosmopolitan* magazine tells women how to be "foxy to get more romantic acts from men." The article argued that women must teach men how to be romantic and that women need to do the unusual to be effective teachers. For example, it was suggested that women might write to their partners and invite them to a romantic date at a pricey restaurant and movie. The article acknowledged that males should be liberated to the point that they understand how to be romantic and the role it plays in relationships. But "Men . . . are taught to be task oriented; early on, they learn that what they *feel* is less valuable than what they achieve or what they can *provide*" (p. 94).

The June 1990 *Esquire* ran a series of essays on "The American Wife." Her role as "bitch," "best friend," "the little woman," "honey," "Evita," "the shrew," "princess," "the ballbuster," and the like were touched on by several writers. While the pieces were humorous and informative, few significant challenges to these stereotypes of the wife were raised. The reader was implicitly encouraged to assume that such qualities were there and form the foundation for relating to women as wives.

Advertisements also perpetuate gender stereotypes. Those that associate wonderful sexual activities or possibilities with a product are the worst culprits.

It is clear that rather unmovable gender considerations continue to play a major role in how corporations treat their employees. While their observations and evidence may be dated, researchers Thomas Cash and Louis Janda reported in the December 1984 *Psychology Today* that personnel managers thought that women whose clothing looked less feminine were more competent. These scholars speculated that very attractive women often get the "pink collar" jobs in corporations, jobs traditionally dominated by females.

According to a July 21, 1991 (Section A, p. 6) *New York Times* commentary, a male corporate CEO will sometimes seek a "trophy wife," a beautiful, often accomplished younger woman whom the successful man "acquires" on remarriage, after a relatively long marriage to a first wife—who just happened to greatly facilitate his success. The prize wife certifies her husband's status and dispels the notion that men peak sexually at age 18!

The "trophy wife" concept reflects the different scales used in judging the value of women and men in this culture. Beauty is one of the main scales for judging women, while wealth is a primary scale for judging men. (See Hatfield and Sprecher, 1986, for a discussion of the beauty stereotype.)

Gender stereotyping is also revealed in humor bashing the opposite sex. Consider these recent male-bashing jokes (from the August 25, 1992, *Chicago Tribune* wires):

What's the difference between government bonds and men?
Bonds mature.

What does a man consider a seven-course meal?
A hot dog and a six-pack.

Why is it a good thing there are female astronauts?
So someone will ask directions if the crew gets lost in space.

Youth readily display gender stereotypes in their conversations about the other sex. Below is a list of things teenagers said they dislike about the opposite sex. They may be seen as an innocent form of poking fun at the opposite sex, but they also involve stereotypical elements that have persisted in spite of major societal changes. Girls said:

1. Boys go after you, then dump you once you like them.

2. Boys never have good gossip.

3. Boys ignore you until you get a different boyfriend, then all of a sudden want you.

4. Boys don't understand why girls are so paranoid about their looks. (But if boys see an ugly girl in a magazine, they'll make fun of her.)

5. Boys don't understand that women are still discriminated against. (Boys rarely have to take typing tests.)

6. Boys don't introduce you to their friends or their parents.

7. Boys are intimidated by girls with strong opinions. (Boys laugh when you're enraged.)

8. Boys underestimate the importance of Valentine's Day, birthdays, and anniversaries. . . .

Boys said:

1. Girls have keychains that jingle.

2. Girls always go to the bathroom in packs.

3. Girls act like they think they're hippies (The '60s are over.)

4. Girls always ask "Am I fat?" (This bugs every guy because half the time the girl looks like she weighs about five pounds.)

5. Girls like to make big problems out of everything. They thrive on dilemmas.

6. Girls love to name-drop. (Why does every chick brag about who she knows?)

6. Girls want to analyze you. (Girls stay: "In a lot of ways you're still a little boy. You're still very immature. I think it's Freudian." Girls think Freud is a magician.)

8. Girls can't handle silence for more than two minutes without turning to their boyfriends and asking them what they're thinking about (from the November 1992 issue of *Dirt* magazine, pp. 3-4).

As a further illustration of gender stereotyping, consider these relationship-related stereotypes presented in my university-level class on interpersonal relationships. Women said about men:

They love you in the beginning of a relationship when you're smiling and happy. But the minute you let them know you have problems and you get depressed, they're gone.

They're expert at playing "Ditch your wife." You visit some mutual friends, and the next thing you know, the guys are going out for a beer.

Why do guys say they're interested in girls for their sense of humor, intellect, and personality, and then turn around and go out with the girls with good looks and totally "fake" personalities?

And men say of women:

They put down their looks, figure or intelligence, ostensibly out of modesty. They play the martyr for no reason. They pique your curiosity about something, then clam up just to see you twist in the wind. They use coyness, cuteness, and diabetes-inducing sweetness to get what they want, sexual or otherwise.

How come, no matter how hard we try, we can't compliment you on how good you look without your getting the impression that all we care about is sex and your body?

I am not contending that such stereotypical points necessarily are deleterious to close relationships between the sexes. They probably do not help, though, either. They seem to be part of the fabric of social experience most individuals are exposed to from early on in their lives. What seems necessary is much more dialogue early on between the sexes regarding what each is like and about the substantial variability within, as well as across, sexes. Courses focusing on stereotyping and relationships at the elementary school level might well assist in stimulating this dialogue.

The Two-Career Relationship

Partly because of the economy, in the 1990s most relationships involve two-career couples. According to the U.S. Census Bureau, in 1990 a record 53 percent of working mothers returned to their jobs before their children's first birthdays. In 1976 less than a third of working mothers did this. For members of two-career couples, making contributions to family, relationship, and work, not to mention their own needs, represents an imposing agenda.

Consider the following account by a woman, age 28 (as reported by Rubin, 1983):

> We agreed before we were married that we would share it all.
>
> I was already on my way up in the agency. I was in advertising . . . and about to be a big success; I'd just landed my first account a couple of months before we got married. . . . We had it all figured—we'd both work, have our careers, and at home . . . we'd both take care of things there, too. We didn't know; God, we were dumb. . . .
>
> It's easy, all right, until the kids come. Then watch out. Our biggest concern was child care. It was hard with one kid, but with two it got to be such a constant pain and strain that I finally decided I had no choice but to leave work for the next few years. I thought I'd be able to manage it if I could work half time, but that's a no-go in advertising. Now I piddle around with some freelance stuff at home—nothing much. (p. 173)

Finding affordable, high quality day-care arrangements for the children of working parents (or the single parent) is one of the most taxing problems facing families today. Well-run day-care centers have plenty of room for toddlers and older children, but often have waiting lists a year long to accommodate babies. Those who have the money often hire nannies and au pairs to take on much of the early child care. These workers may live in the home of their employers and care for the children for periods longer than the typical workday. Thanks to the divorce and separation rate, grandparents and other relatives are increasingly shouldering part of the load of day care and socialization of children, especially in single-parent families.

A vigorous debate is taking place regarding whether the mother should stay home with the children during their first few years of life. More traditional analysts have suggested that it is essential for the mother to do so (Johat, 1990). Part of their argument is that the mother is the primary caretaker—and always has been—and that the child must form an attachment with her early on in order for normal psychological functioning to occur. Otherwise, the child may feel abandoned. They have related this argument to Bowlby's (1969) influential theorizing on the child's sense of loss and bereavement when a parent dies.

On the other hand, other analysts have argued that there are many sound ways to handle the children's care during their early years that do not force the woman to give up her career, or take a disadvantageous break from it, and stay home. Writers such as Scarr (1984) have contended that those who want to maintain the more traditional arrangement pine for "the good old days" that are gone forever. What about the father and his child-care rights and responsibilities? What about good day care? Each can also contribute strongly and positively to the child's early care and socialization. These writers also have argued that the woman's ability to pursue her own career and self-actualization is essential not only to her psychological well-being but also to the psychological well-being of her children and husband.

In addition to the women who leave successful careers in order to raise children, there are those who concentrate on careers that would readily fit with child rearing. For instance, some women have begun cottage industries, such as selling and marketing products at home using a phone and personal computer. So-called mommy wars have occurred in the 1990s between women who stay home and those who try to continue full-time work and employ day care for their children. One 36-year-old mother, a former political campaign consultant who had returned to the home to raise her child, was quoted recently as follows: "I feel like I'm a disappointment for the women who have worked so hard to broaden opportunities for other women. . . . I'd wake up in the morning and I'd look at my daughter and I'd look at the list of phone calls I was supposed to make and they didn't seem that important" (quoted in Lynda Richardson, "Mommy wars," *Chicago Tribune,* February 7, 1993, p. 4).

Lengthy commuting to jobs is another problem facing many families in the 1990s. The commute in a large suburban area could last as long as one or even two hours each way. Even more trying, some couples see one another only on weekends; during the week they reside near their jobs at some distant location. In *Commuting Marriage* Gerstel and Gross (1984) discussed some of the problems facing people in commuting relationships. For example, they reported the following comment from a woman in a commuting relationship:

> Here are these two single divorced men who I would like to say to: "Come over to supper," and they would not have to think about it because I am married. But there is something in the situation that doesn't allow that. They are really confused about how to relate to me. I'm not single, but my husband is not here. (p. 95)

According to sociologist Arlie Hochschild's (1989) book *The Second Shift,* as of the mid to late 1980s women in dual-career families with children continued to carry a far greater portion of the responsibilities associated with running a home and raising children. Hochschild followed 150 two-career couples to find out what happened when they came home from work. He found that, overall, women carried a heavier burden. They were more likely than their mates to wash the dishes, dress the child, and stay home with the sick child. As a result, they had little if any leisure time. Hochschild suggested that for many men the concepts of fairness and respect in division of labor seemed to be impersonal moral abstractions imposed on love. He said that over the long run, such inequities would lead women to divorce their husbands. In the minority of couples who indeed exemplified more egalitarian arrangements, the husband's contributions were greatly appreciated and contributed to a wife's sense of being loved.

There are notable exceptions to the conclusions of Hochschild's work in the news. The most recent addition to the U.S. Supreme Court Ruth Ginsburg has noted the important role her husband Martin, an attorney, has played in facilitating her career by staying at home and taking care of domestic needs. One area where equity is increasing is family relocation. More and more, husbands are following wives who have strong careers in progress and who must relocate. Traditionally, it was the wife who followed the husband. In an August 18, 1993, *USA Today* article, reporter Julia Lawlor interviewed a number of men who had left their jobs to follow their wives as they relocated. The primary factor in their decision was economics. It was estimated by Mobil Oil Corporation that a man generally will not move unless his wife stands to make at least 25 percent more than he does. In the United States today, three in ten wives in dual-earner families earn more than their husbands.

On top of their jobs, many families' members today are incredibly busy with activities—school, athletic events, clubs, music and the arts, physical fitness, PTA, boy scouts, etc. They hardly see one another during much of the typical week. Some psychologists have contended that there is a disconnectedness that exists in these families, who have provided little opportunity for casual talking and visiting, problem solving, and planning together as a unit. The development of intimacy takes time, and these families do not have any.

Aaron Latham, author of *The Urban Cowboy,* has emphasized the male's need to consider family above career in making decisions about work and schedules. In the following perceptive statement, he discussed the dilemma of juggling responsibilities in two-career marriages:

> Any marriage, especially the two-career marriage, is a juggling act. . . . And the important thing to know, as you're juggling everything, is which of the balls are rubber and which are glass. And your family is a glass ball and your health is a glass ball, and your career is a rubber ball.
>
> When you are juggling, if you drop the glass ball, you're not going to get it back. But the rubber ball, if you drop it, you'll get it back. (quoted in *The Dallas Morning News* interview with Diane Jennings, Aug. 21, 1988, Section E, "High Profile")

Gay and Lesbian Close Relationships

In the last decade, gay and lesbian individuals increasingly have been "coming out of the closet" in declaring their sexual orientation and in asserting their rights in the political arena. Despite early beginning progress in social science research examining issues in gay and lesbian close relationships, we still have a paucity of evidence available as to whether most of the principles and issues of close relationships discussed in this book are applicable to gay and lesbian relationships.

There has been one large-scale national study comparing different types of couples along dimensions such as their sexual patterns, satisfaction, and orientations toward work and financial needs. This study was reported by sociologists Philip Blumstein and Pepper Schwartz in their book *American Couples* (1983). The method involved comparing samples of gay, lesbian, cohabitating heterosexual, and married heterosexual couples. Although the samples are as good as any in the literature for such a complex set of comparisons, they were relatively small and mainly drawn from a few large U.S. metropolitan areas. Also, the evidence is quite dated in that it was collected in the late 1970s before the AIDS epidemic, which greatly altered patterns of dating and sexual behavior. In the study, gay men indicated they had engaged in sexual relations with a relatively large number of partners. However, after AIDS, with the adoption of safer sex practices, including having fewer sex partners, it is unclear whether there is much difference in the number of sexual partners that gay and heterosexual men have over a lifetime.

With these caveats in mind, it is instructive to consider some of the differences among the different types of relationships reported by Blumstein and Schwartz:

Lesbians emphasized to a much greater degree than did other types of couples the importance of each partner communicating and sharing emotions. They most strongly appreciated and represented the egalitarian relationship; all of the other types of couples ran their domestic lives less equitably. Also, lesbians emphasized the value of each partner working and developing a career. Thus, they often felt conflicts, similar to those of dual-career heterosexual couples, in how to find the time and energy to make strong contributions both to the quality of the relationship and to their careers.

Blumstein and Schwartz found that heterosexual married couples in the study reported the greatest amount of deception about sexual relations outside of their primary relationships. As might be expected, all types of couples showed high degrees of possessiveness when they feared their partners might be having a meaningful affair. Married couples and lesbian couples both stressed the importance of monogamy, whereas gay men did not. Lesbians, alone, tried diligently to make sure that the partner who made more money was not accorded more power and decision-making ability. Also, as compared to married and cohabiting couples, gay and lesbian couples divided housework according to practical considerations—who was at home more or who had the most time to do chores. Heterosexual married and cohabiting couples showed more traditional patterns, with women doing the bulk of housework.

Blumstein and Schwartz concluded their book with this interesting observation:

Looking at marriage and its alternatives, we see advantages both in the institution and in nonmarital forms. As we look at the impact of being male or female, we see no evidence that historic gender-role traditions and restrictions help solve *all* issues for couples. We believe that the time for orthodoxy is past. Neither, however, do we reject the idea that gender differences may be valuable for a couple in certain areas of life together. Gay couples face problems that arise from 'sameness' of gender [e.g., they had noted lesbians' difficulty in deciding who would lead in many decision-making areas, including sexuality]; these give us an indication of where it might be wise for partners to be different. Heterosexuals face problems that arise from their "differentness"; these give us guidance about where it might be better for partners to be more alike.

There is, of course, no perfect composite picture that will fit every couple's needs. . . . As the institution of marriage loses its predictability for heterosexuals, and while homosexual couples have no institution to enter, each couple will have to establish guidelines for making gender work for, not against, the possibility of a lifetime relationship. (p. 330)

Laurence Kurdek has compared gay couples with lesbian couples on various relationship dimensions. His studies have looked at moderately sized samples (e.g., 100-200) of couples in the Midwestern region of the United States. In general, Kurdek and his colleagues have found that gay and lesbian couples are more similar to each other than they are different from each other. Noteworthy findings include the following: (1) Lesbian couples perceive more rewards from their relationships than do gay couples (Kurdek, 1991). Kurdek suggests that this difference may reflect lesbians' stronger emphasis on expressivity and nurturance. (2) As research has found with heterosexual couples (Rusbult, 1983), dissatisfaction with a gay or lesbian relationship predicts its later dissolution (Kurdek, 1992). (3) When couples stay together over an extended period, both gay and lesbian couples report increased satisfaction, emotional investment, and perceived reward, and report decreased perceived costs (Kurdek, 1992). (4) Lesbians and gay men report receiving more emotional support from friends than from family and less support from family than do heterosexuals (Kurdek & Schmitt, 1987).

We now are seeing a major increase in research evidence about how gay and lesbian couples function. Much of it reveals considerable similarity in the way homosexual and heterosexual couples function (Rohrbaugh, 1992). For example, research has shown that gay and lesbian parents do just as well as, if not better than, heterosexual couples in parenting activity. Reviews of available evidence in

McWhirter, Sanders, and Reinisch (1990) reveal no evidence to suggest that the psychosocial development of children with lesbian or gay parents is compromised in any respect. Aspects of sexual identity, such as gender identity and sexual orientation, do not appear to differentiate children of lesbian and gay parents from children of heterosexual parents. Further, problems experienced in lesbian or gay blended families are similar to those in heterosexual blended families (e.g., rejection, jealousy, and conflict between children and stepparents; Lewin & Lyons, 1982).

A 1993 book entitled *Love Match* (Birch Lande Press) by Sandra Faulkner with Judy Nelson described Nelson's seven-year relationship with tennis star Martina Navratilova. Nelson describes herself as a typical Texas girl who became a beauty queen, married a doctor, had two children, and divorced her husband when she discovered he had been having affairs. Soon after her divorce, Nelson met Navratilova and started a relationship that involved their traveling together around the world. Navratilova ended the relationship in the 1990s, resulting in a "palimony" suit by Nelson that was settled out of court. Nelson's account points to many similarities in style of interaction between her marriage and her lesbian relationship with Navratilova. In an interview with *Chicago Tribune* writer William Currie (August 29, 1993, Section 6, p. 3 "Womanews"), Nelson suggests some of these similarities:

> In my marriage, I had him [her ex-husband Ed] to take care of
> . . . [and after becoming involved with Navratilova] you do
> indeed take care of her . . . . Her coach said to me, "She plays
> tennis. All we want her to do is focus on that ball. You do
> everything else."

Nelson also indicated that while they were involved with her, both of her partners had carried on affairs. But she suggested that her relationship with Navratilova was much more aboveboard than her marriage had been. She said: "We talked about a lot of things before the relationship ever began seriously. . . . You know—about making choices and taking risks, the quality, the freedom that I felt in our relationship that didn't go on in my relationship with my husband."

Nelson discussed the stigma she faced in the 1980s in her Texas hometown when her relationship with Navratilova was widely publicized by the media. She indicated that she received the full support of her children and parents. Nelson is now in a relationship with author Rita Mae Brown, with whom she shares a farmhouse and business in Virginia.

In the 1990s lesbians and gays still face discrimination. However, the greater acceptance of homosexual relationships by the general public and the greater willingness of individuals in such relationships to discuss them should soon lead to a better understanding of similarities and differences between heterosexual and homosexual close relationships.

The New Male

The February 1993 *Chronicle of Higher Education* listed 28 new and recent books on men and masculinity. The *Chronicle* (p. A6, article by Scott Heller) argued that the Marlboro Man, an icon of strength and stoicism, is a fading image in the psyches of a segment of 1990s men and that these books reveal the diversity of qualities exhibited by the "new male." Many young adult men have been raised in single-parent families by women, and a smaller number have been raised by two women living together. These men appear to be less compelled to adhere to some standard of masculinity that prevailed a couple of decades ago. An increasing number embrace qualities such as openness to emotions and greater expressivity of emotions. These works also emphasize males getting reconnected with their fathers. Books that represent this new spirit of manhood include Liam Hudson and Bernadine Jacot's (1991) *The Way Men Think* and Samuel Osherson's (1992) *Wrestling with Love.*

It may be true that these "new males" are still a distinctive minority in this country. But their number is growing. Popular television shows about males such as *Seinfeld* are portraying males as exhibiting a variety of gender qualities. The 1990s may be a time in which many "new males" begin to feel more freedom to carry out an array of social roles in their relationships. They also seem to be trying to balance intimacy with independence. They appear to be supportive of women's quest to find a similar type of balance. More than men ever have before, they appear to value their relationships, both with their close heterosexual or homosexual partners and their close friends.

Another type of "new male" is on the scene in the 1990s. He is the warrior. Writers such as Bly (1992) have led a men's movement that embraces some of the qualities of the "new male" mentioned above, such as expressiveness, but also emphasizes the "natural" warriorlike qualities of the male. According to this view, males can be empowered by bonding experiences with other men in which they express their uncertainties, fears, longings, and other interior feelings that too long have been suppressed. They do not talk about sports and politics in these ritualistic ceremonies. The warrior is hurting, often from too many disappointments with his relationships and "the way the world works." To cope, he must go back partially to his nature (warrior— one who uses his violent energy for constructive personal growth; see Moore & Gillette, 1992), while simultaneously learning new traits such as the ability to express his feelings.

The men's movement involves much more than I have described. It may be here for some time to come, since the women's movement continues today after beginning in earnest in the 1960s. Each movement will be better off in the long-run if it spawns and nurtures communication across the gender divide. At present, the men's movement seems to involve a lot of work on male-to-male communication and empowerment. Optimistically, I am hopeful that a maturing of the men's movement will ally it with a twenty-first century women's movement that beckons conciliatory interaction.

CHAINS DO NOT HOLD

A MARRIAGE TOGETHER. . . . IT

IS THREADS, HUNDREDS OF

TINY THREADS,

WHICH SEW PEOPLE TOGETHER

THROUGH THE YEARS.

—Simone Signoret

5

LOVE AND
THE MAINTENANCE
OF CLOSE
RELATIONSHIPS

The Struggle To Study Love

The scientific study of the social psychology of love is a twentieth century phenomenon. Until the end of the late nineteenth century in the United States, human love usually was unequivocally linked with obeying God's will in marriage. There was little recognition of passionate love. In fact, other than early studies by sociologists on love within the context of the family, the first systematic study of love by social psychologists did not begin until the 1960s. Pioneers such as Ellen Berscheid, Elaine (Walster) Hatfield, Keith Davis, George Levinger, Steve Duck and Bernard Murstein began to develop this topic in the 1960s and 1970s. But they encountered much criticism from the mainstream psychology fields and from grant review committees, who often wrote their work off as commonsensical, or too "soft."

Berscheid and Hatfield's work on love, which probably involved the most influential and ground-breaking early research, was singled out in the 1970s by Senator William Proxmire of Wisconsin for one of his "Golden Fleece Awards" which he bestowed upon those who received grants for work he considered useless. Here is what Berscheid and Walster (1978) quoted Proxmire as saying in criticism of their work:

> I believe that 200 million other Americans want to leave
> some things in life a mystery, and right at the top of things we
> don't want to know is why a man falls in love with a woman
> and vice versa. . . . So National Science Foundation—get
> out of the love racket. Leave that to Elizabeth Barrett Browning
> and Irving Berlin. Here, if anywhere, Alexander Pope was
> right when he observed, "If ignorance is bliss, 'tis folly to be
> wise." (p. 150)

That millions of Americans buy books on love and use relation-ship counseling services shows Proxmire was wrong. We want to learn about any mystery, especially one so fundamental to the human con-dition as what love is and why it occurs. Luckily, the senator's view did not prevail. In fact, it may have indirectly sped along some scholars' quests to learn about love. Several additional psychological research projects on love have since been funded by federal agencies. Even if many of the ideas in the close relationships literature may be viewed as commonsensical, there is much to be learned from common sense, as pioneering psychologist Fritz Heider showed in his seminal (1958) work *The Psychology of Interpersonal Relations.* The scholars who founded the close relationships field in psychology deserve great praise. They endured an onslaught of criticism and persevered, so that today the topic is a valid area of study in psychology (e.g., see Berscheid, 1988, p. 360).

A Caveat On The Use Of The Term "Theory"

I use the term *theory* in this chapter with pause. Thus far, most of the approaches that have been referred to as theories of love and relating are really no more than a few assumptions, a few hypotheses, and a body of evidence. They are not elaborate hypothetico-deductive mod-els of the way humans operate, as were early theories of learning or present theories in the cognitive and neurosciences. But that is not too troublesome for our present purposes. Many of these conceptions ex-plicitly, or by implication, have something to say about how people love and maintain close relationships.

Definitions

Love Love is one of the most difficult concepts to define in the study of close relationships. There is no simple definition. Susan and Clyde Hendrick (1992b), Aaron Beck (1988), and Bernard Murstein (1974) all refrained from defining love in a specific way.

One general idea is that love is an emotion, that it benefits the person who is loved; that it is possible to direct love toward oneself, just as it is to direct it toward another person. Love has also been construed as an attitude involving positive feeling toward oneself or another. People frequently make a distinction between "loving someone" and "being in love." The latter is usually reserved for special, romantically oriented relationships, while the former may be said to apply to relationships with, say, relatives and friends.

In *Courage My Love* (1989) Merle Shain defined love as involving stages: First, there is the highly romantic stage that she suggested is short-lived, lasting usually around six weeks. (Many other theorists believe that romantic love may last a lot longer. However, they typically are referring to love in a general and positive way and not to idealization of the other person, feeling a loss of personal control, and other such illusory qualities.) If the couple stay together, they then go through a more substantial stage, involving much less idealization of the other person. In this more advanced stage, respect (which Shain referred to as "love in plain clothes"), acceptance, understanding, and mutual self-disclosure represent love. If love matures to this more advanced stage, it also involves self-love. Shain quoted the theologian Martin Buber, who contended that there cannot be a "we" until there is an "I" to keep company with the "thou." In this context Shain said, "While it's often easier to flesh someone out with your own creativity and fall in love with what you've made, the real joy is in understanding and accepting and loving what you find" (1989, p. 31).

Bernard Murstein was a pioneer in the study of love, sex, and marriage (see his 1974 book *Love, Sex, and Marriage*). In an essay (1988), he reviewed a number of other observers' definitions. H. L. Mencken called love "the triumph of imagination over intelligence"; Theodore Reik said, "Love is a substitute for another desire, for the struggle toward self-fulfillment, for the vain urge to reach one's ego-ideal"; and Sigmund Freud suggested the succinct definition that love is "aim-inhibited sex." These definitions cloud further our attempt to provide at least one short definition that can hold up against many qualifications.

Ellen Berscheid's commentary in Sternberg and Barnes' (1988) book *The Psychology of Love* is one of the most cogent statements on the multifaceted nature of love. She said:

> . . . love is not a single distinct behavioral phenomenon with clearly recognizable outlines and boundaries. Rather, the genus love is a huge and motley collection of many different behavioral events whose only commonalities are that they take place in a relationship with another person (in that they are caused by and/or affect the behavior of another. . .). (p. 362)

The value of Berscheid's point is its emphasis on behavioral events. Too often, scholars who study love do not define it as involving behavior. How can we know about another's love for us unless we have behavioral evidence?

So far, we have examined definitions that focus on people who are "in love." Beyond these definitions, I like Seymour Epstein's (1993) simple definition: "To love is to derive satisfaction from observing the welfare and fulfillment of the loved one. . . . I know I love you because it makes me happy to see you happy" (p. 109). I would only add that implied in this definition is that the lover acts toward the loved one in a way that enhances this satisfaction and happiness.

Maintenance I define maintenance as work toward keeping a relationship ongoing and healthy. How does love relate to maintenance? My view is that love is probably a necessary determinant of maintenance. But love probably is not a sufficient determinant of people's staying together. It often is part of the package that keeps the relationship alive. Yet, there likely are other factors, too, that may be involved in the maintenance of most close relationships. Why else would people whose close relationships have ended say, "I still love my ex-partner and I always will. I just can't live with him (her)"?

In a recent special issue of the *Journal of Social and Personal Relationships* (1993) on maintenance, Dindia and Canary discussed four goals of maintenance: (1) to keep a relationship in existence; (2) to keep a relationship in a specified state or condition; (3) to keep a relationship in satisfactory condition; and (4) to keep a relationship in repair. I think that these can be reduced to two major goals—*to keep the relationship going and to be satisfied with it.*

Leslie Baxter (1994) argued that maintenance involves coping with the constant change that results from the struggle of contradictory tendencies inherent in relating. This approach makes sense in trying to analyze what lovers do in the ongoing give and take of their relationships. Sometimes they move close to one another; sometimes they distance themselves. They take these steps in countless small and large ways throughout the course of the relationship.

Most relationships, no matter how well maintained, go through highs and lows. However, couples who stay in a relationship that slowly erodes over time are enduring, not maintaining, the relationship. This commonly occurred until the divorce rate shot up in the early 1970s.

Differentiating Between Liking and Loving

Are liking and loving points along a continuum that measures how intensely we feel about another person? Not necessarily. Zick Rubin (1973) suggested that love was composed of attachment (involving passion and possessiveness), caring (involving giving to another), and intimacy (reciprocal sharing between two people). Rubin and his colleagues created different scales to measure liking and loving. An example from their liking scale was "My partner is one of the most likable people I know." An example from their loving scale was "I feel I can confide in my partner about virtually everything." The results of the research showed the two scales to have statistical validity. It was found that, as expected, there was a very high correlation (around .80) for responses to items within each scale—suggesting that the items within scales were reliably similar. On the other hand, the correlations between the liking and loving scale items were quite a bit lower—.36 for females and .56 for males.

A related study conducted in Australia by Cunningham and Antill (1981) showed positive relationships among liking, love, and a personality trait called romanticism. As in Rubin's study, males showed higher associations among these qualities than did females. Why did this occur? One argument is that females make more clear-cut distinctions between liking and loving than do males. This finding has not been pursued enough in subsequent work and remains quite tentative.

Subsequent research on Rubin's liking and loving scales led to some qualifications regarding when men and women differ. Dion and Dion (1976) asked people in different types of relationships to fill out liking and loving scales. They found that only casual daters clearly differentiated between liking and loving. Exclusive daters, engaged couples, and married couples revealed less differentiation. This finding makes sense. The more positively involved people become, the more likely they are to report both high degrees of liking (e.g., "he also is my best friend") and loving (e.g., "I don't know what I would do without his love").

Liking versus loving is a dilemma for most people. We want to be friends with our lovers. An implicit theory many of us entertain is that we *must* first like one another and be close friends in order to develop a close relationship. After we become lovers, we hope that our friendship will endure and that both it and the love we have will grow. In *A Book of Self-Esteem: Revolution from Within,* Gloria Steinem (1992) suggested the importance in her life of the sequence of friendship to lover: ". . . for the first time in my life [I] made a lover out of a man who wasn't a friend first—my mistake, not his, since I was the one being untrue to myself" (p. 265).

Many times, however, people are unsure whether they should cross the line between liking and loving, or between being a friend and being a lover (the classic question posed in the movie *When Harry Met Sally*). Many preserve the friendship and never know if it could have been successfully turned into love. Some friends do become lovers and then successfully return to being "just friends." For someone to have a few former lovers who are still good friends is a great blessing. It may provide him or her with as much social support as having one good, long-term close relationship.

What if we are not sexually excited by a lover? This common dilemma has now been addressed in court. According to an Associated Press wire report, in April 1993, a California jury awarded an ex-husband $242,000 in a civil suit against his ex-wife because she never told him in their 11-year marriage that she was not attracted to him sexually—even though she loved him. This woman had lost her sexual desire for her husband early in the marriage and well before she began an affair with another man. She never told her husband about her loss of sexual interest, or the other man. The jury probably concluded that the wife had duped and humiliated her husband by making him think she was sexually attracted to him.

Conceptions of Love

Styles of Love The sociologist John Lee (1976) argued that there are styles of love. Lee developed his approach based on research in which he asked people to sort through a large set of cards describing relationships and select the ones that fit theirs.

Lee's original work has been extended into a major conceptual approach and body of evidence by the Hendricks (1986, 1989, 1992a, 1992b). They have concluded over a decade of work on love styles and how such styles are associated with relationship satisfaction, conflict, and sexuality. A general assumption made in this work is that people do exhibit the same styles of loving across time and different relationships.

The six types of love posited by Lee and further developed in the Hendricks' work may be briefly defined as follows:

1. *Eros*—characterized by strong sexual desire and intense emotional attachment.

2. *Storge*—comparable to what is called companionate love (see below), it involves a slow, affection-oriented pace of relating, emphasizing the development of friendship before love; mutual need fulfillment also is embraced.

3. *Ludus*—this term means "game" in Latin; it is a nonpossessive type of love that typically does not lead to marriage. It may focus on the conquest of a number of sexual partners.

4. *Mania*—an obsessive, jealous, possessive, and dependent

style of loving. It is highly stressful and involves many peaks and valleys in emotion (see Tennov's "limerent love," described in Chapter 3).

5. *Pragma*—characterized by keen awareness of one's market value and comparison level. Love is maintained for practical reasons.

6. *Agape*—embraces altruism, or unselfish concern for other (see later discussion of communal love). Love is freely given without expecting anything in return; also, this style may involve a spiritual component that focuses on communion and other nonphysical aspects of relating.

As might be expected, the Hendricks have found that relationships often involve mixtures of these styles of loving. Their work has increasingly moved from love styles in dating relationships to love styles in more advanced, long-term close relationships. Some of their more interesting findings using this approach include:

1. Males report themselves to be more ludic than do females. Why? Maybe it is simply because many males buy into the stereotype that men play a game in relationships until they get what they want—sex usually. And they may see themselves playing such a game in multiple relationships simultaneously.

2. Women report themselves to be more storgic, pragmatic, and manic than do men. The Hendricks suggested that many women have been socialized to marry someone who is a love partner and can also provide economically for them.

3. Men and women score similarly on eros; both females and males believe they are passionate in their close relationships.

4. Eros lovers have been found to be more disclosing to their partners and able to elicit self-disclosure. Eros lovers appear to be sensitive to the important role of communication in sexuality and relating.

5. Ludic lovers score relatively quite high in desire for excitement and novelty. Ludic lovers also have been found to be more extroverted in their behavior.

6. Manic lovers were found to be sensitive and emotionally expressive, but they also showed higher defensiveness, aggressiveness, and neurotic tendencies.

7. For ongoing close relationships, partners have been shown to have considerable similarity on their storge, mania, ludus, and agape scores. In terms of relationship satisfaction, men appear to favor women who are high in eros and agape; whereas women's satisfaction was unrelated to their partner's scores on eros and agape.

This body of work on love styles has stimulated research and theory on how people love one another. We still do not know, however, just how durable love styles might be. If research were conducted with a senior population, would we find, for example, that there are 88-year-old men who still are "erotic" lovers to the day they die? Let's hope so!

Companionate Love vs. Passionate Love Walster and Walster (1978) and Berscheid and Walster (1978) first explored the idea of companionate love and distinguished it from passionate love. They contended that the core features of companionate love are friendship and desire to be together. Companionate love involves low-key emotions and becomes very common as people age.

Passionate love, unlike companionate love, is theorized to have a large component of physiological arousal (or feelings of "chemistry"). Couples may combine companionate and passionate love, sometimes emphasizing one more than the other. Passionate love, like romantic love, is especially likely to occur early in a relationship. As a couple grows together, they may have a solid base of companionate love, but also enough continuing spark to have periods of passionate love as well.

While for most of us simple companionship may not do, we nonetheless would be well advised to consider the value of a mixture of romance, passion, companionship, and friendship in our close relationships. Such a mixture coupled with the dose of reality that comes with experience and careful thinking about relating may help a couple avoid the disillusionment that is common among those who have experienced only romantic or passionate love. Tennov (1979), whose work on limerant, or highly romantic, love was discussed in Chapter 3, argued that companionate love likely is a far more lasting form of love than either passionate or romantic love.

Triangular Theory of Love Robert Sternberg's (1986) triangular theory of love suggests that there are three major components of love: intimacy, passion, and decision or commitment. Intimacy includes self-disclosure through sharing emotions and stories with one's partner; passion involves erotic interest in another; commitment involves making a decision to stay with your partner and to defer this type of relationship with other potential partners. When all three elements are balanced, the most complete form of love—consummate love—exists. According to Sternberg, that hardly ever happens. Usually people emphasize one or two elements, and these may not be the same ones emphasized by their partner. For example, it often is argued that men emphasize passion while women emphasize intimacy. If left unresolved, this divergence could lead to conflict.

Other types of love in Sternberg's conception are: Infatuated love (involving high passion but low intimacy and commitment); romantic love (involving high intimacy and passion, but low commitment); empty love (involving high commitment, but low intimacy and passion); companionate love (involving high intimacy and commitment, but low passion); and fatuous love (involving high passion and commitment, but low intimacy). Sternberg's component analysis has been well received by scholars of close relationships. More work needs to be done to determine how partners' sharing or not sharing the different love emphases affects satisfaction in their relationships.

Attachment Styles and Types of Love Philip Shaver and Cindy Hazan (1988, 1994) developed the provocative idea that people's adult style of love relates closely to their attachment styles developed in early interaction with their parents. Their theory is premised on Bowlby's (1969) work in developmental psychology. Bowlby posited that over thousands of years, humans have evolved to fear being alone, especially when in a novel, dark, or dangerous environment. Bowlby hypothesized that the young child who experiences attachment (protection, support, and nurturance from parents, particularly the mother) feels secure to explore the environment. On the other hand, the young child who experiences attachment only some of the time or who suffers complete abandonment will feel insecure in dealings with the environment.

Shaver and Hazan's main assumption is that people learn attachment styles early in their lives as they interact with their parents and then carry these styles over to adult close relationships. In their research, Shaver and Hazan asked people to select the attachment style that best characterized their adult close relationships. About 50 percent selected the *secure* style of attachment ("I find it relatively easy to get close to others and am comfortable depending on them and having them depend on me"). Approximately 25 percent chose the *avoid-*

ant style ("I am somewhat uncomfortable being close to others; I find it difficult to trust them completely, difficult to allow myself to depend on them. I am nervous when anyone gets too close . . ."). And approximately 20 percent selected the *anxious or ambivalent* style ("I find that others are reluctant to get as close as I would like. I often worry that my partner doesn't really love me or won't want to stay with me").

One of the major difficulties with Shaver and Hazan's approach is that it would require longitudinal studies lasting many years to strongly establish a link between early experiences with parents and later experiences with adult lovers. Thus far no such research has been conducted. Another problem is that people may exhibit different attachment styles in different relationships, and they may not be aware of their variance in styles.

Communal Love   Based on an impressive body of evidence, Judson Mills and Margaret Clark (Mills & Clark, 1982; Clark & Mills, 1979) theorized that "communal love" rather than "equity" usually guides interactions among married and unmarried couples, family members, and friends. When equity governs a relationship, people think in terms of getting exactly what they deserve from a relationship, given their contributions to it (Walster, Walster, & Berscheid, 1978). They give to others with the expectation that their giving will be reciprocated. In a communal relationship, on the other hand, each person is concerned about the welfare of the other and wants to benefit the other, especially when the other has a need for such a benefit. The parties are following what Pruitt (1972) referred to as the norm of mutual responsiveness. The fact that people in close relationships often remove the price tag from gifts they buy one another, said Mills and Clark, is evidence that they usually do not follow the principle of equity in their resource exchanges. The researchers further contended that participants in communal relationships are seldom guided by traditional laws of equity in their feelings for one another.

It seems likely to me that many close relationships involve elements of both communal love and equity. I would postulate that, when a close relationship is highly satisfying to both parties, a lot of communal love will be displayed in the behavior of both parties.

Exchange Theory and Love   Foa and Foa (1974) developed an exchange approach emphasizing the "societal structures of the mind." According to the Foas, as part of the socialization process, people learn what is acceptable to give to or take away from one another in various types of relationships. In their view, the resources people exchange have different degrees of "particularity" and "concreteness." Love is the most particular resource; it matters a great deal from whom we receive love. Money is the least particular and most concrete resource. The resources of status and services are less particular than love and more particular than money. As the Foas view societal norms of exchange, only particular resources can be exchanged for particular resources. People learn that concrete resources such as money should not be given in order to get particular resources such as love. To get love from another, someone must give love, or possibly status—which the Foas have shown to be close to love in the way people think about exchanges. An intriguing proposition of the Foas is that when one gives love to other, one experiences a kind of love from the very act of giving.

Destructive Forms of Love   Love is not always a positive state or emotion. The following types of love are problematic both for oneself and one's partner.

Obsessive Love: As discussed in Chapter 3, Tennov (1979) posited that some people, whom she called limerant, are more subject to romantic and obsessive love than are others. When a devotion to romance and a high degree of obsession regarding another converge, the stage is set for destructiveness. The obsessed person spends so much time thinking about, directing affective energy toward, and acting slavishly around the loved one that he or she feels miserable.

At the heart of obsession is a type of projection featuring the incorrect belief that a person you love and care for returns these sentiments. The sociologist William Goode (1959) made the following statement about this type of projection: "Love is the most projective of drives; only with great difficulty can the attracted person believe that the object . . . does not and will not reciprocate the feeling at all. Thus the person may carry the action quite far, before accepting a rejection as genuine" (p. 38).

The following is an excerpted account taken from Tennov's (1979) report of the conclusion of a love affair between a man and the respondent, an obsessed young woman:

> When I found Danny's letter in the mail box, I actually staggered. I was afraid to read it; my premonition was strong. My hands literally shook as I opened it. . . . It was just one short sentence saying, "Let's call it quits because it's really over for me." It was total, final, the end.
>
> I don't remember how I made it upstairs except that I was in a state of true shock. . . . I hardly breathed. It was as if, if I remained absolutely motionless, it would in some magical way not be true. . . . Then I considered actions . . . like going after Barbara (the woman toward whom Danny's interest had shifted) with a knife or throwing myself out the window. (p. 147)

Though not unusual, such obsession is one of the most dangerous, self-destructive hazards of romantic love. When a lover is obsessed, there is a feeling of helplessness and of losing oneself in another, even when the loved one does not reciprocate. Obsessive romantic love is a narcissistic type of love that degrades you, cannot produce a happy outcome for either party, and prevents you from contributing to the world at large. Tennov (1979) eloquently said of the obsessive limerent: "The limerent endures painfully intense suffering as daydreams smash against the rocks of events, until hope can only be built from the rubble through interpretation" (p. 61).

Infatuation, Need, and Control Disguised as Love: Epstein (1993) analyzed situations in which destructive tendencies masquerade as love. In his discussion of infatuation, he seemed to be referring to a situation in which an individual believes that he or she is "in love" with another person even though there is little basis for that love in the interaction they have had and the loved one may be showing little or no such affection for the infatuated lover. The infatuated lover may be basing his or her feelings on projections about the loved one's signs of love. Infatuation does not involve careful consideration of the other person's true feelings and needs. Rather, it involves idealization of the other person's qualities.

Epstein argued that infatuation is related to automatic, often irrational, thoughts. It is as if you have just encountered the person for whom you have always longed—the person of your dreams. Thus, as in the typical romantic love scenario, you begin to idealize this person, and it may be some time before the "real other" is clear to you.

Epstein contended that need and control create similar illusions. Need refers to the belief common among lovers that they cannot do without the idealized other person, who makes them complete. As Epstein perceptively suggested, one cannot attain a secure love relationship if one is not secure enough to relinquish the relationship.

Love as control is the flip side of love as need. In love as control, the lover expresses his or her insecurity by not being able to love the other without trying to control the other's thoughts and actions. Domination by the lover becomes a frequent pattern when love as control is being played out. In truth, the person who must be in control is exhibiting anxiety about their vulnerabilities. Epstein also noted the "control through guilt" strategy in which lovers try to keep a loved one bound to them through a sense of obligation or guilt. "If you are the right kind of person, you will take care of me and never leave." "Can't you see how much I care about you?" (subtext: You should be ashamed that you cannot appreciate how much I care for you.)

Usually, the love objects of people who are infatuated, needy, or controlling will in time extricate themselves from the situation. Unfortunately, we also see in the news almost daily instances of obsession culminating in violence.

Ideas and Theories Pertaining to Maintenance

Commitment There has been valuable work directed toward distinguishing commitment and love. Following an influential theoretical analysis of commitment and love by Harold Kelley (1983), Beverly Fehr (1988, Fehr & Russell, 1991) conducted a series of studies designed to compare commitment and love. One of her studies asked respondents to list characteristics of these two states. There was some overlap in the characteristics noted, but there also were key differences. The responses for love centered around the experience of a positive emotional state and emphasized the qualities of caring and intimacy. The responses for commitment centered around the experience of making a decision and emphasized the qualities of loyalty and responsibility.

Chicago Sun-Times writer Diane Crowley told a writer to her "Dear Diane" column that "Without a commitment, there may be no love." Crowley was responding to a 40-year-old woman who had been involved with a man for two and a half years, with no sign of marriage in sight. Crowley also said:

> What seems to be spooking Ben [the woman's lover] is commitment, which is the next step when you are "in love." Your undemanding relationship has stayed spectacular because you and Ben have maintained a certain distance from each other. Now you want more closeness, but Ben feels squeezed. He wants to continue the no-strings-attached arrangement—more than friendship, but less than marriage. . . .
>
> If commitment has become a must-have for you, tell Ben how you feel.
>
> If it's clear that what you've seen is what you're gonna get, it may be time to seek true love elsewhere. (March 9, 1993, Section 2, p. 1)

Crowley mentions marriage, but people do not have to be married to be committed to each other. Census Bureau estimates indicate that there are a few million unmarried couples living together in the United States. Such couples often indicate that they are making a commitment to one another through their love and other forms of committing behavior (e.g., living together, being known as a "couple"), and that a formal commitment such as marriage is unnecessary.

As Kelley (1983) implied, commitment pertains to a person's attitude and behavior indicating that he or she will continue in a relationship (as the sayings go, "through thick and thin," "for better or for worse"). Perceived commitment usually depends on various types of behavioral evidence that let a relationship's participants believe they are a couple (Beach & Tesser, 1988). As Caryl Rusbult's important work in the 1980s (e.g., Rusbult, 1983) has shown, when people make investments of time and resources in a relationship, this contributes to their partner's perception that they are committed to it. An engagement ring may symbolize a commitment, but more important may be more subtle indications that one's partner is committed. According to Rusbult, global satisfaction with a relationship is another determinant of perceived commitment.

Hinde (1979) wrote of the "private pledge" as one process by which commitment develops. This pledge may be an explicit act, such as a promise of fidelity. More often, however, it is part of the implicit unfolding of understanding between the individuals. Frequently, people look for evidence that their partner will be exclusive sexually and in terms of closeness and will spurn other romantic possibilities. Ambivalence may develop about whether one's partner is the best one available, or whether one's partner is being faithful. If these fundamental issues are not carefully considered, they can eventually erode a close relationship.

Trust   Trust is vital to a close relationship. Trust is essential for commitments to be made in close relationships. Trust is also necessary for people to engage in what Altman and Taylor (1973) referred to as social penetration. In the process of social penetration, people get to know one another through self-disclosures that increase in depth over time and that tend to be reciprocated by their partners. As Kelley and Thibaut (1978) have suggested, trust is the exchange of actions or messages that over time reduces uncertainty and increases mutual assurance that the close relationship will endure. John Holmes and his colleagues examined the dynamics of trust in close relationships. In so doing, they have developed the concept of trust as a dispositional quality. That is, people are viewed as having varying degrees of trust that they hold about their partner and his or her acts across time and different situations. Rempel, Holmes, and Zanna (1985) developed an 18-item trust scale that covers a range of trust-related experiences. This scale measures a person's perceptions of his or her partner's predictability, dependability, and faith in the future of the relationship.

One finding emerging from this work and reported by Holmes and Rempel (1989) is that highly trusting couples tend to be more positive than couples who are low in trust in their attributes (i.e., ascriptions of what caused an event to occur) and feelings about their partner's behavior in past situations of conflict. Holmes and Rempel suggested that highly trusting couples take a broader perspective on their partner's behavior and do not judge particular actions (e.g., that may be negative for the relationship) out of context.

Holmes and Rempel also analyzed the typical course of the development of trust in a close relationship. They argued that initially "trust is often little more than a naive expression of hope" (1989, p. 192). Later, however, the extent of trust in the relationship becomes part of its defining fabric. Couples may have a little or a lot. Couples may need regular reassurances regarding their trust. Partners may test one another's trustworthiness on occasion.

Issues of fidelity and trustworthiness are some of the most wrenching in a close relationship. Consider Tereza, Tomas's lover in Milan Kundera's (1984) profound love novel *The Unbearable Lightness of Being*. Tereza recently has had sexual relations with someone other than Tomas and is threatened with possible blackmail when someone takes a picture of her and the other person in intimate embrace:

> What would happen if Tomas were to receive such a picture?
> Would he throw her out? Perhaps not. Probably not. But the
> fragile edifice of their love would certainly come tumbling
> down. For that edifice rested on the single column of her
> fidelity, and loves are like empires: when the idea they are
> founded on crumbles, they, too fade away. (p. 169)

Much of what we know as both trust and commitment in close relationships may boil down to the "maturity" of the couple. George Levinger (1983) recognized this:

Beginnings of relationships are marked by the partners' experiences of novelty, ambiguity, and arousal. In contrast, middles are accompanied by familiarity, predictability, and the reduction of cognitive and emotional tension. The smoother the functioning of a marriage, the less will be the partners' self-consciousness of their ambivalence. (p. 336)

To me, maturity is a combination of experience and ability to adapt. We learn, for example, the value of being reliable and dependable, having a broad perspective in judging ourselves and others, and showing our love and commitment.

Similarity in Attitudes, Beliefs, and Values

As discussed in Chapter 3, similarity between partners in their attitudes, beliefs, and values plays a vital role both in getting people together initially and in the maintenance of their relationship (Byrne, 1971). Most of us have a certain degree of dissimilarity with our partners in these areas—e.g., we might support different political parties—but can still maintain our relationship. However, when partners differ in their central beliefs—such as a strong belief in human kindness and altruism (Rokeach, 1960)—it is unlikely that their relationship will last.

Byrne and Murnen (1988) remind us that people often change to varying degrees in their attitudes, values, and beliefs over time. They may not change together. Hence, their similarities may change and the relationship may end.

Sexual and Physical Attraction

For satisfaction to be high in a relationship, it is helpful for sexual and physical attraction to exist over its course. Many people maintain relatively high levels of attractiveness to and for one another over the course of the relationship. In fact, some people grow to view their partner as sexier and more attractive as the relationship progresses. However, people sometimes stay with their partner long after lust and physical attraction are gone. They may be satisfied with the friendship, companionship, and other aspects of the close relationship. So while continued lust may help, it may not be necessary for the maintenance of a long-term relationship.

Sexual and physical attraction may lessen some over a couple's lifetime (with lots of peaks and valleys). Further, members of a couple may reveal different aging patterns, such that one may look youthful for many years, while the other ages quickly. These kinds of bodily changes may affect the attraction people have for their partners and their desire to remain in the relationship.

The Little Things In close relationships, we learn over time to value the little things in our interactions. Steve Duck and his colleagues (1991) have provided evidence about the value of daily talk, even "small talk," in sustaining confidence and satisfaction in a close relationship. In a useful book entitled *How to Live with Another Person* (1974), David Viscott listed little things that can strain a relationship. I have adapted some of the items on his list to create the following list of small behaviors that may contribute to healthy relationship maintenance:

—not hogging the bathroom
—calling when you must come home late
—respecting a closed door by knocking first
—noticing when your partner shows caring
—saying thank you for your partner's helpful acts
—kissing or hugging as a greeting and kissing goodnight
—listening to your partner
—engaging in eye contact when you have conversations

—paying attention to your partner at a party or social occasion
—taking time to ask your partner about his or her day
—smiling and laughing together
—crying together

Close relationships are delicate entitles—not unlike the "fragile edifice" of Tomas and Tereza's love in Kundera's novel. So often their decline occurs subtly and insidiously over time. We cannot readily see the changes, but they are there in the minds, emotions, and behavioral patterns of the people involved. Just like the days of our lives, we need to view and treat close relationships as precious parts of us that can fly away, with finality, in an instant.

I endorse the Hendricks' (1992b) conclusions about love. They said:

> It seems clear that no one volume or theory or research program can capture love and transform it into a controlled bit of knowledge. Love is too complex for that, and even simple questions such as the relation of love to sexuality, cannot be given simple answers. . . . An ultimate purpose in research on love is to help enrich the vocabulary of love such that everybody will have a more variegated, yet integrated conception of love than has existed in past eras. . .
>
> Romantic love may not be essential to life, but it may be essential to joy. Life without love would be for many people like a black-and-white movie—full of events and activities but without the color that gives it vibrancy and provides a sense of celebration. (1992, p. 117)

I would argue that love for others that is well conceived and communicated is one of the major positive ways a person can contribute to and connect with other people. Martin Luther King spoke of such love when he said, "Love is the only force capable of transforming an enemy into a friend." This reasoning is similar to another poignant conclusion offered by the Hendricks: "When we love and are loved in return, we are somehow 'more' than we were before. . . . When we are loved in the bestowal sense, without rules or conditions, loved for exactly who we are at this moment in time, then we are somehow free to become closer to what we might ideally wish to be" (1992, p. 117).

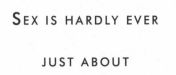

SEX IS HARDLY EVER

JUST ABOUT

SEX.

—Shirley MacLaine

6

THE
VARIED
MEANINGS OF
SEXUALITY

IN MY SEX FANTASY,
NOBODY EVER LOVES ME MORE
FOR MY MIND.

— Nora Ephron

Far from being simply a biological process, sexuality emerges from the circumstances and meanings available to us. Sexuality teaches us a lot about ourselves. It is the source of some of our greatest fears and embarrassments and, at the same time, the source of some of our greatest moments of ecstasy and hope for life. It can represent a time of intense connection to another person—and especially another mind—but it can also represent a time of despair and detachment.

Defining Terms

In our conversations about sexuality, we sometimes talk as if sex pertains only to the act of sexual intercourse, or coitus. This act, however, is only one part of a larger constellation of acts, thoughts, and feelings that define sexuality. McKinney and Sprecher (1991) edited one of the first books that explicitly treated sexuality as part of a close relationship. They offered the following definition of sexuality: "Although this book is about erotic arousal and genital responses, it is also about a lot more. We use *sexuality* very generally to refer to sexual behaviors, arousal, and responses, as well as to sexual attitudes, desires, and communication" (p. 2).

I would also endorse an aspect of sexuality that the sociologist Ira Reiss (1986) emphasized in his book *Journey into Sexuality*. He contended that the essential elements of sexuality are self-disclosure and pleasure. A relatively full sexual relationship involves two people's in-depth communication about their lives, their past loves, their understanding of sexuality, their hopes and fears as they pertain to sexuality.

I do not embrace the term *making love* because I think of love as a state that has durability and depth and evolves rather gradually in a close relationship. Sexuality is probably a necessary but not sufficient part of that evolution. Sexual relations may contribute to love, but they do not "make it" in any substantial sense. Terms like "having sex" or "engaging in sexual relations" are not much better. They limit the scope of the act to the physical activities, and that is unfortunate. As for the euphemisms "to go to bed with" and "to sleep with," sexual relations may occur in places other than a bed, and sleeping might not occur at all.

Definitions and words matter. We ought not confuse them and obfuscate further the vital differences between what occurs during the sex act and what occurs more generally in close relationships. Weber (1993) comments that people *need* to talk about sex, but because it is such an intimate topic, our words are either obscenities or quaint evasions.

A Historical Sketch

The evolution from 1830 to 1980 of sexuality as a public topic has been described and analyzed in a book entitled *Romantic Longings* (1991) by the sociologist Steven Seidman. From the mid to late 1960s to the present, people in the United States have generally shown considerable openness about sexuality and have also experimented with different sexual life-styles to an unprecedented degree. According to Seidman, however, this evolution sometimes has been analyzed as standing in marked contrast to other periods. Seidman suggests that there has been a continuity in the evolution of sexuality and that sexual attitudes and behaviors during periods well before the 1960s were significant precursors of contemporary ones.

Early in our country's history, the Puritans and their successors emphasized a standard of moral purity and constancy in all that people did. They stressed moderation in sexuality and placed severe constraints upon erotic pleasures. Sensual motivations were thought to disturb the emotional and moral constancy they sought. The Puritans believed that their main duty was to serve God. For the Puritans, sex had value only within marriage. Sexual activity outside of marriage was severely condemned. Marital sex was therefore essential in order to prevent an individual from becoming lured into the sins of improper sexuality, including extramarital sex. Sexual activity within marriage was expected, not only to produce legitimate offspring, but also to bring mutual comfort and pleasure. Because of this, Seidman suggested that the Puritans were not so prudish, after all.

Seidman said that marriage during the Victorian period, which took up much of the nineteenth century, was a consensual arrangement based on love. In marriage, sex was not restricted to a procreative function, but was valued as a sign of love and as a domain of sensual pleasure. Sex meant coitus to the Victorians; noncoital sex and masturbation were proscribed during this period. Victorianism represented less a departure from Puritanism than a continuous development of the American intimate culture. The Victorians almost obsessively acknowledged the presence and power of sexuality and unequivocally embraced the value of sex *within marriage*.

As the twentieth century began, attitudes and behavior began to shift swiftly toward more diversity in sexual practices and openness about the topic. No longer would everyone believe that sexuality should be expressed only within marriage. No longer would people necessarily think that partners must be in love to have sexual relations. No longer would people necessarily believe that sexuality was either a duty to be performed within marriage or a spiritual communion. Rather, the meaning of sexuality was, for many, becoming broader to encompass sex for purely pleasurable reasons and with different partners.

Seidman noted that from the 1920s through the 1950s, surveys reported a dramatic increase in nonmarital sexual activity. Interestingly, Kinsey's (1953) famous analysis of female and male sexuality suggested that the number of men going to prostitutes for sex decreased around the 1920s, indicating that after that point men did not need to find prostitutes as much for sexual gratification. His research suggested that there was a major rise in premarital sex by middle-class women in this period. Kinsey found that, while only 14 percent of the generation of women born before 1900 reported premarital coitus, almost 40 percent of the generation born after 1900 reported premarital coitus. During the first 20 years of this century, there also was a dramatic increase in the divorce rate, the spread of venereal disease, and public awareness of homosexuality.

Kinsey (1953) found that sexual activity and attitudes changed radically after 1900. Oral-genital sex was accepted more often. More and longer foreplay was endorsed, as was deep kissing. People experimented with many sexual positions other than the classic missionary position, and they increasingly had sex while nude. Erotic fulfillment began to be seen as necessary for successful love and marriage.

In the last two to three decades this society has become much more open to discussion of sexuality and to diverse sexual practices. During the 1950s, "heavy petting" was expected as part of dating, but not coitus. The period from the mid 1960s to the present saw the widespread acceptance of coitus and other forms of sexuality as a part of dating experiences. The number of sexual partners women had grew at an exponential rate starting in the 1960s (but possibly decreased in the mid 1980s because of AIDS worries). Still, there are residues of the Puritan and Victorian ethos within our psyches regarding sexuality. Indeed, some people within this culture still choose to conduct their intimate and sexual lives in ways that parallel what was advocated during Puritan and Victorian times.

A fascinating topic for which little if any research evidence exists concerns the impact on a person's close relationship of having had many lovers before marriage. Although they do not provide direct evidence about this question, Janet Reibstein and Martin Richards suggest in their book *Sexual Arrangements* (1993) that couples and their parents are increasingly spending a lot of money on weddings as an implicit statement that the couples now are ready to settle down and are off-limits to previous lovers. Will having had many past lovers influence an individual to be more or less faithful in marriage? On the other hand, will a person who has had few past lovers be more likely to engage in affairs? Such questions are especially ripe for study at this time, given the diversity of past sexual experience that people may bring to marriage.

As Weber (1993) observes, the media has played a major role in the evolution of the openness about sexuality in our culture today. We seem to have an unending appetite for talk shows that explore all aspects of private lives. The types of "openness" and "exploration" that we encounter in the media, however, too often are sensationalistic and simplistic, while serious analysis of sexuality, intimacy, and close relationships is minimal.

In the 1990s, have we moved back toward the "heavy petting" period because of our fears? Consider this introduction to an article in *Self* magazine, July 1988, entitled "Sex Without Sex" by Stella Resnick:

> While it may seem as if the last 20 years have broadened our perspective on sex, in some ways we've become more narrow-minded. In the Fifties, "going all the way" was off-limits, but people could "make out" passionately for hours. The Sixties changed all that: Gone were the hours of sensual buildup. Intercourse became the focus of every sexual encounter.
>
> One side effect of this that we're still feeling today: climaxes that are too often anticlimactic. (p. 98)

Essentially, this writer is bemoaning the loss of the endless build-up period before sex. She even goes on to argue for lovemaking without sex—a perfect antidote to the AIDS scare. It is by no means clear that people are deferring sexual behavior in the 1990s in light of concerns about AIDS. However, fear has become part of sex to a degree unprecedented in the recent history of humanity.

Early Encounters

How does sex feel to the novice? Sexuality is at its most vivid and visceral to the person experiencing it for the first time. Unfortunately, there has not been much research or writing on the meaning of eroticism in adolescents' lives (e.g., see Jessor, Costa, Jessor, & Donovan, 1983). It seems clear from available data, however, that young people are first having sexual intercourse at earlier and earlier ages. According to Zelnik and Shah (1983), in the early 1980s 23 percent of female adolescents and 37 percent of male adolescents reported that they had engaged in their first act of intercourse by the age of 14. The writer Frank Conroy poignantly portrays this early sexual experience in a July 1987 *Esquire* article entitled "How Sex Feels."

> And then one night, parked in some out of the way place, in the darkness, loopy and trembling from hours of kissing, his hands warm from her flesh, his head filled with the delirious scent of her, he begins to realize that the impossible event may well be about to occur. She has agreed to move to the back seat. Once there, things move along rapidly. Ever since he turned off the ignition the boy has been swept along by forces he can barely keep in check, the full power of which he must conceal from the

girl, lest she be frightened away. He has pressed forward, but carefully, so as not to overwhelm her tacit right to control the tempo of events. Rather a gentle escalation, instinctively done, without guile, all the more remarkable considering that he is literally drunk with sensation and would have to think hard to remember whether it was Monday or Tuesday. He is in the midst of a storm, a great storm, and some kind of automatic pilot is guiding him. In the dark, chasing the girlness, he has almost forgotten the girl. He has been obsessed with getting her in the back seat, but by the time it happens his perception of her has narrowed to the point where he misses the fact that she actually wants to get in the back seat. He thinks it has all been the storm. His storm. His blindness is almost complete.

When he enters her it is a revelation. Nothing has ever felt so right, so profoundly, self-evidently right. He is in alignment with powerful forces, and in some curious way his own reality seems reconfirmed, as if a fraction of the power had stayed with him, become part of him.

Afterward, he is almost entirely absorbed by his own emotions. It seems a brand new world, after all. But stirring now, faintly, as he watches the girl straighten her clothes, comb her hair, is the truly exotic idea that he might have something in common with her. (pp. 205-206)

Conroy's piece is a fictional essay. But it probably portrays more effectively the actual feelings of many young men in their first sex act than would a real account. But how does the girl feel? We could be horrified by the apparent selfishness of the male in "having his experience" without much regard for the female's experience. Maybe, however, we should be patient with him—this step was only his first on the way to learning (hopefully) to appreciate the mutuality of sexuality and intimacy and the necessity of trying to understand and honor a partner's feelings, too.

It would be helpful if a similarly adroit female essayist would write a comparable account for the young female. We need to know whether she also experiences some type of magical epiphany. If so, perhaps this initial experience transcends gender boundaries. Or is she turned off the experience—not uncommon for the female at this point because of the male's inexperience and failure to be sensitive to her needs? Does either of them think of "safe sex"?

Stereotypes Regarding Sexuality

Throughout the history of this country, stereotyping of people following certain sexual lifestyles and myths about sex have been a salient part of the intimate landscape. Stereotypes are negative attributes about others, usually groups of others. They are usually based on little knowledge or evidence and often are quite simple in their construction and unaffected by evidence to the contrary (e.g., "She is an 'easy lay.' " "He is a 'womanizer.' ").

Throughout history, women and their sexuality have been the targets of the most vicious stereotyping. Such stereotyping goes along with societal customs, religious doctrines, and laws that long have sought to control women's reproductive activities. (Even in the 1990s some men may fear and try to control women's reproduction and everything they do or feel in the area of sexuality.) Labeling a woman a "slut," for example, degrades her and sends a powerful message to other women that they should not take actions that would warrant such a label. So we label and stereotype to try to control others.

Perhaps the most widespread stereotype that gets applied to both females and males is that they are *promiscuous* in their sexual behavior.

This photograph from *Basic Instinct* connotes the manipulativeness of sexuality.
Photography by Ralph Nelson/Tri-Star.

The notion of who is and who is not promiscuous often is problematic. Most people who have had different numbers of partners and types of sexual experience likely discriminate among partners and situations. They do not engage in coitus with just anyone.

There is a lot more to the labeling of women in the sexual arena. Over the course of history, women have been given such contradictory labels as "goddess," "madonna," "witch," " Earth Mother," "temptress," "nursemaid," "priestess," "slave," and "sex object." They have been viewed sometimes as sexually insatiable "nymphomaniacs" and at other times as frigid. Women have been considered the weaker sex, the domineering sex, the gold-digging sex, and the castrating sex. Although such labeling is not as bad as it used to be, and people sometimes show unfair and pejorative views of men, women still bear the brunt of it.

As a small piece of evidence that the sexual double standard is still in place, consider what one 21-year-old woman told author Lillian Rubin (1990): "I'd never tell my boyfriend how many guys I've slept with. . . . It upsets me that I can't be honest about it because it's not the way I want this relationship to be. But I know he'd feel terrible about it because I've heard how he talks about other girls. I don't want him to think I'm a slut, because it's not true" (p. 119).

Rubin herself spoke eloquently of the double standard when she said, "Interesting, isn't it, that even though more than two and a half decades have passed since the sexual revolution brought women a new measure of sexual freedom, there's still no word in the language that doesn't reek with pejorative connotation to describe a woman who has sex freely" (p. 110).

Gender Differences in Sexuality

At present, there is a tremendous amount of media coverage of sexuality, and much of it focuses on gender differences. As an illustration, in June 1993 *Mademoiselle* published a summary of the results of a survey of over 2000 men and women regarding their sexual experiences and attitudes. Prominent findings were: (1) 26 percent of the women could not recall the first and last names of everyone with whom they had had relations vs. 51 percent of the men (presumably this result derived in part from the fact that men, on average, still have a greater number of sexual partners than do women); (2) 9 percent of the women vs. 34 percent of the men indicated that they would have more sexual partners "if it were not for AIDS" (this result reinforces the idea that men are more likely to want more sexual partners than do women but that members of both groups are being more cautious now); and (3) surprisingly, the proportion of women indicating that they do not get enough sex (50 percent) was close to the proportion of men saying they do not get enough sex (63 percent).

Another interesting reflection of our current focus on gender differences in sexuality may be found in a book entitled *The New Male Sexuality* (1993) by psychotherapist Bernie Zilbergeld. This author suggested that more and more men are seeking therapy because they want to learn how to satisfy women sexually. He argued that the media and various social commentators have mercilessly criticized men's traditionally insensitive approach to female sexuality and that essentially "love and sex are becoming feminized" in the 1990s. For men who grew up in the 1950s, a whole new world of opinion about what is valuable and meaningful in sexual behavior has emerged. Men increasingly have heard the message that if they are knowledgeable and sensitive about sex, women tend to enjoy it much more, and, in turn, close relationships become more satisfying in general.

Zilbergeld's findings from his clinical practice reflect a positive change in how men relate to women. But most writers today are not as optimistic about gender relations. A quote in Seidman (1991) attributed to Dana Densmore (in an article in *Radical Feminism*) says a lot about the presumed psychological gender differences in sexuality:

Intercourse, in the sense of the physical act . . . is not necessarily the thing we [women] are really longing for. . . . Physically, there is a certain objective tension and release, at least for a man, when excitation proceeds to orgasm. With a woman even this physical issue is much less clear. . . . The release we feel . . . therefore is psychological. . . . We then enjoy the pleasures of closeness. (p. 139)

Densmore's logic fits with a thesis popular in some circles that connects female sexual values with intimacy, not necessarily sensual pleasure, and that views sexuality, humor, tenderness, and commitment as vital to satisfying sexual relations. On the other hand, male sexuality is seen as being dominated by the genitals, body centered, selfish, and as emphasizing control. This reasoning is much too general and is also marginally sexist. On the other hand, it does challenge men to examine their sexuality and whether it degrades women.

Echoing Densmore, authors Giler and Neumeyer (1992) argued that there are legions of women who have had a series of close relationships and feel betrayed by the sexual revolution. Some have been married, many have dated or been involved in live-in arrangements of varying lengths. They are sexually sophisticated but ambivalent about their goals for an optimal close relationship. Most want a committed relationship, but one that provides a balance of intimacy and independence. They often feel now that sex for sex's sake is shallow and without sufficient meaning. They seek a more profound bond, and are dubious of sexual intimacy as a way of producing emotional intimacy and commitment.

One of the hallmark analyses of gender differences in sexuality was the book *Re-making Love* (1986) by Barbara Ehrenreich, Elizabeth Hess, and Gloria Jacobs. The authors argued that a sexual revolution had occurred for women, starting in the 1960s. They wrote provocatively about how much they thought women had changed.

. . . if either sex had gone through a change in sexual attitudes and behavior that deserves to be called revolutionary, it is women, and not men at all. This fact should be widely known, because it leaps out from all the polls and surveys that count for data in these matters. Put briefly, men changed their sexual behavior very little in the decades from the fifties to the eighties. They "fooled around," got married, and often fooled around some more, much as their fathers and perhaps grandfathers had before them. Women, however, have gone from a pattern of virginity before marriage and monogamy thereafter to a pattern that much more resembles men's: Between the mid-sixties and the mid-seventies, the number of women reporting premarital sexual experience went from a daring minority to a respectable majority; and the proportion of married women reporting active sex lives 'on the side' is, in some estimates, close to half. The symbolic importance of female chastity is rapidly disappearing.

It is not only that women came to have more sex, and with a greater variety of partners, but they were having it on their own terms, and enjoying it as enthusiastically as men are said to. As recently as the 1950s, America's greatest acknowledged sexual problems . . . was female frigidity. Some experts estimated that over half of American women were completely nonorgasmic. . . . But in 1975, a *Redbook* survey found that 81 percent of the 100,000 female respondents were orgasmic "all or most of the time." (pp. 2-3)

Re-making Love was not about love, as most people conceive love. It was about sexuality. Further, despite brief mention of the fear sweeping the United States in the 1980s in connection with the AIDS epidemic, this book does not do justice to how people's libidos have been chilled by this fear.

Communication and Sexuality

Lillian Rubin (1983) suggested that females frequently find males to be wanting in communication of intimacy. She argued that women desire intimacy that is born of verbal expression—whether or not it occurs during sexual episodes. Rubin said: "The problem, then is not *how* we talk to each other but *whether* we do so. And it's connected to what words and the verbal expression of emotion mean to us, how sex and emotion come together for each of us" (pp. 101–102).

Rubin was writing in the early '80s, a time that may represent a distinctly different era in gender relations. Nonetheless, she stressed that men too often engaged in "high sensation-low emotion" sex, while women preferred emotionality and self-disclosure to be central in their sexual experience.

In a more recent analysis of gender, communication, and sexuality, Cupach and Metts (1991) contended that two major generalizations hold when one examines the research literature: (1) A couple's quality of communication is closely linked to the quality of the relationship; and (2) a couple's skill in communicating about sexuality is instrumental in maintaining sexual satisfaction and general satisfaction in the relationship.

We do not have research evidence on how couples talk about sex. Despite this lack of information, we do assume that people interested in having sex often do talk about it first. In 1993, Antioch University established a new sexual harassment policy stipulating that explicit consent must occur before sexual overtures are permitted!

Leslie Baxter (1987) perceptively argued that the typical close relationship does not feature direct communication about sexuality. Rather, it involves the construction of a web of ambiguity in which people signal their desires indirectly. If this is true, Antioch is indeed asking a lot of its students.

Why is this indirectness so prominent in communicating about sexuality? First, it fits into the romantic mindset that guides much early relating and sexuality. Males, in particular, learn that they will disturb the erotic mood if they talk too much about what they desire to do. They learn to rely on signals such as mood music or having a drink. Women probably learn the same scripts, though they may believe that males should take the lead. Second, as Goffman (1959) emphasized, people are often worried about the embarrassment of a direct rejection. Indirect, usually nonverbal signals, let them save face.

One of the few lines of research that has much to say about talking and sexuality was carried out by biologist Timothy Perper (1985). He provided a number of reports by men and women regarding how they seduce persons in whom they have sexual interest. Such behavior may have little relevance to how we talk about sex in established relationships, but it does show how indirect we tend to be in more casual relating. Perper called it "oblique sexual discourse." Here is what one 19-year-old man said about his practice of seduction:

The idea here is simple. There are steps that one follows which lead up to the actual act. No words are desired or necessary. A positive response to one step allows the next step to be initiated, and this continues until she conveys to me the desire to stop the progression. I find it no problem to know when she would like to stop. If we don't stop, we arrive. (p. 178)

Women showed a little more interest in talk about the relationship prior to sex, but they also exhibited considerable indirectness. Here is what a 19-year-old woman said:

I would influence this person by asking how he viewed the relationship at this point. I would feel out what he says; then I would give little hints like: How would you like to come over to my place or your place for a drink? I then think he would get the hint and act accordingly. (p. 179)

Evolutionary Psychology

Sociobiology, or evolutionary psychology, has become a popular means of analyzing human sexual behavior in the 1990s. Its arguments are presented in texts, journal articles, social science conventions, and talk show discussions. This school of thought has adapted parts of the theory of evolution to try to explain male and female dating and mating practices.

The first work that presented the sociobiology position was *Sociobiology: The New Synthesis*, written by biologist Edward Wilson in 1975. Other works from this school include biologist Donald Symons' (1979) *The Evolution of Human Sexuality* and psychologist David Buss's work, which has been published in several journals (e.g., 1989a, 1989b). Buss has been the most active in adapting ideas from Wilson's original work to the domain of dating, relating, and sexuality.

Evolutionary psychology is concerned with how events are related over thousands of years, how the organism and psyche have evolved. In simple terms, evolutionary psychology proposes that males and females have different genetic wiring. Throughout the long hunting-and-gathering phase of human evolutionary history, the argument goes, the sexual desires and dispositions that were adaptive for one sex were a ticket to reproductive oblivion for the other. The most controversial implication of this evolutionary reasoning is that the social double standard (i.e., men can have outside sexual relations, but women cannot) is almost built into people's genes. The evolutionary psychology position is that men tend to have multiple sexual partners as a way of increasing their odds of paternity. On the other hand, women will be more discriminating, since their motivation is to find someone who will be a good caretaker. A final controversial implication of the evolutionary psychology position is that males and females possess different brain anatomy and functioning that contribute to their sexual differences.

Evolutionary psychology emphasizes the biological transmission of genetically programmed patterns of behavior. It does not give a lot of weight to the environment in influencing human action, nor does it focus on the so-called proximate causes of behavior embraced by many in the close relationship field. These include a person's particular patterns of thought, feeling, and perceptions of his or her partner's behavior.

Although evolutionary psychology is strangely mute regarding why some people develop homosexual preferences, it argues that male homosexuals often show behavioral patterns that support the theory. The "American Couples Study" by Blumstein and Schwartz (1983) provides evidence that by far, homosexual men have the greatest number of sexual partners. Symons in his 1979 book suggested that the number of partners gay men had in the San Francisco Bay Area in the late 1970s averaged in the hundreds; 28 percent had had more than 1,000 sex partners in their lives.

Buss (1994) has applied the logic of evolutionary psychology to male-female close relationships. For example, he predicts that in general, males will prefer to have relationships with women who are youthful and reproductively vital (so that they can bear offspring). they also should prefer women who can give the male confidence in his paternity, who are physically attractive (and, hence, who should have attractive offspring), and who show intelligence, social skills, and resourcefulness (cues regarding the female's parenting abilities). On the other hand, females in general should prefer males who show the ability and resources to support offspring. These males may have a lot of status and money and buy the woman gifts, as well as show qualities the woman believes would make them good fathers. If they are younger, these males may show a lot of ambition and industriousness—indicating that they have good potential to attain resources. Strangely, it is not argued that women will also prefer physically attractive and youthful mates. Presumably, resources are their main agenda. Buss has provided data that he contends support the above hypotheses.

Buss and Barnes' (1986) early studies at the University of Michigan were concerned with the tactics of mate attraction. They probed intrasexual (within gender) tactics of mate competition. In one study college students attributed to three persons whom they knew actions that these persons had taken to make them more attractive to the opposite sex. For example, a student might list a woman's wearing a stylish short dress as one tactic, or a male's bringing flowers to his date.

As Buss and Barnes predicted, males emphasized displaying resources and bragging about them while females emphasized staying well groomed and clean, wearing stylish clothes, and using makeup. In a second study, these data were replicated with a sample of young newlywed couples. In a third study, college students were asked to assess how effective in attracting a member of the opposite sex were the tactics that had been listed by previous respondents. The data again supported Buss and Barnes' hypotheses. The female tactics rated most effective were good grooming, sense of humor, sympathy to the male's troubles, and showering daily. Male tactics seen as effective included good humor, sympathy, good manners, and spending a lot of time with the female.

It is not clear that these results are related to evolution. The sex differences found may be the result of people's scripted approach to answering the questions that were asked. For example, because such an emphasis is everywhere in the culture, a female may think that she should emphasize her looks when she notes characteristics that males will appreciate. Similarly, a male may believe that the "best" answer is to emphasize his status and resources when he indicates qualities that females will like.

How does having a good sense of humor relate at all to evolution? Maybe it is valued because people face many pressures in their daily lives, and a good sense of humor in another person helps lighten their feelings of stress. But such reasoning focuses attention on environmental factors and not evolutionary processes.

Let's consider one additional perspective on Buss and Barnes' data. It is possible that older males and females (usually in their early 30s and beyond) converge quite a bit in the qualities they desire in their mates. Today, both sexes probably look for similarity in beliefs, attractiveness and health, resources, and occupational success or promise in a close relationship. If this convergence occurs with experience in dating and mating, it suggests again that younger people's report of what they want may be culturally scripted. They may not know what they want early on and need experience to find out. This type of argument emphasizes people's reactions to their environment and does not require any reference to evolutionary processes. It deserves to be evaluated in future research.

More generally, the assumption of a built-in tendency by males to be more oriented toward having more sexual partners than females usually leads to a lot of discussion, as well it should! One criticism of this assumption is that it is a justification or apology for a double standard of sexual conduct. Another criticism is that males who inseminate many females should be the least certain as to the paternity of their offspring, assuming that these females will also be inseminated by other males. On the other hand, if simply having more offspring was the main goal of male sexual behavior, inseminating more partners should enhance that probability. If paternity was the male's main objective, he must make sure that the female he inseminates is not inseminated by other males—fidelity to her may be one such tactic. Another challenge to the double standard is that if a female has a number of sexual partners, it is unlikely to have any detrimental effect on her ability to take care of her offspring. It might even provide her with a better sampling of possible partners from which to choose. Finally, it should be clear that men and women have sexual relations for a variety of reasons other than reproduction. In fact, they often have sexual relations with the intent to avoid reproduction.

It is unfortunate that, to date, evolutionary psychologists have not tried to blend their ideas with those embracing so-called proximate processes. Certainly, evolution has played a major role in the unfolding of those proximate processes. Psychologist Sandra Bem (1993) discusses the importance of interactions between the environment and evolution in her book *The Lenses of Gender*. Bem argued that the sociobiology position is one of "biological essentialism" (i.e., the belief that biology is destiny). She said that arguments derived from this position have failed to recognize the powerful role of situational context in interacting with or moderating biological gender differences. She said:

> . . . the interaction between situation and biology is insufficiently theorized; hence, the theorists jump too quickly to the conclusion that either sexual difference or sexual inequality is the product of biology alone. . . .
> The failure to theorize biology in context has fostered wild and premature speculation about the existence of profound differences between the sexes in the biology of their genes and their brains. (p. 29)

Fidelity in the 1990s

It is likely that the number of sexual partners people have while they are single has decreased at least somewhat from its high in the late 1970s and early 1980s. Weber (1993) mentions a scene from the movie *The Big Chill* that humorously addresses how fear of sexual disease affects fidelity. In this scene, several women, who are former college friends now in their 30s, are musing about the realities of making relationships work. One who has recently remarried comments, "Well, I know Richard will always be faithful to me."

"Wow!" responds another woman, "that committed, huh?"

"Oh, no," says the wife, "fear of herpes."

Such notions notwithstanding, available evidence suggests that infidelity in marriage is alive and well in the 1990s. Hite (1987), Bringle (1991), and Buunk (1991) and other writers and scholars have estimated that married people continue to have affairs at a relatively high rate—from about 25 to 70 percent of all married people, depending on the study you choose. The very high percentage reported by Hite is suspect because her sample was limited to the readers of a particular magazine who responded to a request to write to her regarding whether they had been faithful.

Other researchers have come up with much lower figures. Tom Smith, at the National Opinion Research Center at the University of Chicago, found that only 1.5 percent of people surveyed in 1989 reported that they "cheated" on their spouse in the last year. This percentage is suspiciously low. How do we know that the respondents felt comfortable reporting whether or not they had engaged in affairs (or were doing so)? How do we know they were not concerned that their spouse would discover their answer to the question about affairs?

It is not clear whether there are many people who continuously have affairs throughout their marriages. Apparently, some may have one long-term lover on the side. There are some who have one or a couple of brief affairs and then stop. The data are hardly precise, in part because of people's reluctance to talk about their affairs with researchers; and people also sometimes distort their reports of affairs.

In an August 11, 1991, article in the *Cedar Rapids Gazette*, Mike Kilen wrote about how he found a group that put on parties involving recreational sex. One of the people he interviewed indicated that he met interested couples through advertisements in adult magazines; he then made sure that they were married, disease- and drug-free, and knew the rules of party etiquette, specifically that "no means no." He also indicated that while men mostly initiated interest in joining, women quickly became the most enthusiastic members. This parallels reports from "swinging" groups in the United States and abroad from the late 1960s onward (Buunk & Van Driel, 1988).

Mary Batten (1992) in *Sexual Strategies* argued that the tradition of adultery is a long one in human existence. She traced it back to a high point in the time of the troubadours of the thirteenth century. The troubadours were young French noblemen who became traveling poets who roamed about celebrating the value of romantic love and the passions of different women. Batten claimed that the love portrayed by the troubadours was centered on adulterous passion and hostility toward marriage. Batten argued that romance novels reinforce the double standard because they often focus on fantasies about forbidden relationships. She contended that the romance novels, like a drug, may yield temporary, illusory relief from one's close relationship problems; but in the long run, it provides neither ideas nor encouragement to help women deal with the real problems of their relationships.

There are writers and quasi-therapists who now argue that on occasion—as when a marriage is "dead"—affairs may be healthy. Such a message was offered by Dalma Heyn (1992) in *The Erotic Silence of the American Wife*. Based on interviews with her friends and acquaintances, she argued that women who have been forever loyal and self-sacrificing while the husband fools around outside the marriage are now giving themselves permission to look outside the marriage for sexual relationships. She argues that women have dalliances for the same reasons men do: they feel neglected or their sex life is not good.

Critics have been quick to raise concerns about any therapeutic position that might be construed as recommending affairs as a way of making a primary relationship better. If the primary relationship is "dead," why not officially end it, rather than developing some other complicating relationship? Further, as many have noted, while having an affair may be fun at first, it ultimately may adversely affect not only the primary relationships but also bystanders such as children.

Humans being what we are, we will probably continue to be attracted to the "greener grass" of outside relationships. Whether or not fidelity is essential for happiness and success in close relationships has been debated for decades. The passage that follows, from Edward Carpenter's (1896) *Love's Coming-of-Age*, shows that almost 100 years ago, there were critics of monogamous marriage. The essence of Carpenter's critique was the rather romantic idea that monogamy stunts love and the human spirit:

A marriage, so free so spontaneous, that it would allow of wide excursions of the pair from each other, in common or even in separate objects of work and interest, and yet would hold them all the time in the bond of absolute sympathy, would by its very freedom be all the more poignantly attractive, and by its very scope and breadth all the richer and more vital. . . .

It has been the inability to see and understand this very simple truth that has largely contributed to the failure of the monogamic union. (p. 123)

Accounts of Singles' Sexual Behavior in the Age of AIDS

Has sexual behavior among singles really changed that much in the 1990s as a result of the AIDS scare? Apparently it has changed in some ways, but in other ways it parallels the sexual behavior of singles in the 1970s. As anecdotal evidence, let's consider the following accounts by singles collected by the magazine *New Woman* (September 1989, interviews conducted by Karen Friefeld):

Charlie, 28, public relations executive, Jersey City, New Jersey: I've been living with someone for a couple of years, but I don't necessarily equate love with fidelity. And I've found that the fact that I am in a committed relationship makes me more desirable: women who are paranoid about AIDS look at me as risk-free.

Not long ago, for instance, I met someone at a convention who I'd had a long business relationship with over the phone. We went out for drinks and decided we liked each other. . . . We went back to my hotel room. I made two drinks and she commented on the view, but from then on there wasn't much conversation. In the midst of what you would call foreplay . . . she said: "I heard something to the effect that you're living with someone. . . . This is fun, but now I want to sleep with you, and we can."

"We can [he said]?"

"Yes, I'm on the Pill," she said. (p. 48)

Beverly, 34, writer, Lawrence, Kansas: I don't think AIDS has sculpted my lifestyle. Living in the Midwest, one feels isolated from the crisis—I don't know anyone who has AIDS. But I really think it's my age. I don't get a lot of pleasure out of sleeping around anymore.

. . . Now I'm looking for someone permanent. I don't know if I've found him, but I recently began living with someone. We met last year, through friends, at a bar. I was just breaking up with someone I'd been with for two years, so I didn't want a relationship right away, and I wouldn't sleep with him for a month because of that. . . . But then I realized I was in love with him.

We were sitting on the roof, watching the sun go down, when I told him I wanted to sleep with him. . . . Afterward, he told me he'd had an AIDS test. I just laughed and said, "well, I didn't." . . . I just know I'm not going to get AIDS. (p. 49)

William, 28, political correspondent, Washington, D.C.: I figure I've slept with roughly 100 women. A lot of them were "incidents." I haven't cut down since the AIDS scare, either. I think because, as they get older, women are more eager.

I do have sort of a reputation, and because of it, two years ago . . . I went for an AIDS test. Now I say, "Yeah, I was tested, I'm clear," and it eases their minds.

Ever since I was tested, I have not had sex without a condom. (p. 49)

Ruth, 29, air-traffic controller, Palo Alto, California: I like the more traditional sexual climate AIDS brought about. A few years ago, I slept with someone just to prove to myself that I could go out and have fun. But it wasn't fulfilling.

Last year, I started dating John, a man I work with. He wanted to have sex after about four months, and I was panicked because of the AIDS epidemic. I knew him fairly well, but not well enough to say, "How many people have you slept with?

Can I have references?" He had been married, but he also had been single for a while. So I said, "I don't feel comfortable. I'd like to have sex, but I'd like to be more sure we don't spread anything." I suggested we go for AIDS tests. . . . Although I'd only slept with five men in my life, I was concerned, because I thought one of them might have been bisexual.

When I got the results, it was a great relief. . . . Two days later, he called me with the same news. . . .

I went on the Pill, but he also uses a condom. The only reason I can think of is that he's waiting for a commitment. We've been together a little over a year now and I feel much more comfortable with myself. I think this is the way it's supposed to be done (p. 50).

These accounts show the diversity in the sexual attitudes and behavior of the singles world of the 1990s. There is considerable sexual activity. Some people are now diligently checking out their partners before commencing sexual activity. They also may be sure to always use condoms. Others, however, are asking few questions and avoiding condom use, sometimes because their partners have been in a relationship for a lengthy period, and sometimes because they simply believe that given their circumstances, they will not get AIDS.

The Need for Education and Public Dialogue

In our society we do too little open, thoughtful talking about sexuality as it occurs in the context of relationships. There is hardly any information on whether teachers in the 1990s are systematically educating their classes about sexuality and relationships. There are usually courses on one or the other, but seldom are the courses offered together. Sex education at all levels emphasizes anatomy and functioning. Seldom, though, do such courses attempt to link sexuality with the thoughts, feelings, and behaviors associated with close relationships.

From all reports that I have heard in over 20 years of teaching students in their late teens and early twenties, most parents are more negligent than schools; they skim over these topics, or avoid them like the plague. They may teach the young person about birth control or condom use. But it is rare to hear about parents openly and knowledgeable discussing the various issues of sex and relating with their children. Young people do see television and movie depictions of relationships, and these may attempt such discussion, but usually they are simplistic and unrealistic about difficulties that may be encountered.

However, there are reasons for optimism. Courses at the university level—but not at the secondary school level—that link sexuality, relationship, and family matters are plentiful now. Good, thoughtfully written books are appearing every day. The children of the 1990s, too, have learned a lot from observing their parents, who often are re-entering the dating world even while their children are dating. Some parents are discussing these issues with their children openly and with maturity. Consider the following words of wisdom contained in a letter sent by a mother to her son, who was about to become engaged in his early 20s:

Sex. For lack of a better word, I call this section "sex." I dislike the word. It is so harsh and impersonal and animalistic. But "intercourse" is not adequate; it denotes only a small part of the sexuality between husband and wife. . . .

Married sex is much less important than most young people in the first throes of romantic love think it to be. It is something you do sometimes because you want children, but most of the time because it feels good, or because the situation seems to demand it, or because your partner expects it. But sex is not just something you do, it is something you are—male and female—alike in many ways but different in crucial aspects.

There is a cliché that women make love when things are right and men make love to make things right. The problems bred by that small difference are immeasurable. I recall the many nights I would go to bed, exhausted from a sixteen-hour day of physical work, resentful that I had gotten little or no help, dehumanized by a day or many days with no adult interaction or conversation, and as we crawled into bed, I would think, if he tries to make love, I'll scream.

But that dear man, unaware of the anger I was feeling or perhaps feeling guilty for his lack of attention or help, would respond as men tend to respond by reaching over and trying to make things right by making love. And I, out of some sense of duty, or simply not wanting to hurt his feelings, would acquiesce, even managing to act as if I enjoyed it, but inside hostility would be brimming over.

Talking to young wives, especially mothers, I have found this to be a common complaint and the source of great marital discord. Women want and need to be tenderly courted. Make a promise to yourself now that you will never initiate love-making with Patty if you haven't first spent time in real conversation with her—listening to her problems and pain, taking her feelings seriously. . . .

But it takes time and experience and perhaps luck to sense those moments and respond. I read once that it takes a couple an average of two years to achieve sexual adjustment. I don't know what that means. Sexual adjustment is not something you achieve and then possess forever after. Each act is a new experience, a new challenge. (letter shared with the author by a student in his class)

PEOPLE CHANGE AND FORGET TO

TELL EACH OTHER.

—Lillian Hellman

Chapter

7

PASSAGES: CHALLENGES TO RELATIONSHIPS OVER TIME

EVERYTHING THEY KNOW

THEY KNOW TOGETHER—

EVERYTHING, THAT IS, BUT ONE:

THEIR LIVES THEY'VE LEARNED LIKE

SECRETS FROM EACH OTHER, THEIR

DEATHS THEY THINK OF IN THE

NIGHTS ALONE.

—Archibald MacLeish,
"The Old Gray Couple"

In trying to analyze human lives and close relationships, we perhaps forget that they are not static; what exists today may change drastically tomorrow. This chapter takes its title from Gail Sheehy's *Passages*, a well-known book for the general public about change in the individual. It will address the ways in which relationships change over time, and how these changes affect the partners. Why do we need the concept of passage in studying close relationships? My answer is that the concept of passages keeps our focus on the omnipresent process of change. We can learn much about ourselves and others by listening to, interacting with, and observing people at all ages and stages. Surprisingly however, there have been only a few scholarly works that probe changes over the course of an individual's lifetime—and even fewer that trace the life of a couple. Sheehy's book will be discussed at various points.

For our purposes, a passage will refer to a clear-cut cycle or season in the life course. It is a period, not necessarily of long duration, that differs significantly from previous or subsequent periods. During a passage, events occur that are of major consequence in an individual's or couple's life. For example, just as we speak of individuals' mid-life passage (and the related "mid-life crisis"), similarly we may speak of couples' "middles," to use Levinger's (1983) term. Events happening during a couples' middle period (roughly after several years of a close relationship) often differ markedly from events transpiring at the time of meeting and making a commitment.

The changes observed in an individual's life and relationships may resemble changes other have experienced. Thus, the idea of a passage sometimes implies a norm, indicating how people generally have behaved, thought, and felt at a particular point.

How long is a passage? Focusing on the individual and not necessarily the couple, Daniel Levinson (1978) suggested that new developmental tasks (e.g., starting a family) come along regularly in life and that no cycle can last more than seven or eight years. But this number seems fairly arbitrary. It might make sense for an adolescent to go from dating to marriage in a relatively short time. An individual's mid-life, however, might readily be conceived to stretch from the age of 30 to the age of 60.

Passages may contain various social scripts, sets of learned behaviors and attitudes. The divorce script, for instance, is a common part of the middles cycle of many couples' lives.

In speaking of scripts, Hulbert (1993a) made an interesting point about women having less clear-cut scripts than do men. She said:

> Men have had a relatively straightforward "script" to follow; career progress provides obvious benchmarks of attainment in comparison to peers. Until recently, the script for men has been so clear-cut that men generally have not had to construct their lives consciously through the young-adult years. By contrast, women of every cohort have consciously had to consider how to fit together their own abilities, interests, and values, their changing networks of relationships, the changing gender-role norms and expectations, and the changing structure of opportunity. Women have constructed and reconstructed their lives more actively while moving through the young-adult years. As a consequence, they seem to arrive at midlife with a stronger and more integrated sense of self than men do. (p. 429)

Closely related to passages is the concept of a turning point, a powerful event that changes someone forever. One example occurs in Robert Waller's 1992 novel *The Bridges of Madison County.* The protagonists Francesca, a farm wife, and Robert, a traveling photographer, fall in love and have a passionate, "once-in-a-lifetime" affair that lasts but a few days. Then Francesca returns to being a wife and mother and Robert leaves town. Both go on to lead separate lives, pining away for one another for decades until each has died. They also rejoice, however, in having had "one true love experience." Although it lasted a short period, their interaction changed their lives. Therefore, it was a major turning point for both persons.

Valerie Bentz (1989) argued that people use turning points such as broken marriage plans and health crises to become mature. She referred to turning points as "axial events." Bentz's ideas were based on autobiographies from and interviews with 53 women who were mostly in their late 20s and older. They were questioned about major influences in their development. Much of the focus of the women's commentaries was on the "unfinished business of childhood," or unresolved conflicts with their parents and other significant persons in their early years. She wrote:

> The ghosts and spirits of childhood haunt and inspire us throughout our lives. In order to become mature, it is important that we rid ourselves of the ghosts of immature parents and others. The women in this study have broken significant ground in doing this in their own lives. They found that by remembering their childhood, and by writing about it and discussing it with others, they could catch up with some of these ghosts and exorcise them. (p. 249)

What frequently defines a turning point is that it comes out of the blue and shakes to the core our taken-for-granted world. It is the type of event that makes us say afterward, "Every minute that we live is precious and should be treated as such." It is an event, such as the sudden loss of a loved one, that stops us dead in our tracks and stirs our emotions in ways that are unpredictable and uncontrollable. It then lives on in our memories and our most self-revealing stories and in the images and symbols that populate those stories.

When we divide a life into passages, we do not do justice to the enormous variability that individuals and couples exhibit. Further, we may imply that there is little flexibility for movement away from what is normative, or what typically occurs during a particular period. For instance, although many couples experience major relationship conflict near some middle point (sometimes corresponding to the birth of a first child), many do not. Enough do to treat this period as one to watch. But such treatment should not be seen as implying that there is a lock-step sequence to the development of conflict in our lives.

Also, the idea of passages may suggest a certain order of change, but often such an order does not exist. Couples and individuals may jump across segments that others have experienced in a serial fashion. Couples and individuals may reverse the sequence that others have shown.

Another caveat is that much of this chapter concerns passages that middle-class individuals and couples may go through. This is the population that research focuses on. What do we know about the passages and close relationships of people who from early in life know only destitution and poverty? What abut those people who live much of their lives in institutions for the disabled or mentally ill? A March 1993 fire in a single-room-occupancy hotel in Chicago killed 19 older individuals. In the analysis of the cause of the fire, the life-styles of some of these victims were discussed in the media. They involved periods of homelessness and little contact with relatives, or even friends or associates. What do we know about the passages of millions of people in their 20s and beyond who are spending much of their lives in SROs, homeless shelters, cardboard boxes, or on sidewalk heating grates? Unfortunately, little. And no one seems to care very much that we know so little.

A Popular View of Passages

Passages-type analysis of relationship events is often presented in popular literature. It may be presented in the form of what to beware of at various points in a relationship. As an illustration, let us consider a recent analysis presented by Dr. Georgia Witkin in the April 4, 1993, issue of *Parade Magazine*. Dr. Witkin suggested that there are eight major periods in a close relationship (she wrote mainly of marriage), which correspond roughly to the number of years that the relationship has been ongoing.

Witkin's first phase is "Year 1: The Honeymoon." In this period, she contended that intimacy means sex for most couples. Frequency and intensity are high, and most couples say they are satisfied. Witkin said that gender differences in communication and intimacy styles become evident during this period: "She wants more emotional intimacy with their sex; he wants more experimental sex with their intimacy. She wants to talk about feelings; he wants to talk politics" (p. 12).

Witkin's description of this period is a lot like Rubin's (1983), which was discussed in Chapter 4. Recall that Rubin believes that early in the relationship, the female often encounters the male's reluctance to be emotionally expressive and to listen to her "troubles talk."

In the second period, which Witkin labeled "Years 2 to 5: A Balancing Act," the couple is faced with the challenge of balancing self-disclosure and privacy, invasion and isolation. She argued that during this period, some couples pull each other so close and share so many secrets that they suffer claustrophobia. She offered a special caution about the powerful self-disclosure process: "Your fantasies about others and past exploits may be forgiven but never forgotten. Be guided by consideration and respect for your partner's feelings—and by common sense" (p. 12).

The third period was labeled "Years 5 to 10: Finding Time." Now daily life becomes especially hectic, and subtle but crucial processes may begin that will be problematic for the relationship a little later. This period frequently involves parenting and all the work and time that go into this role. It also may be a time in which one or both partners try to juggle a fast-paced career with emerging family needs. Witkin advised couples to be sure to devote time to intimacy during this period. She espoused viewing intimacy as an island of pleasure that may act as an antidepressant in the midst of life's many stresses. She advised against making sexual demands, but stressed the need to allot time for one's partner and showing affection.

In the fourth period, referred to as "Years 10 to 20: Beware of Boredom," Witkin suggested that the routine nature of a long relationship may come to be its downfall. It may come to involve little intimacy/sexual activity. She suggested that sexual activity may be reinvigorated during this period by "trying teen sex" (perhaps making out in the backseat of your car), or "romantic sex" (which might involve building a fire and cuddling on the rug in front of it). She noted that women probably would have to help men achieve this new atmosphere or relearn the fun of foreplay.

Witkin defined the fifth period as "Years 20 to 30: The Dangerous Decade." In this cycle, romantic interest may begin to climb again, partly because of the "empty nest" syndrome. Couples may rediscover each other romantically when, finally, the kids are launched into the world. Also, during this period, Witkin posited that outside affairs may be a peril for the couple, with some men, in particular, experiencing a mid-life crisis and seeking reassurance about their aging faculties through an affair.

"Years 30 to 40: Renewal" was the sixth period described by Witkin. She said, "These can be wonder years, because a second childhood—a time to play together—is possible" (p. 13). She goes on to argue that emotional intimacy during this time may be more expressive, honest, and sensual.

Witkin described a seventh period as "Years 40 to 50: Too Much Togetherness?" These are the typical retirement years, when people frequently complain of being together too much and getting on one another's nerves. She suggested that they should negotiate some "breathing room." As with all of the other periods, Witkin contended that sexuality should be a regular, normal part of this period.

Witkin's eighth cycle was described as "Years 50+ . . . and Many More!" She argued that emotional intimacy during this period may literally keep you alive. It stimulates morale, mental stability and is associated with better nutrition and health care. Witkin noted that many surveys suggest becoming "good friends" along the way is crucial to getting this far.

Witkin's article should be of value to many couples. It is based more on common wisdom than it is on research evidence. But such a basis is fine given her objective of alerting people to the major sequence of periods and issues that couples may experience. One major difficulty with Witkin's analysis is that it really does not help couples figure out how to become close across time. Her brief portrayal leaves the couple in the first period, for example, in an isolated existence in which each partner does not know how to meet the intimacy needs of the other. Her statement aptly presents the gender dialogue dilemma but points toward no positive change process. Just one such process would be the man's learning to be more emotionally expressive with his partner, because he gains personal release from such an experience while at the same time giving her more emotional satisfaction.

Another problem is that many of us will never experience that many years with the same romantic partner. With a divorce rate since the mid-1970s of around 50 percent, people in mid-life who have divorced at least once, but who are now re-married, are not likely to reach their fiftieth anniversary, the "golden anniversary," with their current partner. They simply won't live that long!

Witkin overgeneralizes by failing to take into account the movement back and forth between, and skipping over, marital phases couples may experience. Young couples, for example, may move quickly from their honeymoon phase into a dangerous period in which mid-relationship-type events, such as affairs, occur. Couples may also move through all of the stages that Witkin posited well before the 50-year mark. Or a couple may point to a day or a week in their relationship that was so difficult and ripe with potential calamity that it seemed like a year to them.

Witkin is also insensitive to some complex modern realities. Many two-career couples wait until their 30s or even 40s to begin raising kids. Thus, unlike in Witkin's stages, they may be only half-way through child rearing during their third decade together.

Nor did Witkin address the fact that many couples do not have children. Their lives together will likely reveal dynamics different from those of couples who do have children. Rubin (1983) noted that the preponderance of research evidence suggests that couples without kids are more satisfied with their relationship than are couples with kids. (However, this type of generalization does not do justice to the many nuances of how children affect relationship satisfaction. For example, "without kids" may mean that a couple has raised kids already and that the children are out of the household. In such a case, the couple may be newly free to travel and do things that they could only dream about while their kids were being raised. Couples who never had children may or may not feel regret and that they missed out on something important. There are many other factors that we understand only in part that may mediate the effects of children on relationship satisfaction.)

Other Views Of Passages

Youth A 1984 UPI headline screamed out LONELINESS HAUNTS "NEW GENERATION." Based on Megan Marshall's (1984) *The Cost of Loving,* the article that followed suggested that many women in their 20s who grew up with women's liberation and sexual liberation were finding life lonely. This loneliness resulted from the new responsibilities associated with their greater opportunity for work, different life-styles, and sexual diversity. This piece went on to say that many women now preferred more traditional approaches to relationships, including being a housewife and facilitating the man in his career. In part, this preference was based on these women's fears about getting involved in a career and missing out on starting a marriage and family in their 20s. They were also worried about the apparent shortage of available men for marriage, as we discussed in Chapter 3.

I doubt that the thesis of that 1984 report still holds for a great many women in the United States. The desirability of career development and the satisfaction of work outside the home, not to mention the frequent need for dual career incomes to make a living, are deeply embedded within young women's mind-set about their futures. Certainly there are some who have given up the "rat race" to become stay-at-home mothers. But the movement away from this role has been very significant in the last two decades, which influences the passages both for young women and men of the 1990s. Those passages continue to reflect the strain of trying to balance work and relationships. This is a time of vast "cultural sea changes," as they were described by *Washington Times* writer Suzanne Fields in a March 25, 1993, article portraying the turmoil and uncertainty facing the young in the 1990s. For American teens, this historical period is associated with high rates of poverty, drug use, suicide, crime and homicide, sexually transmitted disease, and unwanted teen pregnancy.

People who are dating and forming close relationships in their turbulent adolescent years and early 20s face some special events. They may just be beginning to cut their ties with their families of origin. They often are concerned about school, college, careers, and most of all, their own identity and goals. On top of this is nature's plan that they begin to date seriously and to make their first moves toward mating. Their biological readiness is often far superior to their psychological readiness for mating. Yet try they will.

Sheehy (1976) wrote that love at age eighteen is largely an attempt to find out who we are "by listening to our own echo in the words of another" (p. 96). Teens often become obsessed with their lovers and smother them with their possessiveness, usually a direct result of their insecurity. Carol Gilligan (1982) argued that young women often confuse identity with intimacy, defining themselves through relationships with others.

A common sequence of events for marriages of people age 17 to 19 is as follows: getting married (usually without parents' approval); having a child within a year or so; having major marital problems; being divorced within three to five years; and rejoining the mating game. Cherlin (1992) estimated the divorce rate among married teens to be as high as 75 percent. Sheehy (1976) described the teen marriage as a "jailbreak marriage." It involves fleeing parents and their rule in the teenager's life. The teens' aim is to get out of the home, and they may only vaguely understand the person they are marrying and what it would be like to spend a good portion of their life with that person.

On the other hand, what if a couple waits until age twenty-four or -five (the national average point) to marry? Will they avoid the common quick divorce passage often experienced by married teens, which has been estimated to be as high as 75 percent (Cherlin, 1992)? They surely have better odds. But even if they are older and more experienced with close relationships, the complexities of a long term union are such that they still have a lot to learn. Recall the many issues discussed in the meeting chapter about readiness for a close relationship. I would venture that the best biological-psychological readiness for marriage does not take place until one has had *a lot of experience dating, considering marriage—including doing and talking about intimacy and what it means to achieve closeness.* Most individuals likely would not be able to develop this level of experience until they had reached at least their mid- to late-twenties.

Many people say that they do not want to wait until their 30s to start a family because they want to be relatively young parents. This is a very reasonable desire. However, if they rush this stage much beyond their experience and age, this passage might cause great early heartbreak. For this type of heartbreak cannot be readily avoided simply by listening to and watching their parents relate (assuming their parents have a good relationship), reading of relationship books, listening to marital counselors, and so on. Perhaps it can be avoided only after they have moved into a more middles period when they are hopefully *a lot* wiser about close relationships.

Many young people experience the following passage: A young man and woman, each neophytes in the love arena, begin dating and engaging in sexual activity around the age of seventeen. Then one of the partners breaks off the relationship after a certain period—say six to eight months. However, the other partner desperately wants the relationship to continue. He or she may feel that life is not worth living without the relationship and may threaten to harm the former lover or commit suicide if this person does not return.

Obsessed love often happens when young people do not have much experience in dating and relating and may cherish the presence of someone special in their lives to make them feel complete and give them stability. The breakup is acutely difficult for teens who, for a variety of reasons, feel that they do not have options for other possible mates. The psychology is one of uncontrollable loss. The insecure young person has not developed the resiliency that usually comes through experience in dating in order to withstand feeling that only dire options exist.

The type of insecurity that is at the heart of obsession will pass and change to security if the young person takes the loss as a challenge to develop personal identity and goals of higher individual accomplishment. The person has to recognize that other passages will occur and that, with learning and patience, he or she may perceive more control when next faced with difficulty.

People in their 20s also have illusions regarding close relationships, as discussed by Sheehy (1976). Men and women at this age often project their needs onto the person whom they love. They invent their version of the loved other. The man may view his partner as a mother when he needs mothering, a child requiring his protection, a beautiful seductress who proves his merit and potency. He may also see her as his therapist (with whom he can discuss his work problems) and his guarantor of a degree of immortality because she will bear his children. Similarly, the young woman may create in her mind a male partner who is very successful, growth oriented, sensitive, caring, sexy, dependable, and who will take care of her intimacy needs. Given these projections of their partner's many assets, both the male and the female may view themselves as without question "in love." As Sheehy and other commentators have noted, however, the love of people at this stage is often characterized by lust and a hunger for approval more than by an in-depth appreciation of and respect for another person.

Sheehy said that such illusory expectations may be necessary to give us a sense of excitement and the power to overcome life's obstacles. As we grow older and wiser, we learn to compromise and to take a much more realistic look at ourselves and our partners.

People in their 20s may feel caught between their goal of becoming independent and their quest to find someone with whom they can have great intimacy. This conflict may be especially difficult for women who want careers but who also want a husband and a family.

One of the most interesting observations emerging from Levinson's (1978) study of the evolution of young men's lives is that to be successful, a person needs a dream. The dream involves one's hopes for career success and how one links those hopes with domestic pursuits, such as marriage and a family. Levinson and his colleagues said that to achieve their dreams, men in their 20s needed a mentor in whose footsteps they could follow as well as an anchor in their personal life. The best such anchor, they maintained, is a "loved women" who could help define and carry the dream and create a life within which the dream could have a place.

Levinson, whose study focused only on male respondents, did not emphasize the reciprocal need that exists for women to have a dream and the role of men in helping them pursue it. It is likely that these factors are instrumental in many women's successes. The 1993 U.S. Supreme Court appointee Ruth Bader Ginsburg has credited much of her professional success to the supportive home life created by her husband, Martin.

Sheehy (1976) made this observation about the critical role women have played in helping men fulfill their dreams:

> If women had wives to keep house for them, to stay home with vomiting children, get the car fixed, fight with the painters, run to the supermarket, reconcile the bank statements, listen to everyone's problems, cater the dinner parties, and nourish the spirit each night, just imagine the possibilities for expansion— the number of books that would be written, companies started, professorships filled, political offices that would be held, by women. (p. 157)

Fortunately, a new day has arrived for many women in the 1990s. Some husbands do stay home now and/or attend to many of the chores mentioned by Sheehy.

"Middles" Couples

In the middle of the journey of our life I found myself in a dark wood, for I had lost the right path.

—Dante

Mid-life is a frequently discussed passage in part because members of the well-populated "baby boom" generation are going through it now. Authors such as James Hollis, in his book *The Middle Passage* (1993), Ross Goldstein, in his book *Fortysomething* (1990), and William Bergquist, Elinor Greenberg, and Alan Klaum, in their book *In Our Fifties* (1993), have discussed what people can expect from around age 30 to age 65. Levinson (1978) found that 70 to 80 percent of the men he interviewed found the mid-life transition around age 40 to 45 to be tumultuous and psychologically painful, as many fundamental aspects of their lives came into question.

What events characterize the middle period of an individual's and a couple's lives? Biological changes include the aging of the body and its faculties, a diminishing of many of the athletic skills in which people often take pride, and menopause in women and a related reduction in reproductive capacity in men. Social changes often include the transition of one's children toward adult status and independence, beginning the grandparenting role, and greater travel and exposure to new peoples. Deaths of relatives and friends tend to become more salient, and one begins to give greater attention to personal mortality. Somewhere in mid-life, we often increase our reflective and retrospective activity and become most curious about our roots and why we are the way we are.

The middle period is a time of personal and interpersonal prosperity for many people. They may have settled into a stable and satisfying family life and may finally have the financial resources to go places and do things that they could not afford earlier. They also may have more perspective on life, its brevity, and the need to focus their energies on what matters to them most. In 1993, a few months after his father had been murdered by two teenagers in a robbery, 30-year-old basketball superstar Michael Jordan stunned the sports world by announcing his retirement. While still brilliant on the court, he had played for nine years, won three world championships, and accomplished all that he could as a basketball player. But the death of his father, with whom he was very close, had shattered any possible illusion that his loved ones would be with him for many more years. He wanted to redirect his focus to his family and to be afforded a greater opportunity to lead a private life—a life not always in the glare of the media and public eye. Jordan said what mattered most about the decision was that "I am at peace with myself."

In the middle period, many of our early expectations about the course of our lives may be revised. We become aware that most things we once thought were critical are not that important. Losses may begin to pile up. Yet, we also may have developed more patience and greater equanimity in dealing with whatever comes our way. In her autobiography *Changing,* Liv Ullmann (1976) wrote of feeling such equanimity in her mid-life after recovering from a stormy seven-year love affair with Ingmar Bergmann. She said, "Many of my dreams were never to be fulfilled, but I had found what I had never dreamed of; reality can be magnificent even when life is not" (p. 197).

Goldstein (1990) discussed how people in mid-life may experience considerable burdens such as financing the educations of their children and contributing to the welfare of aging parents. In fact, the competing demands of work, children, and aging parents on mid-life couples has given rise to the term "sandwich generation," because of the pressures of trying to juggle these demands. For many families, there is precious little time for intimacy and thoughtful interaction. Probably the greatest burdens fall on the wife in a dual-career relationship. Unless the couple is diligent in allocating domestic responsibilities, the wife may fall prey to trying to be the caretaker for husband, children, and parents, while she continues pursuing advancement in her career and follows her personal interests. She may succeed for a time in being "superwoman," but in the long run, she may lose herself and her health in the process.

These burdens of mid-life can contribute to depression. As Martin Seligman (1991) has argued, there is often a great loss of hope and faith among people at this stage. It might be thought that people in mid-life would be at the height of their creative powers and optimism for making their worlds better. Ironically, though, many are not; many have been crushed by the weight of stressors such as divorce, death of spouses or children, and financial disasters. Similar to Bellah et al. (see Chapter 1), Seligman contended that this depression will not be relieved unless people learn to reduce their quest for material possessions and quick gratification and redirect their energies toward facilitating the lives of others—toward giving to their families and communities.

Why are affairs so common in the middles period? Hollis (1993), arguing from a psychoanalytic perspective, suggested that affairs are often carried out by people trying to deal with unfinished business from an earlier developmental passage. He contended that the undeveloped agenda agitates the unconscious until the person acts (or "acts out"); sometimes an affair is the outcome. I think that there is some truth to that. Affairs can just as easily happen for other reasons, including the quest to fulfill needs for intimacy not being met in the marriage, boredom in marriage, of a "flash of chemistry" coupled with the justification that "you only live once."

It sometimes does not take much for an affair to occur, especially with women and men working closely together for many hours each day. An individual who engages in an affair is not necessarily uncommitted to the primary relationship. He or she may want the experience but not want to make it a habit. However, affairs rarely make primary relationships stronger. They may be a sign that the primary relationship is in trouble.

Major losses begin to occur more often in our middle years. One of the most daunting is the loss of a child. To use Blieszner and Mancini's (1992) term, such a loss is out of the normative sequence. In the normal course of events, we do expect to lose our parents but not our children. The loss of a child may serve as a catalyst that brings other, previously latent, problems to the forefront for the couple. The loss may stagger each parent, who must then struggle to address his or her own individual healing. At the same time, the parents need to recognize that the relationship itself may be on the line. They cannot hole up and grieve without regard for their partner and how their individual grief affects the relationship.

The loss of a close relationship may be particularly disastrous if one person tries to block out expression of feeling about the loss. Weber (1993) suggests that such a loss can turn an intimate partner into a stranger. Typically, the male may withdraw and, perhaps trying to be stoic, act as if he is moving on with his business and life in a normal way. Meanwhile, the female may desperately seek a confidant. If the male partner is not there at this critical point, the relationship may suffer a fatal blow. The best path would be for both members of the relationship to confide in one another during this grieving period, which may last for the remainder of their lives—but most powerfully for a few years.

Separation and divorce is a quintessential middles passage. It is well scripted too. The following is a typical example: A young man and woman just out of college get married and begin a dual-career life; they have two children, one in the third year and one in the fifth year of marriage; they hit thirty; young couple have conflict over a litany of issues, including the wife's concern that her husband was having an affair when she was pregnant with their second child; the young couple—not so young anymore—tries counseling, but to no avail; they decide to try "trial separation" in their eighth year together; the trial fails; wife files for divorce; a custody battle ensues; finally, wife and husband agree that a semi-joint custody arrangement, in which the husband has the children in the summers, would be best initially; ex-wife and ex-husband have been renewing their dating activity since their "trial separation"; after dating a dozen or so women, some of whom are ten years younger, ex-husband meets a woman five years younger at work with whom he begins to live and then marries in the second year past divorce; after dating three or four men at work, ex-wife is introduced by friends to someone a little older than she is and they begin a relationship; ex-wife and new lover get married in the fourth year past divorce; each ex-spouse now forms part of blended family with her or his joint-custody arrangement and the different custody arrangements of the new people whom they marry; each now is in her or his mid 30s; they have come a long way!

The following comments from Becky, a 31-year-old woman (taken from John Kotre and Elizabeth Hall's [1990] *Seasons of Life* describing her decision to leave her husband, fills in some of the psychological detail for the divorce scenario outlined above.

I think I was just trying to get across how desperate the situation was. Finally, one night in the middle of a terrible fight, I left home. I went to my girlfriend's house and stayed there for two weeks. I had made the break and I had no intention of going back. Bill didn't know where I was. Didn't have a phone number to get in touch with me. And I had nothing.

[When we were first together] Bill and I were in love. We couldn't wait to get married. I thought he would provide for the family and I would stay home and bake cookies and make homemade bread. . . . It wasn't like that. . . .

Probably two months into the marriage I had thoughts about leaving [but she didn't, and two years after the marriage, they had a boy, followed by a girl a year and a half after that]. . . .

I stayed home and Bill became the provider for the family. Neither of us was happy. We considered a divorce, but we chickened out when we started to feel what it would be like to split the family up.

[After spending two weeks at her girlfriend's house, Becky and her two children moved to an apartment.] Somebody lent me an air mattress, and I slept on the floor for a couple of months. It seemed unreal that my life could go from being so comfortable—you know, it was a normal married life when we weren't fighting—to only having two rooms and no food and no money and no idea of where I was gonna go or what I was gonna do. Not even a way to wash the clothes" (p. 230).

I totally lost my identity. . . .

I started to realize that I was actually going through a grieving process, and all of this was normal. . . . So that helped, and I think it was then that I started to recover. (p. 232)

In Kotre and Hall's discussion of this divorce passage, they noted that Becky and her kids have stabilized their lives, although she is not dating much yet. Bill is helping with child support, and they have a friendly relationship. Becky is going to college and is optimistic about their future. Bill has been seeing other women, but he is not yet thinking of remarriage. Becky noted her difficulty in seeing her ex-husband with other women: "There's been a couple of times when it's really hard for me to see pictures of him with them. He looked happy, you know?" (p. 234).

Now let us turn to an account of a woman at a somewhat later point in the regrouping phase after divorce. This woman tells of the apprehension involved in developing a new life and self-confidence and of the sequence of events leading to her new close relationship:

> About a year after my divorce, I decided I needed to take a look at how I was going to live as a single person. I decided to go to graduate school. I could have stayed nearby. A more exciting option was a school 2,500 miles away. I decided to go with my feelings.
>
> But the end of my first year of graduate school in social work, I was quite different from the child bride I had been in 1966. Then, if you didn't have marriage plans by the senior year in college, you were pitied.
>
> I returned to school in 1975. Times had changed. I felt a wonderful sense of accomplishment in my new independence, and I felt excited about possibilities.
>
> I savored the privacy I had living alone. I had returned home to a private part of myself I hadn't experienced since I was a teenager. . . .
>
> But now, a year later, I also felt ready for a new relationship. And this time I knew what I wanted: a companion, a best friend, someone who would be there if I needed support, someone who shared my interest in camping and traveling.
>
> "Am I crazy?" I wondered, as I entered the room on campus where the Friday-night singles gathering took place. I felt more comfortable when I learned that we would meet in discussion groups first; dancing was scheduled later in the evening. . . .
>
> [She goes on to tell about noticing at the dance a thin, bearded man with a sensitive face sitting at the edge of the dance floor.]
>
> I walked over and asked him if he would dance. "No," he said. "Why don't you sit down here on the floor with me and we can watch people."

When the song ended, he suggested we get a Coke and sit at a table. . . . Four hours later we were still sitting in the same spot. Most of that conversation is lost on me now. My memory instead is of two people who had found commonality in dreams, values, needs, and interests.

As we walked to the parking lot I thought, "I hope this person will become my friend." I didn't know what to expect. . . . We got to my car and he asked me if I wanted his phone number. "That's different," I thought.

Fifteen years later, I remain with my best friend Rich, now my husband. ("One Day It's Time to Turn Dreams into True Living," by Linda Converse, *Chicago Tribune,* March 28, 1993, Section 6, p. 8.)

I would suggest that the general aspects of these accounts are common to this passage in the middle period. Many people have similar stories to tell. For all, this cycling through loves in mid-life is frightening, filled with uncertainty but also laden with possibility for the future.

The reigniting of a love affair with a long lost sweetheart from one's youth illustrates well the fact that at the psychological level, close relationships never totally end; they live on in our memories, thoughts, and how they have influenced our lives.

Stories abound in the 1990s about people meeting at reunions or in chance encounters and renewing lust and love after 20 or 30 or more years of absence. Or in some instances, after many years of wondering about the old love, a person will reach out and try to renew contact with the lover from the past. Sometimes both parties have been divorced; in some cases, their reunion might lead to their divorcing their spouses in order to be together; in still other cases, a brief affair will occur but no lasting close relationship will ensue, and the individuals may remain in their primary relationships. Let us examine a few accounts of reunions to try to understand better how young loves that have long been gone can reappear and reignite sparks of passion many years later.

First, here is a January 23, 1993, letter from a woman to Dear Abby (from *Chicago Tribune*):

> Dear Abby: Can you stand another "lost love" story like the one about the woman and her American airman? [She signed her letter with the name of a popular song of the '40s, "It's Been a Long, Long Time."]
>
> She asked if she should try to locate her old love whom she had not seen since World War II. It was about the same time I was involved in a very intense, but brief, relationship. It ended because I had a commitment that had to take precedence over our love.
>
> For the next 40 years, my old love was never very far from my mind, even though I had no idea whether he was dead or alive.
>
> Then, recently, in an unbelievable stroke of fate, we met face to face, and all the intensity of our feelings for each other came flooding back.
>
> Sounds like a happy ending, right? Wrong. We are still committed to others. Nevertheless, we are both aware that the old flame never went out completely. (Section B, p. 6).

Abby did not have a response. We might predict that if one of the people involved loses a spouse later in life, this person will try to renew contact then.

Why did the old feelings come flooding back to this woman, as they do to many others? Hollis (1993) suggested that by the middle period of our lives, we may have many past loves for whom embers of feeling still smolder and with whom it is possible to reconsider a close relationship. In psychoanalytic terminology, we are still cathected to (or have strong unconscious emotional connections to) past loved ones, and such connections can become so powerful that they begin to play a role in our current close relationships.

Let us examine another illustration of the dilemmas of rekindling old loves, taken from a February 21, 1993, *Chicago Tribune* "Tales from the Front" column. Marcy and Rich went steady in high school in the 1960s, but then went their separate ways as young adults, each getting married and having children. Then in the 1990s, Marcy received a phone message from Rich, who had gotten her number from a mutual friend. Rich was not divorced and "was just wondering how she was." He was living in a nearby state and left his phone number. Marcy reacted with shock. Cheryl Lavin, who writes the column, described the sequence from there:

How could this guy be gutsy enough to call her at home? Wouldn't he wonder what he was stepping into? What if her husband heard the message?

But Marcy knew Rich. . . . His whole personality was like that . . . confident, a little brazen, happy.

Now Marcy can't get her mind off him. She went through some old boxes and found the letters he wrote her in high school and college. . . . "I was afraid that if I called I would see him, and if I saw him I would have an affair with him," she said.

Marcy's marriage suddenly seems empty. . . . Should she call? She's snapping at her husband, even her kids. She wishes that she had never heard the phone message, but now that she has, she can't think of anything else.

"I keep telling myself that life was OK until that Friday night that he called, but then another voice says, 'It [her marriage] was boring, it was humdrum, it was lonely,'" she says. "I'm putting myself through hell and I don't know what will make this end." (Section C, p. 6)

Marcy's marriage may be somewhat lacking, and Rich seems to offer the promise of excitement and something better. But there might be great costs if she got involved with him. Her mental conflict over what to do will likely take a toll on Marcy unless she resolves it—either by trying to work on her marriage to make it more satisfying, or choosing to become involved with Rich. If she becomes involved with Rich, a likely scenario is that she will get divorced but she and Rich will discover that they are not so compatible either.

The final account I will present is of a couple late in mid-life who reunited after 30 years. Unlike other stories, this one ends happily. The participants were somewhat older and maybe ready for the chance meeting and commitment. Readiness may make all the difference.

From the Associated Press, by Jessica Baldwin, April 18, 1993:

London—Sylvia and Jerry Wylie's romance began amid boisterous V-E Day celebrations.

But 29 years and two attacks of cold feet intervened before the English Land Army girl and the Texan bomber pilot tied the knot.

Their photographs—one as a couple in uniform, holding hands and standing stiffly for the camera, the other of relaxed, casually dressed 68-year-olds—are part of a "Forces Sweethearts" exhibition at the Imperial War Museum.

The Wylies . . . keenly recall that day when Jerry and the navigator on his B-17 Flying Fortress sauntered up to Sylvia and her sister, Myra, in Bedford, about 50 miles north of London.

"We had lots of fun just sitting and talking. Time slipped away and we missed our transport back to the hostel. . . ," says Sylvia.

As the time came for Jerry to return to Austin, the two 20-year-olds were talking about a life together.

But a few months after a "heartbreaking" goodbye . . . Sylvia got cold feet.

Eventually, they stopped writing. Both married, had two children each and divorced.

In 1974, emboldened by a few glasses of wine, he wrote to her.

"I had the urge to write and I wanted to before too much life went by. I wanted to try and settle the thing in my mind. If she was happily married then I'd be happy," says Jerry. . . .

Sylvia reached into her purse for that letter, four pages that began, "How to begin a letter started 100 times that is 10 years late. . . ."

That led to a reunion, at the same railway station [from which they had parted in England].

"He ran and I ran and we met in the middle of the road and hugged, with traffic going all around us," she says.

She refused a proposal then, but accepted a year later.

After living in Texas for 10 years, they returned to England.

The Elderly

Grow old along with me!
The best is yet to be,
The last of life, for which the first was made:
Our times are in His hand
Who saith, "A whole I planned,
Youth shows but half; trust God: see all, nor be afraid!"
   —Robert Browning's "Rabbi Ben Ezra's"

Senescence begins
And middle age ends
The day your descendants
Outnumber your friends.
—Ogden Nash's "Crossing the Border"

You know, the physical aspect of aging is so sneaky. It doesn't just hit you—boom—overnight. It starts in your twenties, really. It's the stamina that goes first. And I can tell you, it really takes you by surprise. In a way it's like a flower, where first the petals start to droop. And then the leaves start to change, and slowly the flower just wilts away.
—Mikhail Baryshnikov

Schaie (1988) divided people aged 60 and older into three groups: those in their 60s and 70s, who are quite similar to persons 10 to 20 years younger in the way they live their lives, although they may be retired from their primary line of work: those in their late 70s and early 80s, who still live in their communities, but whose health may be beginning to fail; those in their late 80s and beyond, who are likely to be in failing health, frail, and in nursing homes. Thus, like the middles passage, this one may span a number of decades.

The "senior years" continue themes of earlier periods and perhaps introduce a few new ones too. As we have seen in earlier chapters, many older persons help their grown children raise their grandchildren. Often their children have divorced, have custody, have to work to make a living, and cannot afford other means of child care. The adult children may move back to their parents' home with the grandchildren for a period of time, making for three generations under one roof. So this parenting passage is, in effect, a return to a period that most seniors left some 20 to 30 years before. It can create problems because these older people, who usually are retired, often expect to be

As MacLeish's poem suggests, "everything they know, they know together . . ." © *Copyrighted 1993, Chicago Tribune Company, all rights reserved, used with permission.*

relaxing and enjoying travel or other pleasures they did not pursue during their earlier life.

Ironically, some grandparents face a reluctance on the part of a son- or daughter-in-law to allow them to see their grandchildren. Usually, such a situation has evolved from a difficult divorce and custody battle. This has become a legal problem in the 1990s, with suits filed to try to force custodial parents to allow such visitation.

The issue of searching for identity remains salient in the later years. At 65, for example, people may have to come to grips with retiring and losing identity associated with their former profession. They may have the feeling that society no longer has any use for them, now that they are not part of the work-a-day world. Or they may have to get used to a new career.

The older adult is confronted regularly with the mortality of family members, friends, and self. For many people in their 70s and 80s, the death of associates, and the attending of funerals and memorial services, is a regular event. Thus, grieving may become a routine part of life. The individual may have to become somewhat inured to loss so as to balance the magnitude of these events against the need to stay positive about living. Of course, people in this passage often anticipate the loss of their closest other—their spouse or lover. Who will go first is a disheartening question that confronts couples at all ages, but particularly elderly couples.

People in their 60s and 70s may divorce, as quite a few have done in recent years. Or their partner may die, leaving a still healthy mate. So getting back into the dating scene may become as important for the older person as it frequently is for the person two to three decades younger.

Romantic close relationships involving partners of very different ages happen frequently. They may lead to great satisfaction, but there are perils. Here is one account of a mating across generations:

When Marion fell in love with Jerry, she felt she had found the father she never had but always wanted. Jerry was an older man, sophisticated, cultured, and eager to take care of her in every way. He even offered her financial security. When they got married, she was not only in love but, for the first time in her life, she felt safe and secure. And she was, for a time. But then she began to realize that he had his own insecurities, too, and expected to turn to her for comfort and support when he was stressed-out at work, and especially if he didn't feel well—which began to happen frequently. When he had his heart attack and needed even more care, her world seemed to fall apart. He could no longer fulfill her expectations, so she felt deserted and betrayed. (from Barbara Silverstone and Helen Hyman's, 1992, *Growing Older Together,* p. 58)

Regardless of age disparity, it is hazardous to try to find a father in your husband, or to try to find a nurse in your wife. Silverstone and Hyman go on to provide a number of very useful suggestions for couples who are aging together, such as what to do if their sex life becomes unsatisfying to one or both partners. While there may be no great answers to such questions, they may be best approached by open dialogue well before they become of acute importance.

Discrimination against people based on age can occur at any age. The older person, however, is a particularly common target for systematic bias and stereotyping. We sometimes use terms such as "geezers" and "old hag," usually without consideration for the way it feels to be the target of such labels. Care in the use of language is one antidote to ageism, because language can influence how we perceive others and consequently how we treat them. Equally important are the assumptions we make about what older people can and cannot do or how they should behave. For example, we need to be open to the possibility that older people can fall in love, be very sexual, get married, raise children again (or grandchildren), get divorced, then do it all over again. Creative, vital contributions can be made in many kinds of work and other endeavors, regardless of one's age. And many people in their 70s and beyond have learned that exercise contributes to physical, mental, and relationship health.

Because people in this culture are now more attuned to sound health practices as they age, the definition of "old age" is no longer clear. People born in 1900 expected to live to be 47. Life expectancy in 1993 is about 76 years and climbing. There are many positive role models for older people. Entertainers such as Bob Hope and George Burns have performed for many generations of Americans and are going strong in their 80s and 90s. Movie stars in their 50s and 60s, such as Jane Fonda and Elizabeth Taylor, continue to dazzle with their looks, health, and youthful life-styles and mind-sets. Writers, editors, and journalists, including James Michener and Helen Gurley Brown have also set high standards for productivity and successful personal lives for people in their 60s and beyond.

People who age well can still develop new skills, have new thrilling life experiences, and forge new identities well beyond a point at which we formerly believed everyone should be headed to the nursing home. Paula Hardin (1993) described how she obtained a Ph.D. in education in her early 50s and established a consulting service in Chicago that helps people in their 40s and beyond discover new identities for themselves. In an interview in the *Chicago Tribune,* she said, "Some people stay with adolescent values all their lives. . . . They don't get to the midlife stage so they can find what is the meaning of being 40, the fullness of being 50 or the joy and power of being 60 or 70" (May 9, 1993, "Tempo" section, p. 2).

In this chapter, I have tried to make the case that recognizing these passage-like stages helps us to understand how we move through major transitions in life—even though there is tremendous variation in both the course of our close relationships and in our individual lives. Over the years, our expectations for various stages have changed enormously. Most people in the United States are now living over a decade longer than were people at the turn of the twentieth century. Passages for people in their middles are stretching out even longer than the 30- to 60-year span that was once used as a yardstick. In light of people's enhanced health and nutrition practices and improved modern medical technology, the stretching of these passage-like stages is likely to continue.

Throughout these passages the major developmental tasks at very different age ranges appear to be similar. We are usually seeking to achieve positive human states such as happiness, contentment, tranquility, and a feeling of accomplishment. Similarly, we mostly try to combat negative human states such as hopelessness, depression, despair, guilt, fear, and anxiety. We continue to work toward these ends both in our individual lives and in our relationships. Until death, we search for an identity that gives us pride and our lives value. For most of our adult years, we seek—sometimes implicitly—to complete unfinished business and resolve matters of the heart and mind that have burdened us since we emerged from our families of origin. For most of the journey, we try to affirm our autonomy, while at the same time we quest for intimacy—reaching out in an often futile attempt to know and be known by another human being. Just as in Chapter 4, femaleness and maleness in the end come together under a common "humanness." The various cycles and seasons of a person's life devolve quite simply to the very basic, yet very imposing process of trying to find meaning and closeness with others in an ocean of change.

THE SORROW OF THE LOVER

IS CONTINUAL, IN THE PRESENCE

AND ABSENCE OF THE BELOVED:

IN THE PRESENCE FOR FEAR OF THE

ABSENCE, AND IN ABSENCE IN

LONGING FOR THE PRESENCE. THE

PAIN IN LOVE BECOMES IN TIME

THE LIFE OF THE LOVER.

—Sufi master Hazrat Khan

Chapter

8

DISSOLVING
AND DIVORCING

THEIR LAST NIGHT TOGETHER WAS LIKE ANY ONE
OF A THOUSAND OTHERS, IN MANY RESPECTS.
HE SET THE ALARM, AND SHE PUT THE CAT OUT.
THERE WAS THE SUDDEN COMPULSION TO
RECONSIDER. THEY FOUND THEMSELVES STANDING
AT THE TOP OF A HIGH DIVE, SCARED TO JUMP OFF
AND TOO TIRED TO CLIMB DOWN. THERE WERE
OTHERS LINED UP BEHIND THEM, PRESSING AND
NUDGING, MAKING THE LEAP SEEM INEVITABLE.
THERE ON THE PURGATORIAL PLATFORM, THEY
CLUNG TO EACH OTHER FOR THE LAST TIME. IT HAD
NEVER SEEMED SO IMPORTANT TO BE TOGETHER.
FOR YEARS, THEY HAD NOT HAD
THIS MUCH IN COMMON.

—(June 1, 1983, article "Only scars are shared
in a friendly divorce," by Rheta Johnson,
Dallas Morning News)

All close relationships or marriages end, either through death or via the decision to separate, terminate and/or legally divorce. The quotes regarding the couple's decision to terminate their marriage, and the inevitable ambivalence associated with this decision, reflect some of the issues associated with divorce and dissolution.

Viorst (1986) described a number of "necessary losses" we all will experience in life. We will lose our youth. We will probably lose our sexual virginity. Over time, we will part company with many friends and acquaintances. We will likely lose prized possessions and material property. We may lose our financial assets. Eventually we will all lose our health. Each of us will probably lose a close, romantic relationship at some point due to death, drifting away, movement away, dissolution or divorce, or a mutual parting of ways. Indeed, we may lose many romantic relationships. And although each of us may not experience divorce personally, in light of the frequency of divorce, most of us will either experience it directly or indirectly through the effects it has on those close to us. Sometimes, it is almost as difficult for a parent to watch their son's or daughter's divorce unfolding as it is for them to divorce.

Today it is common for people marrying in their 20s to have had a relatively large number of close relationships before marriage. Such experience can be invaluable in evaluating potential partners and other issues associated with relating closely to others. On the other hand, extensive experience with dating, separating, and dissolving can also produce a cynicism about the durability of close relationships. If they marry, then divorce and begin another dating period, they are likely to experience still more losses of this nature.

People who go through this process may feel as if they are having the time of their lives and gaining valuable experience. As times goes on, however, memories of their former lovers may become a difficult part of their everyday existence (Harvey, Flanary, & Morgan, 1986). The dissolution process often exacts a heavy toll in psychological pain, and possibly physical and practical devastation. In addition to the couple, children or close relatives such as parents may suffer.

The U.S. divorce rate has risen to one in two for marriages that began in the last 10 to 20 years. And according to Thornton (1989), in 1962, when a sample of young mothers were asked whether couples with children ought to remain together if they could not get along, one half said they should. But when these same women were asked the identical question in 1985, fewer than one in five said they should. Why? Had the world of marriage, sacred vows, and human commitment deteriorated in that time interval? Maybe. But perhaps in the intervening 23 years, these women had learned a lot about the difficulties of some close relationships. Many of these women were in relationships that dissolved. Some of the relationships involved physical abuse. The human degradation experienced in an abusive relationship is far worse than dissolution and divorce.

Divorce in the 1990s has become a common phenomenon not just here but throughout the world. In Moscow, for instance, people are responding to the extraordinarily difficult economic situation by divorcing at a record rate. According to an April 5, 1993, article by Jack Kelley in USA Today, 75 percent of all recent marriages in Moscow ended in divorce last year, and 62 percent of recent marriages throughout Russia ended in divorce. Social commentators have suggested that this trend is part of Russians' embrace of capitalism and career making. Increasingly, they are foregoing traditional relationships in which the wife stayed at home and raised children. As one 19-year-old woman, married only six months and in the process of divorcing her 21-year-old husband, told Kelley: "Being a housewife is not for me anymore. . . . I want to make something of myself. I want a BMW" (p. 1).

In the 1990s, the stigma of divorce is mostly gone. After a dazzling wedding in 1981, the "perfect couple" Prince Charles and Princess Diana of England separated in 1992. As English tabloids recounted many details of their conflicts and likely extramarital ventures, it became clear to all that this marriage was no fairy tale and would not have a fairy tale ending. The marriage was probably between ill-suited people.

Having been divorced can sometimes be viewed as a asset. For example, people who are single in their late-30s might be viewed as having less questionable relationship histories if they were married previously. The stigma of divorce may have decreased over the last quarter of a century. But the hurt, the long-term pain for participants, and the brutality of the legal aspects of divorce have not abated.

The divorcing time is, as Robert Weiss (1975) suggested, a time of craziness. For instance, there is a tendency for the divorcing individuals to regularly have sex with each other during their separation. Weiss found this activity to be common among his separated sample, regardless of level of hostility in the separation. These partners may still like having sex together—although they otherwise can't stand each other. At this time, it is difficult to give up sexual activity, but it is very problematic to quickly try to find a new sex partner (although that is commonly done). Thus, the otherwise hostile and rejecting partners may find that they still have this need in common.

Although people do make mistakes in close relating, and these mistakes are often central to whether their relationships continue, it makes no sense to call relationships that end in divorce or dissolution "failed" relationships. This term dehumanizes the parties involved. There are, however, no precise standards for success. It could as well be argued that it is the people who stay together in highly distressing close relationships who "fail" rather than do those who "successfully get out" of such relationships.

A major loss such as a close relationship dissolution or a marital separation and divorce initially diminishes the partners' sense of self (Harvey et al., 1992). It may even reduce one's dignity, will, or resources. A dissolution of a close relationship takes physical resources from the principal parties concerned, including any children involved. But probably more potent is the loss of emotional resources. As has been argued by Vaughan (1986) and Spanier and Thompson (1987), the most meaningful step in the dissolving sequence is the *emotional divorce*. This is the act of one partner defining the relationship as dead in her or his mind. Once that decision has been made in marriage, the relationship may continue in a legal sense for a short period or for many years, but psychologically, it has ended.

George Levinger (1992) wrote a valuable commentary on loss of a close relationship. He noted that the extent to which one feels that a close relationship's end is a loss (or a deprivation of personal resources) depends on several factors, including the closeness of the relationship, whether the ending was sudden or protracted, and whether the loss involved a lengthy period in which partners could withdraw and possibly explore new options. As will be discussed in the next chapter, Levinger also suggested that loss by death is different than loss by separation or divorce. Not only is death irreversible but it usually occurs due to physiological causes, such as heart disease; which are quite different from the psychological ones that involve a person's intention and motivation to end a relationship.

It might be thought that divorces are more difficult for people to deal with than are nonmarital dissolutions. We have little evidence comparing the effects of the endings of different types of relationships. We do know, though, that many nonmarital dissolutions can be excruciatingly painful. In fact, as Orbuch (1988) suggested, they may be as painful as, or more painful than, divorce because society does not usually recognize them as experiences that involve great pain. The same is true for partners who decide to separate but not divorce, and then remain separated for a lengthy period (Ahrons, Rodgers, & Rodgers, 1987). They may be searching for new partners, but at the same time they may want to retain the possibility of renewing their old relationship. But they put themselves in a "never-never land" of ambiguous identity, with others feeling confusion about how to react to them.

People at all ages feel pain, confusion, and sometimes despair at the loss of closeness with others. The pain of dissolution can be found among college students who lose a close relationship after only a half year or so (Sorenson, Russell, Hardness, & Harvey, 1993). Although college-aged couples may not have invested many years together or have major assets to divide, they go through many of the same steps of grieving that people who have been married many years go through.

A "Fresh Voices" column in *Parade Magazine,* April 25, 1993, posed the question "Rejection in Dating—Is It Better to Hear from Somebody Else?" to high school students. One male, age 16, said, "When a girl says you could be friends, that's like the kiss of death" (p. 21). Another young man noted another way one knows a relationship has ended: "All of a sudden, the phone calls stop—you know she's sick of you" (p. 21).

Marital or nonmarital dissolution often involves these steps: shock or surprise at the decision of one's partner to end the relationship; denial that it really is happening; rushing to find a new mate or indiscriminate, frenzied dating and sexual activity for a period; and then gradual recovery. However, recovery from all types of loss occurs only after the mind and body have had time to regroup. It is facilitated greatly by staying active and hopeful, and by going over the details of the relationship, what went wrong, and what to do and expect the next time. At some point fairly early in the healing, confiding in good friends is essential to recovery (Pennebaker, 1990; Harvey et al., 1990). Close friends will *really* listen to you, offer suggestions when asked, and may even share their own similar experiences. Francis Bacon had these timeless words of wisdom about the value of true friendship:

But one thing is most admirable . . . which is, that this communicating of a man's self to his friend works two contrary effects; for it redoubleth joys, and cutteth griefs in halfs. For there is no man that imparteth his joys to his friend, but he joyeth the more; and no man that imparteth his griefs to his friend, but he grieveth the less. (F. Bacon, "Of friendship")

If such confiding cannot occur, it may be difficult to readily move beyond grief and professional counseling should be considered. Suppression of the loss (not thinking or talking about it; or distracting oneself to a high degree) eliminates the opportunity to grieve and fully recover from the loss. As James Pennebaker's (1990) research has shown, suppression can be quite detrimental to a person's psychological and physical health over the long term. At the same time, there may be a limit to how much one can confide to certain friends or associates. People who are friendly with a grieving person, but who are not perceived as close confidants, may even desert him or her when they believe the person has either told them too little or too much about the details of the loss (Hunt, 1966).

This discussion has emphasized the similarity in the grieving process after dissolved nonmarital and divorced marital relationships. I have emphasized the similarities in major loss experiences. If a relationship is so short or unimportant to the people involved that its ending does not involve a major loss, then that circumstance is outside the realm of logic articulated here. However, it is also an anomaly in the business of close relationships.

Some couples going through the dissolving experience, including those divorcing, may experience little apparent stress and may in fact move on to another apparently happy relationship soon afterward (or even before if they have been having an affair). But we cannot easily escape doing a degree of emotional work in getting beyond a major loss. Those who move too quickly will have to come back and deal with it later—or the experience is likely to eventually result in psychological or physical difficulties.

Not all conflict-ridden, or highly deteriorated, relationships will terminate. Although it is no longer the case, in decades past it was not common to end a marriage even if there was significant ongoing physical abuse. The main reason that some people elect to remain in a bad relationship is that they have invested considerable feeling, time, and resources in it and are reluctant to conclude that their investment must be lost. As one wife told Ann Landers in a 1989 column:

> I have 21 years invested in my marriage. My husband is a prominent professional man, well respected and admired by everyone. Our children are in college. We have a beautiful home and are considered a loving couple.
>
> The woman "Bob" has been seeing for nine years works for him. She has had two failed marriages and her whole life is her job. I do not hate her. She is taking nothing away from me. She and Bob are never seen together in public. Tuesday night is theirs (in her apartment), so I play cards with the girls.
>
> I have Bob's name, his children, the respect of the community, and more than enough sex. One of these years Bob will decide he has had enough outside activity and that will be the end of it. All I have to do is wait. (*Los Angeles Times,* September 3, 1989)

Weber's (1993) response to this letter was "What is there in this marriage? She says that all she has to do is wait—wait for what to happen? So he comes home dragging his tail behind him . . . and then what?" (p. 26).

Surprisingly, Ann Landers reported that she had received many such letters from women who had decided to stick by their men, even if the men were involved in seemingly interminable affairs. Another wife, for instance, was tired of sex anyway, and her husband was merely "servicing" the lonely widow next door. The concept of investment and its power to keep people for long periods in miserable marriages has been carefully studied by scholars such as Heaton and Albrecht (1991) and Rusbult (1980). While that power may be waning as we embrace present-day relationships based on egalitarian principles, it nonetheless still exists.

The Progression Toward Dissolution

In some instances, the deterioration of a relationship is slow and halting. In others it is up and down, including periods of separation and the resumption of living together or "being a couple." In still others the progression is as swift as a bullet. This latter type of progression is most interesting because it is most puzzling, at least to the person being left. It is as if, "out of the blue," one partner in an otherwise functioning, satisfactory relationship decides that she or he wants out and will take the steps to get out. Of course, this particular type of progression may seem as if it is "out of the blue" to the person being left. But to the other partner or a knowledgeable outsider, the progression may be more gradual and systematic in how it plays itself out. If the couple could communicate about problems, an event such as this never should come "out of the blue."

Based on her years of clinical practice, Kessler (1975) divided the typical psychological process involved in dissolution into seven emotional stages: disillusionment, erosion, detachment, physical separation, mourning, second adolescence (i.e., starting to go through the rituals of dating again, just as one did as an adolescent), and exploration and hard work (which refers to the steps toward establishing a new identity and possibly a new close relationship). Kessler stressed that different people experience these emotions in a different order, that the start and end points are unclear, and that the duration of these experiences differs from person to person.

Research that has investigated thoughts, feelings, and behavior at selected points in the dissolution process (Guttman, 1993) has identified factors associated with dissolution, including the following sampling:

- growing apart in attitudes and interests (or never being sufficiently similar to begin with)

- inability to give emotionally and express personal feelings

- involvement with third parties, as in affairs

- paying too much attention to one's career and too little to one's close relationship

- economic difficulties and major societal stressors that tax people's physical and psychological resources to deal with relationship issues (e.g., after Hurricane Andrew devastated Dade County, Florida, in 1992, the divorce rate there jumped nearly 30 percent. Similarly, in Sarajevo there has been a significant increase in divorce, separation, and abandonment due to the Bosnian war. Because of the conflict among the Serbs, Croats, and Muslims, many close relationships between persons of different ethnic groups have terminated. Also, with no news from their spouses on the front lines, some women have found new partners, while others have left with their children to relocate in a safer country)

- feeling constrained to pursue one's career or lifetime dreams by a marriage

- feeling overly controlled by one's partner, such that people cannot "be themselves" and pursue what makes them happy

- physical or psychological abuse

- no longer being physically or sexually attracted to one's significant other

- the difficulties of caring for children and how that responsibility interferes with attention to relationship needs

- failure to understand a partner's perspective and taking the partner for granted

- the weakening effect of religion on maintenance of marriage (i.e., many couples no longer feel obligated by their religious faith to stay together in a bad marriage)

- "no fault" divorce laws (that first began in California in 1969), which make it easier to get a divorce and lessen the stigma associated with divorce

Divergent Perceptions   In trying to pinpoint the progression of events toward dissolution, it is helpful to study the perceptions of both partners in a relationship. Often there is a complex web of understanding surrounding a close relationship and major events in its history. Within these understandings reside much of what determines how successful the relationship becomes. In the mid-1970s my colleagues and I studied partners' divergent perceptions of their problems (Harvey, Wells, & Alvarez, 1978). We were struck both by the divergence of perception and by the widespread inability to correctly perceive their partner's understanding of what was happening. For example, the female partner in the relationship often would say that she was unhappy mainly because her male partner made no effort to understand how she felt about their emotional life. On the other hand, the male partner would say that his female partner was unhappy principally because he was not earning enough money.

More recent work (e.g., Holtzworth-Munroe & Jacobson, 1985) paints a clearer picture of the importance of mutual understanding, divergences in understanding, and recognition of such divergences as powerful elements in conflict and eventual separation. An interesting finding of their research was that women engaged in considerable attributional analysis regularly during the course of a relationship, but men did this mainly when the relationship was in trouble (see also Hill, Rubin, & Peplau, 1976, for similar findings for a sample of college students). In my own work on couples' attributes, I have argued that if couples are flexible, they can better correct their misperceptions and converge more in their understandings of important issues (see Harvey, 1987).

There now are major research programs devoted to understanding the roles of attributions and cognition in close relationship functioning and dissolution processes. Fincham and Bradbury (e.g., Fincham & Bradbury, 1993; Bradbury & Fincham, 1992) have shown how relationship satisfaction over time is influenced by the positive or negative attributions that partners make about each other's behavior. For example, in considering why they cannot save money, a wife might attribute the problem to her husband's careless use of money, which she perceives as going back to his parents spoiling him as a child. A general review of research on the attributional and thought processes involved in close relationships can be found in Fletcher and Fincham (1991).

If we were certain about the *true* causes of dissolution (as opposed to the *perceived* causes, which may or may not be the true causes), we might better understand the complexity and interconnections between different causes. We might discover that innate biological factors *sometimes* predispose us to relationship difficulty (McGue & Lykken, 1992). For example, a person might be predisposed to being diffident, retiring, and uncomfortable around people. We might also find that these predispositions mainly come into effect under certain conditions, such as when he or she tries to relate to others who are cheerful and outgoing. We could also discover that the formula for how these biological and environmental factors go together would vary over different couples. Thus, as Kelley et al. (1983) argued quite persuasively, the interactive and special bonding qualities of particular couples would also have to be understood.

It is about this time that my students often throw up their hands and go back to studying physics—something that at least one can begin to understand with some certainty after a period of diligent effort. They jump to the conclusion that in the behavioral and social science literature *there are no answers,* merely speculation. I admit that what we know is modest. But the process of inquiry is untiring. We cannot back out because putting together the jig-saw puzzle of human relationships is a difficult endeavor. We need to see this for the challenge it is, and to recognize that we have already made major strides toward a fuller understanding. There *is* a rhyme and reason to our behavior.

Vaughan's Analysis   Sociologist Diane Vaughan (1986) presented an interesting analysis and study of the dissolution process. The research Vaughan reported involved collecting reports from 103 people who were separated or divorced; no former partners of the respondents were included. Across her sample, Vaughan found evidence for predictable stages in a relationship's dissolution. She proposed that "uncoupling" involves:

1. "secrets," or the breakdown of frank communication in at least one area of the relationship

2. "the display of discontent," whereby the initiator, in particular, begins to negatively define one or more aspects of the previously positive relationship

3. the initiator's transition from the role of "partner" to a more ambiguous role of "independent person," while trying to cover up his or her leave-taking

In the "secrets" stage the initiator develops a deep unhappiness with the relationship. The initiator broods a lot, goes through life's paces mulling alternatives, and eventually begins to show her or his discontent. The initiator may not be able to fully articulate the major complaints with the relationship but begins to show anger, perhaps blowing up over small matters. The initiator may also show various forms of passive-aggressive pulling away behavior such as perfunctory sexual behavior or "forgetting" to wear a wedding ring.

For some people, an outside potential romantic relationship may begin to develop at some point. Indeed, such a relationship may be the major secret that leads to other secrets, leading the initiator to make comparisons between the outside love and the present partner (e.g., noticing how much easier it is to talk with the outsider than it is to talk to one's partner). The outsider is a "transitional other" with whom the initiator may discuss marital problems; they may move toward romantic or sexual relations or flirting with the possibility of sexual relations. In Vaughan's sample, respondents who reported such outside activities also sometimes reported guilt, which then often led to further passive-aggressive behavior toward the spouse or partner. Why? Because if the initiator can push the partner into taking actions that are clearly violations of the relationship, then the initiator's guilt about his or her own personal violations can be lessened. Vaughan told of a 26-year-old man, living with a woman for four years, whose account fit this pattern well:

> I could never have left Julie. She was so vulnerable, I just could not do it even though I didn't love her anymore. But I started disappointing her in lots of ways. I realized I was becoming someone that I knew she couldn't like. (p. 101)

Some initiators do not begin affairs but may show other forms of discontentment, such as beginning a secret, separate bank account.

According to Vaughan, eventually the partner who is being left will clearly get the initiator's message, and then the conflict escalates. The couple may go back and forth, deciding whether to stay (or get back) together, but by this point, the dye is cast. Vaughan found that the initiator is clearly the person in charge of the unfolding events. This person feels better about what is happening—maybe not happy, but relieved that soon she or he will be free—than the partner. This finding parallels earlier evidence presented by Hill et al. (1976), who studied the breakups of college student romances. They found that students who believed that they had instigated the breakup reported less severe emotional consequences than did those who did not.

In Vaughan's work, the initiator was already beginning to transform her or his identity from being part of a couple to being single, or perhaps a member of a different coupling. The initiator also tended to make moves toward what Erving Goffman (1959) called "cooling the mark" (i.e., roughly defined as getting the person who is being left to accept his or her fate and not make trouble for the initiator). According to Vaughan, the initiator achieves this by

1. focusing on the negative qualities of the partner
2. indicating a belief that the relationship has been unsalvage-able for some time
3. trying to convince the partner that the relationship was/is beyond repair
4. telling other people the story of the demise of the relation-ship—making it public, thus strengthening one's commit-ment to the ending
5. possibly seeking a transitional partner(s)
6. beginning the process of grieving or mourning. Anyone who has been in a long-term relationship is likely to mourn its loss. Initiators just start sooner, according to Vaughan

On the other hand, Vaughan found that the person being left was often "out in the cold without a clue." This person's life was caving in, and she or he really did not understand why. In this situation, people feel abandoned; they feel that they have no control over something that means a great deal to them—another's feelings toward and decisions about them. What we often do in such situations is to make it worse. We get angry and tell our partner to be gone right away; then we apologize and plead for our partner to come back; then we waiver in our statements between bravado and pitifulness. The truth is we are not in control of the situation—the control is sitting there in our partner's hands. We may start to analyze and recognize aspects of the relationship that should have served as red flags, indicating trouble. Yet, these insights do not make us any happier. We may feel like we are losing our right arm, and there is no way to sew it back on. We feel abandoned by someone to whom we still feel strongly attached.

In his classic study of separating and recently divorced people, Robert Weiss (1975) defined separation distress as "a response to intolerable inaccessibility of the attachment figure" (p. 42). Sure, it is clearly apparent to friends and family which partner initiated the break-up, that person may catch more heat about why the relationship has to end. But compared to the one being left, the initiator has a great head-start toward restoring self, establishing a new identity, gaining control over his or her life, and developing a new close relationship.

It does not follow, however, that people who fear that a relationship will end should rush to get out first. Mutual retreat would be more rational. A couple who discusses their relationship issues freely and regularly can more likely achieve mutual initiation than one who cannot do this. It should be clear from the reiteration of Vaughan's findings that the initiator's aim at a certain point is to take care of self, and not be too concerned about the welfare of their partner. A lot of defensiveness is displayed. The initiator is not necessarily being morally wrong in this approach; but their behavior will hurt the partner to a degree that is unnecessary if a more open style of relating is adopted early on. If such openness could not be adopted, why was the relationship continued further in the first place? Also, we are not told how long Vaughan's couples were having difficulties and the extent to which they may have sought professional help for their problems along the way.

Our discussion, thus far, of the experience of the initiator versus that of the person being left probably does not do justice to the complexity of many breakups. As Weiss (1975) eloquently argued, based on his interviews with individuals in the organization Parents without Partners, the matter of who actually started the dissolution is usually complicated:

> There do seem to be differences in the impact of separation on those who define themselves as leavers and those who define as left, but the differences seem to be more nearly in the character of the resultant distress than in its intensity. In most separations . . . [the] marriage became intolerable for both partners; somehow one partner rather than the other decided finally to call it quits. Sometimes husband and wife alternated in the initiation of preliminary separations. . . . Sometimes a spouse who had been unwilling to accept responsibility for ending the marriage behaved so outrageously that the other spouse could not go on with it. And sometimes a husband or wife who had insisted on separation later had a change of heart and wanted to become reconciled, but the other spouse now refused. In all these circumstances the identification of the one spouse as leaver and the other as left oversimplifies a complex interactive process. (p. 63)

Weiss went on to note that when there is a more clearcut situation, in which one person leaves while the other is left, the leaver may have some advantages but also incurs some major costs. Chief among those costs in Weiss's sample was guilt. He found that leavers may experience harsh reactions from outsiders such as friends of the couple. Further, they sometimes start to question their ability to stick to a commitment and to meet a partner's emotional needs. It should be remembered that Weiss's evidence came from the early 1970s, a time when the stigma of leaving another person (in a marriage, at least) was more substantial than it is now, as separations have become more commonplace.

Writing in the January 1993 issue of *Glamour* magazine, Chip Brown provided another interesting perspective on who experiences the most distress when a close relationship ends:

> . . . as there are two roles in any breakup—the passive part of the one who is left and the active part of the one who leaves—so there are two sorts of accompanying pain: the agony of loss and the distress of guilt and doubt. And in the long run, the first may be easier to bear.
>
> Here, I think is why: The pain of loss heals more quickly and completely than the pain of guilt and doubt does. Loss is loss. When someone leaves you, however much it hurts, nothing's to be done but endure it; once you accept that you have no control and can only embrace what's inevitable, you can go on. Guilt and doubt, on the other hand, have a tendency to fester. You look at yourself in the mirror and see the agent of someone's unhappiness: Was it worth it? Did you make the right choice? Were you being selfish? Will you regret your decision one day in the future and have no one to blame but yourself? (p. 163)

Brown said he had learned to be less consumed by the need for control in his close relationships and to disagree with W. H. Auden's line "If equal affection cannot be, let the more loved one be me." Brown noted that there is much irony in loving and losing: The person who takes the bigger chance by loving too much or too quickly, and who then experiences heartache if the relationship ends, may learn much from this experience and later feel tranquil about the ending. Whereas the person who is more reserved about giving love and who moves first to end the relationship may learn little and be beset with the "drip, drip, drip of regret and doubt" (p. 180). (See Chapter 10 for discussion of the related phenomenon of unrequited love.)

Affairs, Adultery, and Betrayal

I've had four careers over the past 18 years—first as assistant to an editor, then full-time homemaker and mother, then free-lance editor, and now copywriter in an advertising agency. I've lived in five different apartments or houses in three different cities. I've mothered four children with four different personalities. I've had dozens of friends and acquaintances. But in my entire life I've only gone to bed with one man. I don't see why I shouldn't have some variety in this part of my life, just as I do everywhere else. (40-year-old woman's report on why she wanted to have an affair; quoted in Wendkos [1985])

All available evidence suggests that affairs and adultery are very common. They have been well studied in the literature of marriage and divorce (e.g., Hunt, 1966). For centuries, men have been the primary instigators of affairs. They still may have a lead over women in this area, but the difference between the sexes apparently is becoming smaller.

The data on the extent to which affairs occur during marriage vary. One problem is that respondents in studies may give answers that they think researchers want to hear. There is also the question of definitions: Does an affair always involve sexual intercourse? (Probably not; emotional involvement, lusting, and passionate embrace over a period of time with a partner outside the primary relationship might be seen as constituting an affair.) Might a one night stand not be seen as a full-blown affair?

Annette Lawson (1988) reported that men still cheat more than women. In a 10-year-study of 600 adults, married or living together, she found that while 25 percent of the women had had as many as four affairs, 40 percent of the men had had that many. But women are gaining on men. Sixty-six percent of the women and 68 percent of the men in first marriages had had at least one affair. Lawson's figures are higher than typical estimates that 25 to 50 percent of women have affairs, while 50 to 65 percent of men do (Cherlin, 1992). Also, because they were collected before the AIDS epidemic became such a salient factor in sexual liaisons, Lawson's data may reflect more outside sexual activity than actually takes place today.

While affairs may occur at any point during an ongoing close relationship, they are more likely to happen at watershed points, both in the history of the couple and in the individual's own history. One such point is the so-called seven-year itch. After a period of several years of marriage or close relating, one or both partners may begin to stray. Usually, couples in their 20s or early 30s will endure this "itch" period (Blumstein & Schwartz, 1983). Another major watershed is the individual's reaching what he or she perceives to be mid-life, anywhere from 30 to 60 years of age. If one is unhappy with one's close relationship at this point, affairs become more likely. Even people in relatively happy relationships may be more prone to consider an affair in times of acute difficulty. Finally, to speculate, I think that affairs are not as likely to happen when people face a crisis such as unemployment, difficulties on the job, or illness. Ironically, it is often after a couple has succeeded in overcoming a crisis that an affair begins, in the security and presumed comfort of a more tranquil time.

Why do people have affairs? The list of answers typically includes: revenge against one's partner for some alleged wrongdoing, including his/her affair; boredom, frustration, or deprivation associated with the primary sexual relationship; curiosity; enhancement of self-esteem. These answers may be more excuses than true causes.

Janet Reibstein and Martin Richards (1993) said that many people explain an affair by saying they "fell in love" with another person. Reibstein and Richards argued that these people usually view love as a sudden, unpredictable state that overtakes people and leads them into romantic relationships.

Sociologists, historians, and demographers (e.g., Blumstein & Schwartz, 1983; Bailey, 1988) have often emphasized the role of women's greater involvement in the workplace since World War II as a key determinant of the high incidence of affairs in the United States. The idea is that women's desire for more freedom in sexual behavior was unleashed by the other freedoms they had struggled to attain (see also Ehrenreich, Hess, and Jacobs' *Remaking Love,* 1986, for a provocative analysis of this topic).

Most, if not all, people who are engaged in close relationships have thought about having an affair. The following story told by columnist Pete Hamill in the *Dallas Morning News* in 1988 relates poignantly the pain of a woman who had considered affairs but who had abstained.

Catherine was an account executive in an advertising agency. She was very successful. Her husband Glenn was a documentary filmmaker. He was not very successful.

For a long time she had occasional thoughts about leaving him, but almost always dismissed the notion. They had been together 12 years; changing the *status quo* would be too disturbing.

"He was always there," she said.

"If I had to work late on some major presentation and came staggering home at midnight, he was there watching TV, ready with a cup of tea. If I had to go out of town on sales conferences or to work with some client, he was there every night when I called. It wasn't like having Burt Reynolds around, but he was a human being, he had a heartbeat, he was sweet."

They didn't have children. That had been part of the agreement years before. She was going to work in advertising for a few years, and when they had put together enough money they would move for a year to Italy, and she would write a novel.

When I knew her years ago in the Village in New York she was a good poet; she might have written an amazing novel. Instead, she wrote copy for cars and soap and underwear.

"I didn't mind," she said. "I'd married a guy who worked in the expensive film medium in the history of art. All a poet needs is a pencil and some paper. A filmmaker needs cameras, sound equipment, assistants. I got pretty good at what I did; they kept paying me more and more to do it."

"Glenn made some nice movies with the money. They didn't turn a profit—documentaries don't show up in your neighborhood movie house very often. But they were nice."

Over the years Catherine had plenty of chances to have affairs. She turned them all down.

She worked, and for a long time that was enough. Then, a few years ago, Glenn went into a depression.

Finally, she began to think again about leaving him. She formed images of a possible other life; leaving the agency, going to Florence, writing a novel, meeting another guy somewhere down the road.

But then she'd add up the minuses: A year in Florence would cost a fortune, she might have put too many scars on her talent, most of the guys she knew were gay, or married, or drunks. And, most of all, if she left Glenn, he would be devastated.

"I didn't want to hurt that guy," she said. "He was decent and smart and nice, and in that depression of his, he seemed so vulnerable."

Then, a few weeks ago they met in a restaurant for dinner. Glenn was, of course, depressed. They ate in silence. But then, over coffee, he started to talk in a stumbling, uncertain way.

He didn't know how to tell her what he wanted to tell her, he said, but he had to get it said. She waited; he went on. He said he wanted to leave her. He had met a woman, 20 years younger than he was, and she made him feel like a man again. Yes, she was very young; but she was intelligent, sweet, beautiful. He blurted all of this out and then stared into his coffee.

Catherine began to laugh, low at first and then louder, and then in a smothered way, holding a napkin over her mouth. She laughed so hard her eyes filled with tears. Then she called the water for the check, paid with American Express, and stood up. Glenn held her hand.

"Where are you going?" he said.

"To Florence," she said, smiling broadly. She was laughing again as she got into the cab alone. (June 25, 1982, p. 19A)

When the wronged partner discovers an infidelity, the hurt can be devastating. This type of hurt is a principal basis for much of the violence in relationships. Speaking to the long-lasting nature of this pain are some of the people who write in to Cheryl Lavin's "Tales from the Front" column in the *Chicago Tribune*:

Ray: "I told my wife I forgave her, but I haven't. Behind every word I say to her is another one: 'Why'?"

Sarah: "My husband cheated on me two years ago, but the hurt never goes away. It's like my insides died. . . . I can't wait until we're both 85 so then maybe I can relax in our marriage." (November 19, 1988, "Tempo" Section)

At issue in the continuing hurt is one's perception of the partner's trustworthiness. As one 34-year-old woman reported in a *USA Today* survey of readers' experiences with affairs:

My husband had an affair nine years ago, for about six months, after my first child was born. I can't trust him anymore. I am worried sick whenever he is late from work. (quoted in *USA Today,* November 1, 1988)

Men may be less likely than women to forgive their partners for having an affair—even if they themselves have previously had affairs. Janet Reibstein and Martin Richards (1993) reported evidence that marriages are more at risk if it is the wife's affair. They say, "old-fashioned double standards combine with the gender dynamics of marriage to make the price of affairs higher for women than men" (p. 124).

It is possible both to learn from and heal from affairs. By sharing issues and communicating feelings, sometimes in therapy, couples can renew their trust in one another. They may have to start all over, psychologically, but such starts are often made with success. In time, all loss and suffering begins to heal.

Adultery is not the only kind of betrayal in close relationships. Jones and Burdette (1994) have argued that there are many other kinds of betrayal, such as violating the mutually agreed upon understandings for a relationship. This may involve a wide range of behavior, from making fun of one's partner in front of others to putting a murder contract out on him or her.

The Aftermath of Divorce and Dissolution

Deciding to Stay Single In a December 13, 1976, *Time* magazine column, Anne Taylor Fleming addressed the fear of being alone, one of the harsh realities of a period that saw an astounding rise in divorce.

> We all marry, in part, to avoid being alone; many of us divorce when we find we can be just as alone in marriage as before, and sometimes more so. Often, women in crumbling marriages conceive babies not to try to hold a man, as the cliché goes, but to guarantee themselves some company—even that of an infant—when that man is gone. After the divorce, for a man or woman, comes the frantic search for a replacement, a new lover, a dog, a singles club, a stronger drink or drug. Waking next to strangers in strange beds—surely, the loneliest habit—is considered preferable to being alone.

Some of Fleming's points still have currency. Certainly, however, the fear of AIDS has dampened people's frantic "bedding down" behavior after dissolution or divorce.

Divorced people are staying single in larger numbers and for longer periods than ever before. U.S. Census Bureau statistics indicate that 1.5 million people between 40 and 54 years of age were divorced and still unmarried in 1970. By 1991, that figure had risen to 6.1 million (3.6 million women and 2.5 million men). The number of divorced people remaining single is rising because of a number of factors. For women, one well-publicized demographic factor is that there are fewer men age 40 and older who are eligible for marriage than there are eligible women in that age group. On average, women

Divorce can be devastating to all aspects of people's lives.
Illustration by Milton Glaser.

outlive men by a little less than a decade. More men are incarcerated than are women. Perhaps most important is Bernard's (1982) argument: Given the large supply of well-educated, professional, and otherwise well-credentialed single women in their mid-life years, the supply of similarly qualified men is quite small; on the other hand, the number of men with considerably lesser credentials is quite large.

Women in their middle years also stay single for social psychological reasons. They frequently have well-established and nurturing social support networks of confidants and friends. These networks buffer them from some of the adverse effects of single life, such as the brooding loneliness that sometimes affects men who become single during their middle years. Women are more independent financially now than they were two decades ago. And although a great many women who have custody of children from a previous marriage depend on child support, many other women are supporting themselves and their children without help from their ex-husbands. In addition, women also do not define themselves in terms of their husband's career and values in the same way that they did in the past, and they are more likely now to have a strong desire for freedom. As one woman, 50, recently said after her divorce, "I could do anything I wanted for the first time in my life. . . . It was so good feeling free" (told to Jane Gross in an article in the *Chicago Tribune,* December 20, 1992). The abiding complaint among women divorcing after many years of marriage is that the husband was overly controlling. Close relationships with men who do not believe in equality and freedom of expression is a challenge that many women are no longer willing to accept.

Men may be less willing converts to single life (Bernard, 1982), but once they are in this state, they may not readily find women whom they want to marry. One of the reasons often cited by men for delaying remarriage is the major cost in assets and emotional resources involved in getting divorced, including child support. Some men feel that they lost unduly in the divorce decisions regarding property and/or custody of children. They feel "burned." Giler and Neumeyer (1992) reported that men in their 20s may be especially devastated and humbled by divorce. They suggested that these young men may see divorce as a major blow to their normal progression toward becoming fathers and having families. But such reasoning also suggests that these young men will quickly try to remarry and will not remain single very long. As men grow older, they often search diligently for partners because their social support system is not as strong as women's. Men may have lots of "drinking buddies," but they often lack the type of emotionally-involved confidants that women have. These confidants are invaluable during times of stress when people need to unload their burdens and engage in healthy catharsis regarding their losses.

Deciding to Remarry

Love can be a rickety vehicle, loaded with so much of life's baggage, and the trip back to the world of the married is often interrupted by slow-downs, halts, and backsliding.
—Morton Hunt, *The World of the Formerly Married*

Remarriage is the triumph of hope over experience.
—Samuel Johnson

In 1980, of 45 million married households in the United States, 9 million were of remarried partners; that number has now at least doubled. At the same time, 60 percent of second and beyond marriages have ended in divorce in the last decade.

Very few people intend to stay single when they divorce, or after the dissolution of a long-term nonmarital close relationship. They want a new partner who has all the good qualities the first one did not have. Or they may want someone who does not have the negative qualities they perceived in their first partner. Thus, people remarrying usually are saying, "I want a better marriage than the one I had before." They also may be more realistic regarding what is possible in a marriage.

There are usually many issues left hanging from the first marriage. Children and their custody is at the top of the list. New partners might each bring children from other marriages to the new home, necessitating a blending of people, personalities, habits, rules, and expectations. Another problem is that the ex-husband may have to make large child support payments to his ex-wife; thus, money may be tight for his new family, and this may be exacerbated if he decides to have more children.

It is common for emotional baggage carried over from the first marriage to interfere with the new relationship. Many therapists and commentators in this area suggest people should let at least two years pass between marriages in order to mute some of the emotional and practical difficulties lingering from the ending of the first marriage. A period of counseling may be helpful in addressing emotional residue. Some people may experience continued emotional attachment that may continue for years beyond separation or legal divorce. Problems in joint-custody arrangements regarding how children are treated are common. Children can be caught between separated husbands and wives who want revenge and who try to use them to spy on their ex-partner and his or her new lovers.

Experts believe that people who remarry have to be careful to not repeat patterns in the new marriage that were problematic in the first one, such as excessive drinking, staying away from home after work, excessive criticism of one's partner, nagging, excessive rigidity and control, inability to express feelings, flirting with or actually having affairs.

At the same time, many people are quick to end a second marriage when problems emerge that are similar to those they experienced in the first marriage. Furstenberg and Spanier (1987) suggested that the psychology of the remarried person who spots trouble is, in effect, "I've survived divorce before and I will again. I do not intend to put up with this very long." One of the respondents in Furstenberg and Spanier's study discussed this psychology.

I think we also went into our second marriage with the attitude that if she woke up one morning and said "I'm not in love with you anymore (or) it's not the same for me anymore—I've met someone else," I'd say, "God bless" without any animosity. I would try my damnest [to make the marriage work] and hope that she would try the same way, but if we couldn't work it out, then we wouldn't stay together . . . it's a little different from what I thought the first time. I think the way you look on . . . the next relationship—you know, that these things can be terminated—that's a matter of historical record, so there's an illusion that's gone. (p. 192)

Health

The effects of relationship dissolution on the psychological and physical health of the partners and their children often are powerful and long lasting and usually negative. One of the most debilitating aspects of divorce is the legal activity of officially splitting up assets and determining custody when children are involved. These proceedings are usually highly adversarial and may go on for years. For example, in 1992, in one New Jersey suburb, contested divorce trials were so backed up that many people endured three-year delays from the time of filing to the point of the trial. One outraged woman who experienced such a delay said: "This is my life we're talking about . . . It interferes with my social life. If I tell a gentleman I've been trying to get divorced for so long . . . he'll figure I'm some sort of lunatic" (quoted in Bethany Kandel, *USA Today,* February 20, 1992).

Divorce is highly correlated with high rates for suicide, depression, mental illness, physical ailments and illnesses, and mortality (Stroebe & Stroebe, 1986). We do not know for certain that divorce caused these problems. Conceivably, other problems, such as financial difficulties, that precipitated the divorce might be the cause.

The impact of divorce or dissolution is enhanced by certain situational factors. Parkes (1972) argued that a sudden or unexpected termination of a relationship was especially hurtful. Also, Parkes noted that people who share domestic and other practical tasks in a relationship are better able to cope, and less devastated, when divorce or dissolution occurs because they have become less dependent on their partner. The same is likely to hold for emotional independence. Individuals who are highly dependent on their partner to meet their emotional needs or to provide friends and a social network are likely to be affected much more harshly by the termination of the relationship.

Why is divorce or dissolution so devastating? First, it robs us of our innocence. The expectation that the relationship will last "till death do us part" is dashed. The result is often a series of hard knocks on one's self-esteem, sense of control over major events, and overall feeling of competence in close relationships. We also tend to compare ourselves with others whom we perceive as being engaged in solid relationships. Such social comparison (see Schachter, 1959) makes more salient our loss and the possibility that we will never experience such stability. Beyond these blows, the person who loses a partner also loses the emotional support and companionship that usually go along with such relationships. Even in sadly deteriorated relationships, partners may not recognize the extent to which they were attached and, thus, may be bewildered by the bereavement at the loss of this attachment. After all, many partners have been together since they were quite young people. They often have gone through many adversities together. These experiences create an attachment, even if the marital interaction quality is poor and becoming poorer.

Finally, there is a loss of identity. We no longer are Joan's "significant other," "John's wife," or "Mary's live-in partner." The outside world has to learn that the identities no longer hold, and we have to adjust to this change in our own minds. Depending on how much we wanted this role and wanted to continue in it, the adjustment can be difficult. But it has to be done. The sooner the newly single person can recognize the need to change his or her life, perhaps by involvement in support groups and working on self-improvement, the sooner the recovery will be complete. One fortunate result of the high frequency of divorce is that outsiders now exhibit more sensitivity in reacting to news of divorce and may assist a person going through it.

Vivid Memories of Vivid Loves Gone By

People who end a close relationship are left with many poignant and sometimes haunting memories of their past love. These memories may intrude unexpectedly when they are reminded of the lost one. They also may come up in dreams or in conscious attempts to dredge up the past. For some, these vivid memories appear to be a normal part of the continued grieving process. Some continue to obsess about the loss, however, and do not engage in the grieving and resolution processes that are necessary to effectively live one's life and fully participate in future close relationships. Let's look briefly at some research on this topic.

Brown and Kulik (1977) found what they called a "flashbulb memory effect" when they asked people to recall what they were experiencing the moment they heard that President John F. Kennedy had been murdered. People recalled their experience of this news in vivid detail. One person remembered the sensation he felt when his foot hit the concrete step entering Harvard University Library at the moment he heard the news. A similar type of effect has been found for people's reports of their experience at the moment they heard that the *Challenger* spacecraft carrying six astronauts and schoolteacher Christa

Reports of Respondents to Vivid Memories
of Vivid Loves Gone By

Harvey, Flannary and Morgan (1986) asked respondents in their 20s and 30s to anonymously report their most vivid memories of their most significant past close relationships. Here are some of the different types of memories reported:

Beginnings

"The first time we slept together I was living alone in a little house in a tiny town in the middle of nowhere. We stayed in bed for fourteen hours—it was wonderful."

"Our first (almost) sexual encounter, we were at a retreat and in the kitchen, and people kept walking in. It was rather amusing; it was ludicrous."

"I met him at a small party given by our apartment manager . . . our eyes kept meeting across the room . . . When the party was over, we both managed to saunter out the door at the same time. He invited me up to his apartment—I remember sitting in his bean bag chair and listening to the Eagles sing, 'The Best of My Love.'"

McAuliff exploded. My colleagues Rodney Flanary and Melinda Morgan and I (Harvey et al., 1986) wondered if flashbulb-type effects would be found when people were asked to recall their most vivid memories of their most important past romantic relationships.

We asked respondents to recall their most vivid memories of events occurring in their most significant past close relationship. A "vivid memory" was defined as a picturelike image or thought that is lifelike, striking, and evocative of strong emotion. The respondents in

Special Occasions (both pleasant and painful)

"The first time he told me how much he loved me . . . considering he was a married man."

"Being raped by him when he was drunk."

"After seven years, he brought home yellow roses. Trips to New Orleans. Five wonderful days of being together, sightseeing, eating out. Time alone in the hotel room."

"August 15, 1984, the date we intended to marry."

Beginning of the End and Endings

"Receiving the 'letter' January 21, 1978."

"Confrontation with girlfriend and husband. Stated he did not love me; that he loved her."

"I remember the time I caught him throwing rocks at my car."

"Our final interaction was an angry goodbye in the car when I was moving away. Time seemed to stand still for a long time."

this study, mostly in their late 20s through early 40s, had been involved either in nonmarital or marital relationships lasting at least two years, and the length of time since these relationships ended averaged almost three years. We found that women reported more vivid memories of their past loves than did men. The content of some of these memories are shown above. The results also showed that women exhibited more depression regarding the loss of these past loves than did men.

As can be seen in the reports of respondents on the previous pages, highly vivid memories tended to be of first meetings, first sexual experiences, critical conflict episodes near the end, and ending events. While both pleasant and painful memories surfaced in respondents' reports, unpleasant memories were more commonly reported.

In a related study, Ross and Holmberg (1992) hypothesized that women pay more attention to the emotional aspects of interactions with lovers and spouses and hence should have more vivid memories of key past events in their relationships than should men. A strength of this study was that both members of 60 married couples participated in the research. The researchers asked spouses to tape-record descriptions of their first date together, a shared vacation, and an argument between them. They subsequently assessed the clarity of their own recall of each event. As expected, women reported having more vivid memories than did their husbands. Women also attributed greater personal importance to the events, reported reminiscing about them more often, and expressed more emotion in their event descriptions than did their husbands. Later, observers of each couple's reports also judged women's recall to be more vivid.

These two studies converge in suggesting that women have more intense, vivid, evocative memories of events in their past close relationships than do men. Ross and Holmberg imply that this is because women have learned to link closely in their minds critical relationship experiences with strong feelings. Other possible explanations are that women pay more attention to critical events in relationships than do men and that women are more open to recalling and reporting memories of such events.

The Effects on Children

In the 1990s Census Bureau data indicates that 50 to 60 percent of the children in the United States will personally experience the effects of a divorce and one third of the children in this country will live in a blended family by the time they reach 18.

Hetherington, Cox, and Cox (1982), Wallerstein and Kelly (1980), and Furstenberg and Cherlin (1991) have provided data and perspective on the effects of divorce on children. Scholars and studies differ on the nature and extent of the impact that divorce has on children. Hetherington et al. found that while divorce initially created turmoil in the lives of the children involved, by the second year after divorce, their lives had become more normal. Wallerstein and her colleagues found that of the young men and women they studied, as many as one half entered adulthood as worried, underachieving, self-deprecating, and sometimes angry people because of their parents' divorces. Other scholars, including Furstenberg and Cherlin, do not believe that the evidence is that clear regarding the degree of impact on children. They have argued that the parents whose divorce have been studied may have had severe problems well before the divorce. In such relationships, the children were probably also negatively affected by their parents' ongoing problems. Most of the divorced couples studied to date have been involved in counseling and have agreed to answer questionnaires and participate in research as part of the counseling process.

Scholars such as Furstenberg and Cherlin have suggested that there is stronger evidence to support the view that harmful long-term effects of divorce are experienced by only a minority of children. They have found that many young adults are likely to retain painful memories of their parents' divorce. It does not follow, however, that these memories will impair their marriages or other parts of their lives. Further, if their parents had not divorced, these children might have retained equally painful memories of their parents' conflict-ridden marriages. Furstenberg and Cherlin (1991) have proposed that children will suffer whenever there is trouble in a marriage and that it is not particularly helpful for parents to stay together in order to alleviate their children's suffering. These researchers found that children who live with two parents who persistently quarrel over important areas of family life show greater distress and more behavior problems than do children from disrupted marriages.

Looking further, there is evidence that in comparison to their peers from intact families, some children show enhanced levels of functioning in areas such as self-esteem and empathy following a divorce (Gately & Schwebel, 1992). This could be because a divorce may allow these children, who are likely to be older and already possessing considerable maturity, to take on additional responsibilities, such as caring for siblings, that can increase their self-esteem. Further, children who learn that they can rise to the occasion during the adversity of divorce may develop a general kind of strength and courage that will assist them when they encounter problems later in life. Research by Zill, Morrison, and Cairo (1993) showed that one of the determinants of how well children cope with a divorce is their age at the time of divorce. Parental divorce was found to have its most detrimental effects on children younger than age 16 and was particularly devastating for children who were younger than 6. Zill reported that young adults (ages 18-22) from families in which a divorce occurred before 16 had higher levels of emotional distress and problem behavior than did young adults from nondisrupted families.

Children deserve to be listened to when adults are considering the impact of divorce on them. Consider these reports from a 1992 *Parade Magazine* survey of kids' views:

Allison [age 15]: When you decide to get a divorce, definitely tell the kids, "We're not doing this because of you." [It is common for kids to believe they are to blame for their parents' problems.] And be honest with your kids about what's going on.

And don't use your child as a middleman, like, "Tell your dad that I say to send the child support right now." I tell my mom, "Just talk to Dad." I hate being in the middle. Because then my dad will say, "Well, tell your mom I'm not gonna . . . unless she . . ." That's happened so much, and I've gotten so mad about it with both of them that now they do call each other directly.

Sometimes, during a divorce, a parent thinks that everything's okay and, "Oh, Allison's just adjusting fine." But you should give your kids extra attention because all this fighting is going on, and you wonder if they still love you just the same.

Jacey [age 14]: . . . Sometimes my father will say, "Why'd your mother let you go do this by yourself?" He still wants to have the same authority that he used to have when I lived with him. And when I'm with my dad, my mom still wants to be able to say, "Make sure you wear your earmuffs."

Don't make your kids feel guilty about talking about the other parent's house or about things you've done together. Because the other parent is still part of the kid's life. (*Parade Magazine*, p. 5, January 26, 1992)

There are many other issues associated with the impact of divorce on children, including: Does the type of custody (joint or sole) make a difference in the child's adjustment? Does type and quality of visitation for the noncustodial parent affect children's progress? Do different blendings of stepfamilies help or hurt adjustment? The answer to such questions is inevitably "It depends."

It depends on a host of factors, such as whether the parents in a joint-custody situation—or the custodial parent, when only one has custody—provide sufficient security, nurturance, and understanding for their children at the same time that they are dealing with their own postdivorce issues. It depends on how well blended families are functioning and whether or not they have figured out ways to enhance both the group's and the individuals' level of family satisfaction. In her 1994 book *Families Apart,* Melinda Blau discusses ways in which co-parenting can be made to work. Hopefully they will develop meaningful relationships with both parents, new significant others in the parents' lives, and different sets of friends.

Parents' recognition of children's feelings and their need to adjust and move on in new directions with their lives is an essential step in this process. As Wallerstein and Kelly said, "Even though the children may still regret the divorce and continue to wish that their parents had been able to love each other, some of these children may nevertheless grow in their capacity for compassion and psychological understanding" (1980, p. 316).

The Future of Divorce and Dissolution

Despite the hundreds of books and thousands of studies concerned with divorce, evidence suggests that no diminution of the high divorce rate is on the horizon. The divorce rate for second and later marriages is even higher than it is for first marriages. Further, factors associated with dual-career marriages and economic difficulties are likely to contribute to future dissolutions.

Fortunately, we are now more sophisticated in dealing with loss of a close relationship. We have more support groups and counseling services available than ever before, stretching across socioeconomic levels. Support groups such as "Parents without Partners," which was established in 1957 and now has over 250,000 members, help address people's social and practical problems. These groups do not make the hurt and damage go away, but they do allow people to confide in others, to vent their pain, and to learn from and be supported by others who have survived similar circumstances.

I WALKED A MILE WITH PLEASURE;

SHE CHATTERED ALL THE WAY,

BUT LEFT ME NONE THE WISER

FOR ALL SHE HAD TO SAY.

I WALKED A MILE WITH SORROW

AND NE'ER A WORD SAID SHE;

BUT OH, THE THINGS I LEARNED

FROM HER WHEN SORROW

WALKED WITH ME!

—Robert Browning Hamilton's

"Along the Road"

Chapter

9

GRIEVING
THE LOSS
OF CLOSE
RELATIONSHIPS

FOR, ALTHOUGH IT IS TRUE
THAT FEAR AND DESPAIR
CAN OVERWHELM US,
HOPE CANNOT BE PURCHASED
WITH THE REFUSAL
TO FEEL.

—Susan Griffith

■

GIVE SORROW WORDS:
THE GRIEF THAT DOES NOT SPEAK
WHISPERS THE O'ER-FRAUGHT HEART,
AND BIDS IT BREAK.

—Shakespeare's *Macbeth*

This chapter is about the grief that we experience when a loved one dies or a close relationship ends. While death and dissolution are quite different experiences replete with their own psychological dynamics, each represents a degree of loss to the survivor. Both death and dissolution may end relationships that were among the most significant ones in the life of the survivor, or they may end less significant relationships, such as an on-again, off-again 6-month dating relationship. For our discussion here, however, we are assuming that the close relationship was quite significant to the survivor.

Death brings with it a finality that dissolution may not. It may ultimately be a relief to the mourner, especially if there was suffering in the end or the possibility of a long period of decline in the quality of life for the person who is ill. But it may also create guilt and angst for the mourner if they feel that there was much unfinished business. If the mourner is to successfully deal with either experience, it is essential that the individual confront their loss and diligently work toward adaptation to the new realities it has created. These losses and their accompanying grief are universal phenomena that each of us must face. But they offer an invaluable opportunity to reflect and search for meaning beyond our day-to-day lives. Engaging in this time of reflection and then confiding in close others is central to the process of grieving.

Shakespeare's and Griffith's encouragement to share one's sorrow and to not refuse to feel it is marvelous advice. Whether we are dealing with dissolution, death, or some other loss, there is compelling logic and evidence that people will suffer more—both physically and psychologically—if they do not allow themselves to feel and express their pain to close others.

Writing about one's loss can be an important step in recovering from that loss. One of the most touching examples of such writings is found in C.S. Lewis' 1961 book *A Grief Observed*. In this little volume, Lewis presented his jottings and notes written in the aftermath of the death of his wife after a four year marriage. His marriage to poet Joy Gresham was particularly satisfying, both of them were highly devoted to one another and felt blessed because they were able to help each other work through the pain from their former marriages. One reviewer said, "The author has done something I had believed impossible—assuaged his own grief by conveying it . . ." (Anne Freemantle, forward to *A Grief Observed*).

To give you just a taste of Lewis' notes, he said about his wife, "Her absence is like the sky, spread over everything" (p. 11). He said about their happiness in the context of her dying hours:

It is incredible how much happiness, even how much gaiety, we sometimes had together after all hope was gone. How long, how tranquilly, how nourishingly, we talked together that last night! (p. 13)

Or consider the following insight about the ways in which others may react to someone in mourning:

To some I'm worse than an embarrassment. I am a death's head. Whenever I meet a happily married pair I can feel them both thinking, "One or other of us must some day be as he is now." (p. 11)

Those who mourn may feel like an outsider in what might now seem to be a coupled-up world. But feelings of embarrassment and exclusion are often exacerbated further by the sometimes insensitive acts of others. A parent whose young son had recently died offered some sage advice: Do not try to comfort mourners by suggesting that they should not despair. Do not tell them that their loved one was "in heaven and much better off" there. These so-called comforting words are not helpful, but merely glib. Instead, the greatest kindness you can offer is to simply indicate that you are sorry about their loss, and let them know that you are willing to listen or help should that person need you.

Cultural Differences

People express grief in different ways in different historical periods. A powerful analysis of how people grieved in the United States in the 19th century is contained in Paul Rosenblatt's (1983) *Bitter, Bitter Tears*. Rosenblatt examined hundreds of tattered, dusty diaries written by people who had been left behind by close others venturing west and people who had lost significant others to death—often at a very early age. He found much outpouring of emotion and yearning for the lost other. He also focused attention on the extent to which diary and record-keeping were part of the grieving reaction of people in the last century.

Grieving also varies according to culture (see Irish, et al., 1993). For example, an Egyptian mother may remain withdrawn, mute, and inactive for seven years after the death of her child. While her behavior may be judged pathological by Western standards, it is normal in her culture.

In the accompanying flow chart I present a model of how people in the West react to loss. Not all people go through each of the stages proposed, nor do people necessarily go through them in the order proposed. Nevertheless, such a model is important because it shows common reactions—ones that we all are subject to and should accept if they occur. This model was initially developed based on a model proposed by Horowitz (1986).

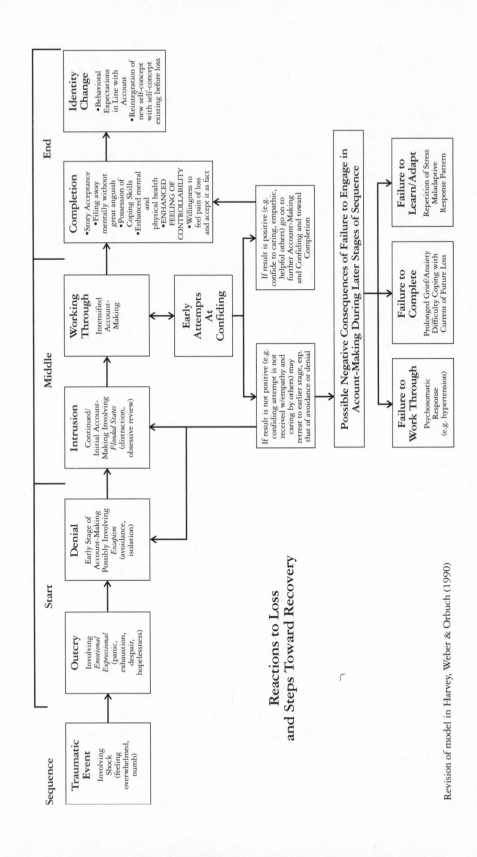

**Reactions to Loss
and Steps Toward Recovery**

Revision of model in Harvey, Weber & Orbuch (1990)

Early Reactions to Loss

The typical early reactions to a major loss include initial shock, feeling numb, the "outcry," as well as a possible period of denial and intrusion of thoughts about the loss. Upon learning that her husband of 18 months had died after a battle with cancer, a 34-year-old woman reported the following reaction: "When he died, I just felt empty, numb. I was in a fog. I couldn't cry. And I felt very vulnerable" (quoted in Alice Steinbach, "A Shoulder to Cry on," *Redbook,* July 1993, p. 43).

People often say they cannot believe the loved one is gone. They cannot sleep at night, or their sleep is fitful—filled with dreamlike images of the loved one. In this state, their minds appear to be fighting against the inevitability of the loss. During the day, they frequently experience flashbacks of images of the loved one and regret that they did not have enough time with him or her, or that some important personal communication with the loved one did not occur—that is, there was unfinished business that they feel a need to resolve.

This early period may last for days, weeks, or months; if it goes on for years, the grieving person might need to seek professional help. The numbing of the mind during the early phase is a natural occurrence. It is as if the mind and one's total self are programmed to shut down (a process sometimes aided by tranquilizers) for a period to let the loss sink in (Raphael, 1982). Then, the next steps in grieving can occur. The outcry may involve periods of uncontrollable weeping. The woman mentioned above whose husband had died of cancer said that she was unable to stop crying. "I was in tears every single day and barely got out of bed on weekends."

The outcry also is a yearning, and sometimes a literal searching, for the beloved. Parkes (1972) identified these elements of this phase of grieving:

- restless moving about and scanning the environment

- thinking intensely about the lost person

- developing a "perceptual set" for the lost person: the griever pays attention to any stimuli that suggest the presence of the person and ignores all those that are not relevant to this aim

- directing attention toward those parts of the environment in which the person is likely to be found

- calling for the lost person

I have personally experienced these reactions on several, daunting occasions in my life. They have etched themselves in my memory both in times of loss by death and in the dissolution of close relationships. They are dark, frightening memories that, once gone, you wish never would return. But you know they will. Loss will recur. It is simply in the scheme of things.

Raphael (1982) reviewed evidence suggesting that continued intense bereavement may be fatal. For example, there is an increase of almost 50 percent in the death rate of widowers over the age of 54 during the first six months of bereavement. Suicide is also a hazard during this early period for the deeply grieving person. Raphael reported national data that showed the suicide rate among a large sample of widows and widowers to be 2.5 times higher in the first six months after the loss than it was in the fourth year and subsequent years.

Intrusion of Images and Thoughts

The experience of intrusion of images of and thoughts about one's lost partner is illustrated in the following excerpt from an article about

University of Illinois basketball coach Lou Henson, whose son, in his late 20s, was killed in an automobile accident in late 1992:

> Last Thursday afternoon in Evanston, a few hours before his Illinois team played Northwestern, Lou Henson picked up a program to examine the Wildcats' roster.
>
> His veteran coach's eyes are trained to look for heights, weights, and experience, the critical basketball facts. But as Henson scanned the lineup, he couldn't help notice that forward Cedric Neloms was born on Nov. 20, 1972.
>
> Nov. 20. The day stopped Henson cold. That's the date, seven weeks ago, that Henson's son, Lou Henson Jr., died in a car crash on a highway not far from his parents' Champaign home.
>
> "It just popped out at me," Henson said. "Things like that come up all the time."
>
> "It comes up every Wednesday night, for that was the day of the week that the younger Henson made his home coaching debut at Champaign's Parkland College. It comes up late every Friday night, for that is when the younger Henson crashed his car. It comes up at 2 a.m. every Saturday—when Henson may still be up watching a tape of an opponent—for that is when the knock came on the door of the Henson's house. (*Chicago Tribune*, January 11, 1993, Section 3, p. 1, article by Andrew Bagnato, "Henson fights grief by looking to No. 600")

Lou Henson is not alone in being unable to escape intrusive symbols of his loss. He will probably experience these intrusions, and even find himself voluntarily reflecting on such images and ideas about his son, until he dies. That is one of the greatest plights and banes of the human mind and memory.

Neither intrusive thoughts nor voluntary reminiscing are detrimental to the grieving process, although they may be continual reminders of regret and pain. A Holocaust survivor, now in mid-life, said about the horrors of losing his relatives and friends and fleeing the Nazis as a 13-year-old in Germany: "I dream about it. I think about it, day or night. . . . It is always with me" (Winter 1991, *United States Holocaust Memorial Museum Newsletter,* p. 2, comment by Arnold Lorber).

Neeld (1990) suggested that reminiscence allows us to maintain an inventory of the key images of ourselves from the past and, therefore, permits us to keep a thread of continuity among them. She further contended that reminiscence helps us realize that the past has not disappeared and allows us to develop goals for the future in the light of past events.

Coming to Grips with Loss

Our model suggests that two of the most effective ways of dealing with major loss are developing an account and confiding in close others about the loss.

The Account   Accounts are people's stories about important aspects of their lives (such as their major losses and successes). They usually contain the account maker's understanding of the beginning, middle, and end of some event or sequence of events. They also frequently contain a set of actors, acts, and behind-the-scenes activities.

We often work on our accounts in our minds, privately. Accounts may be based on memories that are inaccurate or distorted. They thus may have factual as well as nonfactual detail and imagery in them.

Each of us has as many accounts as we have major events that require our understanding. We may work on these accounts for years, and still they are likely to remain incomplete. However, the crucial activity is confronting the issue (e.g., why a lover decided to leave you)—reflecting, analyzing, sifting among images, and allowing oneself to be emotionally moved by this process. The story gives the individual a greater sense of control in dealing with the issue. While the content of accounts matters, it is the process of account making that is instrumental to eventual peace of mind (see Harvey, Orbuch, & Weber, 1992, for various perspectives on accounts).

Robert Weiss (1975) was the first scholar to apply the concept of the account loss. He asked how people in the midst of separation and divorce understand and gain a sense of control over the taxing and befuddling events that are likely to confront. He developed his account analysis through research with a sample of people in the organization Parents without Partners. Weiss argued that although accounts are not necessarily true stories, they usually are perceived as true by the account maker. He said that people often replay (and revise) their accounts in an obsessive way as they try to come to grips with what happened; they also wonder what would have happened if different things had been said or done. Weiss found that husbands and wives in the throes of separation and divorce often disagree in their accounts of why events occurred.

Weiss (1975) offered this statement regarding the practical merit of the account to the account maker:

> The account is of major psychological importance to the separated, not only because it settles the issue of who was responsible for what, but also because it imposes on the confused marital events that preceded the separation a plot structure with a beginning, middle, and end and so organizes the events into a conceptually manageable unity. Once understood in this way, the events can be dealt with: They can be seen as outcomes of identifiable causes and, eventually, can be seen as

past, over, and external to the individual's present self. Those who cannot construct accounts sometimes feel that their perplexity keeps them from detaching themselves from the distressing experiences. (p. 15)

In the general literature today, one of the most common forms of first-person narrative writing concerns people's accounts of bad things that have happened to them or their loved ones. As writer Nancy Mair said in the February 21, 1993, article "When bad things happen to good writers," in *The New York Times Book Review*:

The fact is that the true victim—the person set apart from ordinary human intercourse by temporary or permanent misfortune—has little enough time and even less energy for sniveling. . . . There are hands to be held and basins to be emptied and upper lips to be kept stiff. . . . Self-pity simply doesn't provide an adequate motive for going to the effort of writing a book about the ordeal. But the work, tough as it is, feels singularly instructive. . . . It pricks all of one's senses.

The impulse, at least for someone of a writerly persuasion, is not to bemoan this condition but to remark on it in detail. . . . The process of making sense of a flood of random data also produces the impression of control. (p. 25)

Mair further analyzed this process as therapeutic because it allows for intellectualizing and distancing oneself from the grievous material flooding one's brain.

I believe that there is a deeper mission involved in account making. People who write about major loss are actually groping for an understanding, a meaning for something that has bewildered the mind and soul. They are feeling anew the rush of painful emotions as they write. In this sense, writers are not so much detaching themselves from the events as they are directly grappling with them. The account makers are thus reexperiencing the initial horror, but this time under the protection of a greater sense of control and an empowering desire to do something about the horror—which may be to help others deal with similar situations or simply to demonstrate to themselves that they can survive the loss.

Confiding   Often, people communicate parts of their accounts to their closest friends to gain their perspective, present themselves in a certain light, or simply share their experience. The social interaction process involved in confiding can be a healing process independent of what is said. People are quite vulnerable if, at times of major loss, they do not have confidants in their lives.

Neeld (1990) suggested that the type of confiding interaction that is most helpful after a major loss focuses on problem solving—especially after the grieving person has had sufficient time to experience catharsis (a purging of the emotions) and cry out about the loss. She emphasized the value of confidants who understand the necessity for change and even some risk taking, and who know that progress will not occur in a smooth, straight line.

How and when do we find such confidants? Vincent Foster, deputy White House counsel and President Bill Clinton's friend since childhood, committed suicide in 1993. At the time of his death, it was suggested that Foster was such a close friend to Clinton because they met in kindergarten. Making friends in kindergarten probably is based on insight, intuition, and untaught knowledge. To keep a friend made that early in life until mid-life is a great blessing. Clinton's considerable anguish at the loss of his life-long friend is understandable given his friend's confidant status and the length of their friendship. His grief was intensified because he did not know his friend was so troubled that suicide seemed to be his only option.

Most of us select our closest friends and confidants later in life—perhaps in high school and college. We do so on the basis of a similarity of interests and attitudes. In the course of dealing with personal crises, we also learn that these people are *there* for us. We are indeed fortunate if we reach our later years, or even mid-life, with the same set of confidants we had when we were young. Given their critical role in our well-being, we are luckier still to simply have had one or more such persons in our lives.

In *Opening Up*, James Pennebaker (1990) documents many negative psychological and physical effects associated with the failure to confront one's "devils," or the pain, hurt, and confusion resulting from vital losses and transforming experiences. Pennebaker and his associates found that confiding seems to lead to effective coping. In Pennebaker's conception, it is imperative that people examine carefully their motives and logic in selecting a confidant and in carrying out extended confiding. Too much self-disclosure may overburden the confidant. Further, Pennebaker noted that the confidant must be careful not to internalize the discloser's problems so that they become those of the confidant.

Duration of Grief

Pennebaker also said that in both romantic love and grief there are periods of intensity, plateau, and assimilation. He suggested that the average course for grieving after a breakup runs approximately 18 months. But others believe that the length of time it takes to heal after a major loss is quite variable. In addressing how long one should grieve, several scholars, including Raphael (1982) and Wortman and Silver (1989), have suggested that there is no fixed end point of mourning during the first or even second year.

In another commentary on grieving (November 28, 1992, *Iowa City Press-Citizen,* article by Ian Smith), a physician suggested that people who had suffered major losses should seek professional help if they continued to grieve beyond three months. I felt so strongly about our ignorance regarding the exact nature and duration of the grieving process that I replied in a letter to the editor:

> All that we know about grieving associated with major loss indicates that it is a variable process. Three months hardly is normative for significant losses. A person readily and in a non-dysfunctional way may grieve for years, or even a lifetime, about some major loss. It would be a wonderful condition of the human mind and heart if major loss could so readily be put behind us after a few months. But most of us will find that hard to do, and yet at the same time, many of us will go on in our lives without needing professional counseling. . . . Many a Vietnam combat veteran who is generally doing well in life can tell us about a grieving that may know no end. (*Iowa City Press-Citizen,* December 12, 1992)

Obsessing about vs. Confronting Loss

> Activity, no less than confidence, is deeply connected to the environment of restoration.
> —Norman Cousins, *Head First*

In obsessive memory, we cannot get the lost other out of our minds. For example, a man who has been suddenly and unexpectedly left by a woman after a long-term close relationship may find himself musing about why she left him and imagining her in a new love relationship.

Even if he knows that he has to move beyond her, he may feel compelled to entertain these thoughts and continually slip back to them.

Daniel Wegner (1989) claimed that one of the contributors to such rumination is thought suppression, a mechanism that works only for a short period. That is, when people try to shunt aside an unwanted thought, it does not really go away. He contended that the key to eliminating such thoughts is habituation. Wegner reasoned that by refusing to think about the failed love, people prevent themselves from getting used to the idea. Thus, his recommendation is that every time the painful memory resurfaces, instead of suppressing it, you should think hard about it. Try to come to grips with the pain of dashed expectation and disappointment. Go ahead and get obsessed. Do it big-time. If you do this, argued Wegner, the pain will start to diminish. The idea (that you have lost someone) will start to lose its grip on you. It may even become boring.

The End of the Grieving Process

He has seen but half the universe who has not seen
the house of pain.
　　　　　　　　　—Ralph Waldo Emerson

A new sense of self may emerge when one has finalized an account and come to the end of their grief work. This step in our model is referred to as identity change. We never completely finish our grieving. We simply get to a practical, but absolutely invaluable, point where we can let go and move on—knowing that we will probably have to deal with these matters again.

Stephen Levine (1984) related a similar conception of completion in *Meetings at the Edge,* a book of dialogues with the grieving and dying. He described one man who grieved intensely as his wife lay dying of cancer. Finally, when it appeared that his wife was ready to let go of life, the man seemed to find a type of joy that his wife would not suffer much longer and that he too was ready to let go of her. Levine offered this explanation regarding the relief, or positive feeling, many survivors have when the end is at hand:

> It seems that for those who have worked so hard for so many months or years attending to a loved one and sharing in their death at levels beyond description find the grief somewhat more accessible, even somewhat "easier," if I can use that word in the midst of such pain. Perhaps this is because the mind never quite obscures the depth of the heart connection shared. For these beings, the grief in time more readily sinks back into the heart, where the departed is experienced in his or her essential connectedness and love. Their joy is the joy of completion. Their grief is their loss and their opening to what lies ahead. (p. 153)

Often, the individual who has suffered much has much to give to others. The psychologist Erik Erikson (1963) argued that a great need but also a great challenge facing each of us to try to give back some of what we have learned to others, especially to generations who come after us. He called this contribution *generativity*. Several notable examples of generativity have appeared in recent years. Gilda Radner and Jill Ireland each succumbed to cancer in mid-life. Each wrote about their experiences and appeared many times on TV to discuss their illness and how they wanted their remaining time to serve as an example for others facing terminal illness of continued hope and will to live. Former North Carolina State basketball coach Jim Valvano succumbed to bone cancer at age 47 in April 1993, after a year-long fight that had the nation cheering for him. Valvano established the Jimmy V Foundation for Cancer Research, and he visited with many patients in cancer treatment centers. He said of one such experience:

We're down in the basement. . . . There are no cameras. There are no newspaper articles. Everybody is battling a disease that can take their life. It's a very lonely place. But it's also uplifting because everybody cares so much for everybody else. There's no selfishness down there. . . . I always feel afterward that it's a special role I've been given.

It's for all the people who are struggling, dying, fighting it and trying to have a miracle happen (Charles Chandler's article "Valvano fights so others will win battle he's losing," *Knight-Ridder Tribune News,* April 4, 1993).

Valvano said that he had learned that each day was precious. He believed that every day, you should: 1. laugh; 2. spend some time in thought; and 3. let your emotions be moved to tears—and cry. He said that if you laugh, think, and cry, that is a full day and such activities will benefit you physically, spiritually, and emotionally.

In a brilliant book entitled *Number Our Days,* the anthropologist Barbara Myerhoff (1978) interviewed a group of Jewish Holocaust survivors who were spending much of their final years interacting in a senior citizens center in Santa Monica, California. Most had lost family members and all had lost close friends in the Holocaust.

Myerhoff indicated that some of the individuals she studied had achieved difficult completion over the horrible events that had taken so many of their friends and family. They used account making and confiding to confront painful memories and to prepare for their own deaths. Myerhoff presented this quote by a member of this community who had reached such resolve:

I think this attitude you are talking about, paying such attention to life, is what we mean by a "heart of wisdom," . . . In the psalm it says, "So teach us to number our days, that we may get us a heart of wisdom."

I had a dream the other night. . . . A man of great wisdom, a doctor, told me I had a fatal disease. "You cannot remedy it," he said. "There is nothing I can do for you except to give you this advice: Do your work as well as you can. Love those around you. Know what you are doing. Go home and live fully. The fatal disease is life." (pp. 230-231)

Myerhoff's findings generally are consistent with those of sociologist William Helmreich (1992), who made the first comprehensive study of the 140,000 Jewish Holocaust survivors who came to the United States and the lives they made here. One of the interesting results found by Helmreich was that survivors' marriages were usually quite stable. In 1989 he found that 83 percent of the survivors were still married to their original spouse. Contrary to stereotype, survivors also showed relatively low rates of mental illness and use of mental health services. How did these survivors cope so well with life after having experienced severe trauma—death of loved ones, starvation and beatings, and loss of freedom? Helmreich isolated a set of general traits, some of which were present in all of the survivors. These included: flexibility, assertiveness, tenacity, optimism, intelligence, group consciousness, courage, and finding meaning in life.

Helmreich's report represents a beautiful story of generativity. These Holocaust survivors show in their daily behavior how remarkable people can be in surmounting inestimable suffering and achieving psychic autonomy, integration, and social adjustment.

Stories from the "Wall" The Vietnam Memorial Wall in Washington, D.C., is especially meaningful to parents, spouses, siblings, and children of people whose names are engraved on it. One mother said in a letter she left at the Wall: "I came to this black wall to see and touch your name, and as I do I wonder if anyone ever stops to realize that next to your name, on this black wall, is your mother's

AP/WIDE WORLD PHOTOS.

heart. A heart broken when you lost your life in Vietnam." (Written by Eleanor Wimbish to her son William Stocks and reported by Steve Neal in his column, *Chicago Sun-Times,* August 23, 1993).

The names of two of my friends also are on that Wall. Mine might well be there, too, were it not for the chance fact that I entered the military right out of high school in the early 1960s and had already served four years and begun college by the time the Vietnam War really heated up. The two young men who lost their lives were Army infantry troops and, according to what they told their families and friends, they knew they faced a high likelihood of being killed in the so-called "Tet Offensive" of 1968, one of the bloodiest periods of that whole horrible war, and indeed it took their lives.

Now, one has only to go to the Wall on Veteran's Day, or even Father's Day, to observe an outpouring of mourning that has not been lessened in the last decade. After I made a few trips to the Wall, an act which I recommend to all who grieve any major loss, I realized that great grief will be displayed at the Wall as long as there are generations of people alive who have lost close friends and relatives in Vietnam (see Palmer's, 1987, *Shrapnel in the Heart* for discussion of the many notes and personal messages of grief left at the Wall). Someday in the next century, the grieving at the Wall will be less intense than it is now. The passage of time and the emotional distance that creates will lessen the poignancy; its observers will be more detached from the losses documented there.

The Wall has served as a place to be psychologically near one's lost loved ones. The lifelike statues of young men and women who cared about one another and who sometimes sacrificed their lives for one another, and the black marble wall, which acts like a mirror, all speak to the timeless nature of the cycle of human loss, grief, recovery, and redemption.

The Struggle to Recover English professor Elizabeth Neeld (1990) wrote with great insight about her feelings after her husband suddenly died of a heart attack in mid-life. She described the pain in her early period of greatest mourning and disillusionment, as follows:

> I had lost my identity. As the weeks passed, it became clear to me that an equally devastating loss was the loss of the future I

had assumed I would have. I had expected to have Greg's children. Katie Rachel Pearl . . . Jeremiah Cade. Now there would be no babies. At night I dreamed of brown-eyed sons and curly-haired daughters. At thirty-seven, I mourned those never-to-be children. (p. 59)

Later, as Neeld began to develop a new identity and life, she encountered an additional challenge. She found that others pushed her to be brave and move on with her life. As Neeld implies here, sometimes a grieving person needs to move to her own drum beat and not feel guilty if she has the urge to wallow in the loss:

It's chilly this morning here in Texas. Right now I'm listening to Emmylou Harris and thinking of cold rainy winter days when Greg and I were so content and satisfied and dwelled in the sky called love.

The stew in the pot, his bringing the wood in from the yard, his bare legs sticking out from under his green trench coat—oh, I miss him so much today. I miss the softness, the lack of trying, the not being constantly under the demand called resolving and adjusting. I am so tired of being brave and getting on with it and learning from experience and beginning a new life—all those positive things that you're supposed to do after losing. Instead, I'd like to roll in the rug called "the world's good," the rug called "I love you." (p. 179)

Neeld suffered many periods of severe depression and a recurring feeling that her life was not worth living. After one such period, a Robert Frost poem about a young wife's grief at the loss of her husband flashed into her mind as she drove in her car one day. Here is a part of that poem, which is called "Home Burial."

You couldn't care! The nearest friends can go
With anyone to death, come so far short
They might as well not try to go at all.
No, from the time when one is sick to death,
One is alone, and he dies more alone.
Friends make pretense of following to the grave,
But before one is in it, their minds are turned
And making the best of their way back to life
And living people, and things they understand
. . . I won't have grief so
If I can change it. Oh, I won't, I won't.

Neeld decided she would no longer suffer such paralyzing grief either. She quoted the prescription for dealing with grief-related depression that Carl Jung gave to a friend whose young son had recently died:

> . . . I would seek out one or two people who seemed amiable and would make myself useful to them. . . . I would raise animals and plants and find joy in their thriving. I would surround myself with beauty—no matter how primitive and artless—objects, colours, sounds. I would eat and drink well. When the darkness grows denser, I would penetrate to its very core, and would not rest until amid the pain a light appeared to me. (p. 92, Neeld, 1990)

Neeld's (1990) book represents the culmination of her completion and identity change. She is now remarried and a successful writer. She has done us a major service by creating a book full of courageous self-disclosure and searching for information about grief.

I will end this discussion with an excerpt from a woman's letter to her ex-husband. They had been married for 30 years, then divorced for a few years at the time she wrote this letter. The letter reveals that despite the many negative emotions she had endured, the two of them will always share some sweet memories of their time together:

> You loved me with all your heart, as I loved you. We did the best we could with that love, and the dumb determination that it would be enough for a marriage and a life. With time then to grow into friendship, or trust, or compromise, or comfort? Not that young boy, or the girl at his side. It's for them, and for all the emotions pulled around like an old U-Haul, that I write this letter. I am letting you off the hook, and ask you to let me off any hooks hanging around in your memory, too. I only regret the losses now, where once I raged at them, but don't want them to be all there was. Remember the touch on the cheek, the child, the Notre Dame game we didn't see. (*Esquire,* June 1990, p. 212, "P.S., I loved you" by Larkin Warren)

I hope that these stories of loss and the struggle to recover will give you greater insight into the nature and impact of great loss. I also hope that they will reinforce one of the central assumptions of this book, namely that the human mind and heart are endowed with the will to recover, grow, and give back to others—even in circumstances of bleakest despair and grief. However, we must be allowed to deal with our losses in our own way and at our own pace.

Many well-run support groups exist for people who grieve. These groups can help immensely by providing some perspective as a person tries to put his or her life back together after a major loss. As one person said, "Attending a support group is one way of living the truth. It's saying, 'This really did happen. I really did have those feelings. I know my life will never be the same. I have to be a different person than I was'" (quoted in Alice Steinbach, "A Shoulder to Cry on," *Redbook,* July 1993, p. 43).

The following list of recommendations for the bereaved, developed by the Centre for Living with Dying, has proven to be very useful:

- realize and recognize the loss
- take time for nature's slow, sure, stuttering process of healing
- give yourself massive doses of restful relaxation and routine business
- know that powerful, overwhelming feelings will lessen with time
- be vulnerable, share your pain, and be humble enough to accept support
- surround yourself with life: plants, animals, and friends
- use mementos to help your mourning, not to live in the dead past
- avoid rebound relationships, big decisions, and anything addictive
- keep a diary and record successes, memories, and struggles
- prepare for change, new interests, new friends, solitude, creativity, growth
- recognize that forgiveness (of ourselves and others) is a vital part of the healing process
- know that holidays and anniversaries can bring up the painful feelings you thought you had successfully worked through
- realize that any new death-related crisis will bring up feelings about past losses

I NEVER DREAMED I WOULD
HAVE A LIFE LIKE THIS.
I LIVE IN FEAR—AND IT EATS
YOU UP."

—Dawn Wilson, wife who
has been stalked relentlessly
by her ex-husband; quoted in
Bryan Miller, "Thou Shalt Not
Stalk," *Chicago Tribune
Magazine*, April 18, 1993,
pp. 14-20.

10

THE
DARK SIDE
OF CLOSE
RELATIONSHIPS

THIRTY PERCENT OF THE 4,399 WOMEN SLAIN IN THE UNITED STATES IN 1990 WERE MURDERED BY THEIR BOYFRIENDS OR HUSBANDS, ACCORDING TO THE FBI UNIFORM CRIME REPORT. (ONLY 4 PERCENT OF THE ALMOST 16,000 MEN WHO WERE HOMICIDE VICTIMS THAT YEAR WERE MURDERED BY THEIR GIRLFRIENDS OR WIVES.) MANY OF THE SLAIN WOMEN WERE FOLLOWED, ABUSED AND INTIMATED BEFORE THEIR DEATHS.

—Article by Bryan Miller,
referred to above, p. 16

■

DON'T LET ANYONE TELL YOU TO "LEAVE THE PAST ALONE."

—Incest survivor, who remembered the incest after many years and was writing to Ann Landers, March 13, 1993

The United States is an especially violent country. Just look at our choice of media entertainment, our murder rates, the amount of physical and sexual abuse reported, the number of people who are killed each year by their spouses or lovers, and the violence that sometimes is a part of the divorce process. It is ironic that in closeness we share our most satisfying times with others, but we also share many of our darkest and most horrific moments, moments that are an important part of the American pattern of violence. This chapter will examine the nature of those moments.

Obsessed "Love"

Much has been written about obsession for a past lover or a person with whom the obsessed person has had little contact. An obsession is a condition in which an individual is preoccupied with thoughts of another person. The trouble is that the object of the obsession usually is not interested in having a close relationship with the subject (Beck, 1967). We all obsess to a degree about issues and relationships. However, some individuals cannot readily control their obsessions and it interferes with their lives and the lives of others; that is when professional help is urgently needed.

Obsessed love can occur at any age. Consider the following wire services report on April 26, 1993, headlined "Abduction failure ends in suicide":

Albany, N.Y.—A tennis coach described as obsessed with a teenage player shot himself to death when officers approached after a failed attempt to kidnap her.

Investigators believe Gary D. Wilensky planned to take Jennifer Rhodes, 17, to a mountain hideout he had equipped with an elaborate security system and restraining devices.

Wilensky, 56, used to coach Rhodes, a promising amateur player from New York City. . . .

Wilensky, of New York City, had been undergoing psychological treatment for his obsession until last month and was considered suicidal, although his doctors didn't think he was a threat to Rhodes or her family. . . .

A gunman wearing a sky mask attacked Rhodes and her mother Friday night outside a hotel. . . . The daughter broke away and ran for help while the man beat her mother with a flashlight. . . . When a hotel manager came out and said police were on their way, the man cocked a rifle, jumped into his car and drove away.

Police spotted his car 2½ hours later in a parking lot near the hotel. When police approached, the man shot himself in the head with a rifle. (*Chicago Tribune,* Section 1, p. 4)

It was later discovered that Wilensky had developed a macabre plot to kidnap Rhodes and keep her in a remote house in the Adirondack mountains that had been transformed into an electronic fortress. The house had been equipped with a closed-circuit television system, leather muzzles, and steel chains.

People who knew the tennis coach said that he had become a major figure in teaching private school students to play tennis in New York City. "He had become part of everyone's life," one observer reported to the *USA Today* writer Bruce Frankel in his April 28, 1993, follow-up on the story. It appears that Wilensky had a large following of young women and parents. In 1992 he had been voted "pro of the year" for a three-state area by his tennis colleagues. One tennis colleague said, "He may have been a little bit extreme in the sense of being overly friendly [with the young tennis students]. . . . But I wouldn't have ever expected something like this" (Frankel, Section 1, p. 2). Given his thriving business, rapport with many young people, and following in the city and beyond, Wilensky's behavior is even more mysterious. Or is it?

Let's speculate about the coach's possible motivations. This individual, now in his 50s—still youthful but no doubt thinking about retirement and the latter part of his life—may have seen in this young woman a fulfillment of self that he had not previously experienced. He may have felt that she represented youth, sexuality and sensuality, and someone whom he could mentor and help achieve great things. In some bizarre twist of logic, he may have sensed that his own life would be of little use if she were not in it; indeed, he may have considered the idea of killing himself if she would not accept him as her lover (and he may have communicated that threat to her).

Or perhaps the tennis coach was attracted to the young woman and acted out of compulsion and without reason. Indeed, as former associates of the coach noted on a May 3, 1993, airing of the *Maury Povich Show*, Wilensky had a history of falling in love with very young women, some of whom had dated him over time. Perhaps, then, Wilensky was suffering from a form of obsession that was related to love addiction for young women. Griffin-Shelley (1993) discussed such a behavioral addiction in which someone feels little control over the urge to possess a particular person. The obsessed lover is, in effect, a slave to his or her drive and does not feel free to choose (Norwood, 1985). The loved one occupies the obsessed person's thoughts much of the time. This was the case with John Hinkley, who said that he attempted to assassinate Ronald Reagan in 1981 to impress the woman he was obsessed with—Jodi Foster. Hinkley's love for Foster was an addiction. If he had not fallen for Foster, he may have become obsessed with some other famous starlet.

Unrequited Love

If it weren't for unrequited love, there would be little poetry, less therapy and very few country songs. Unrequited love is a bottomless well of inspiration. . . .

You can topple into unrequited love when you are 18 or when you're 80. . . . Unrequited love is a renewable resource. Anyone who has never experienced it must have slept through life. (Mary Schmich's column in *Chicago Tribune,* September 19, 1993, writing about the 1993 movie *The Age of Innocence.*)

Roy Baumeister and Sara Wotman (1992) depicted the many sides of unrequited love in their book *Breaking Hearts: The Two Sides of Requited Love.* Unrequited love is love that is not reciprocated. As Mary Schmich suggests, we all probably experience this type of love at one time or another—either as the lover or the loved. It may be that at one time the love was reciprocated. Or, as with John Hinkley's love for Jodi Foster, one may feel love for someone with whom one has had no actual relationship.

The state of feeling unrequited love for a lover who has left can vary from normal pining to dysfunctional obsession. According to Baumeister and Wotman, unrequited love can be very painful. This condition can dampen or, in extreme cases, even destroy the self-esteem of the person who cannot overcome it. In the following letter to "Dear Abby," a woman reveals some of the common qualities of an unrequited love condition:

Dear Abby: I am 32 years old and people say I am very attractive. A year ago I started seeing "Alex." He was everything I ever wanted—handsome, intelligent, successful. We were together almost every night, and he even started talking about marriage.

Then last month, out of the blue, he announced that he thinks we're getting "too serious" and we should both start seeing other people. That was the beginning of the end. It's like a bad dream. I can't stop crying. I'm in sales and my job requires my full attention, but I'm in a fog.

My eating is out of control. The night before last, I ate a whole barbecued chicken, a large pizza, and three cheese Danishes.

Abby, I dial his phone number 15 to 20 times a day just to hear his voice—then I hang up. I'm sure he knows it's me. I'm humiliated he would dump me like this. How can I get him back? (September 18, 1991, from *Iowa City Press-Citizen*)

Abby said the woman was suffering from "compulsive behavior," which may or may not be a correct diagnosis. Nonetheless, regardless of the dashed expectations this woman feels, she must figure out how to vent her feelings (this letter to "Dear Abby" probably helped), develop an understanding of her ex-lover's behavior as best she can, and then find positive activities for her healing—such as involvement in a support group for newly divorced/separated persons, enhancement of physical fitness activities, working on a stronger network of friends, writing in a journal, and traveling.

Baumeister and Wotman pointed out that even the object of unrequited love can suffer. This person may become annoyed, angry, victimized, and guilt-ridden in her or his decision, and vengeful toward the person who will not let go. There is no good script for how to reject another person—"it's never easy having to tell someone that you don't love him anymore." The rejecting person also may conclude that getting involved with the other person was unwise in the first place and may question his or her judgment in choosing romantic partners. He or she may also hesitate to become deeply involved with new loves in the future.

Why does obsessed unrequited love occur? One idea mentioned by Baumeister and Wotman is that unrequited lovers maintain an attachment for their lost love. As discussed in Chapter 5, Hazan and Shaver (1987) theorized that people develop attachment styles in adult relationships that mirror their sense of attachment as young children. Perhaps, those who experience unrequited love and become obsessed are more likely to have felt abandoned early in their lives. It may be that they sometimes contribute to their rejection through a neurotic concern about being rejected.

Unrequited love and obsessive love may reflect a failure to accept reality. Often a person who obsessed is repeatedly told by the other person that she or he does not want a close relationship. The obsessed one, however, interprets the message to suggest that he or she must try harder, be a more persistent lover in extending gifts and other symbols of love, and essentially convince anew the other person that the relationship is "right" for her or him. Going back to the tennis coach, we may assume that he too was an undaunted lover, despite repeated indications from the young woman that she did not want to be his lover or even associate with him. Baumeister and Wotman's research shows that over the course of a relationship, the person who ultimately does the rejecting may send many double messages concerning whether he or she really loves the individual who ends up feeling unrequited love.

Baumeister and Wotman suggested that unrequited love often stems from a mismatch in physical attractiveness. This occurs when one person tries to bond with someone else who is more attractive—someone for whom he or she feels great passion and who raises his or her self-esteem and social status. It may work for a time. But over the long run, the "upward achiever" often will not be able to hang on to the relationship. The more attractive person will want someone more similar in physical attractiveness. My own guess is that this role of physical attractiveness in unrequited love may lessen as people age. In mid-life or later, it may continue to play a role but be no more potent than several other factors, such as mismatches in attitudes and beliefs.

Stalking   Stalking involves pursuing another in a threatening way rather than just sitting around moping. Stalking can become violent when the loved one will not accede to the stalker's desire that she or he return to the relationship, or "do what I want you to do."

The stalker—who is usually a male—desires control in his relationships. He apparently feels that his "possession" (his girlfriend, his wife, his child) has been unreasonably taken away from him. He is enraged. He won't stand for it. He cannot control his emotions of anger, desire for revenge, and loathing for the person involved in his loss. He will harm the other person or himself or both before he allows what "he was meant to have" to be taken away.

Gary Wilensky was a stalker. He planned violence toward Rhodes and her mother. He wanted to force her to accompany him and presumably become his lover. In the weeks before the finale of his plan, he began showering her with expensive gifts, and her mother fired him as her coach. His subsequent behavior fits the "obsessed stalker" profile quite well. We may speculate that he took the rejection to an extreme. While he appeared normal to many on the outside, Wilensky's elaborate plans to keep Rhodes captive suggest a seething hurt and anger that he shared with no one. He may have seen his plan both as revenge for the rejection and as a scheme that ultimately would have led to happiness both for Rhodes and himself.

Marriages and nonmarital close relationships in which physical violence occurs often follow this pattern: Early in the marriage or relationship, the husband (usually) hits his wife on occasion. Then the hitting escalates into beatings, and even attempted murder. The wife files for divorce and gets a court injunction to keep her husband away from her. The husband disregards the injunction, sometimes repeatedly, and tracks down his wife and beats her. He then is sent to jail. Consider the following real-life story:

> The system failed Dawn Wilson. Married to Christopher Wilson for just a year and a half and the mother of his child, Christi (now 4), she discovered early on that he was abusive. Even before their marriage, he'd push her around. "After we got married, the real violence started," Dawn says. . . .
>
> When she became pregnant, three months after the wedding, Christopher started having affairs with other women—and using Dawn as a punching bag, hitting her in the stomach and once bouncing a can of milk off her head. After the baby was born, the assaults continued. On one occasion, Dawn fled from a beating to a neighbor's house, leaving Christi behind. Christopher tossed the infant outside, bassinet and all. (Bryan Miller, "Thou Shalt Not Stalk," *Chicago Tribune Magazine,* April 18, 1993, p. 14)

Christopher was sent to jail for six months for abusing his wife. She then moved to try to get away from him and filed for divorce. He was granted visitation rights with his child as part of the divorce degree, and the judge gave him Dawn's new address. Then there were nine more incidents of battery, each followed by a court appearance. Dawn said, "He asked her once, 'Why do you waste your time taking me to court?' He knew he would get away with it" (same article, p. 15). In 1991 Christopher, lying in wait for Dawn as she came home, beat her severely before a building security guard intervened. This beating destroyed all cartilage in her nose and led to four surgeries. This time Christopher was given three years in jail. He has continued to write her threatening letters from there. Even though his sentence has been extended because of these threats, he likely will get out soon. Dawn said that she will not move again and try to hide from him. She said she is afraid he will hurt her family if he cannot find her. She also argued, "I am not the criminal. Why should I have to move? You have to deal with the problem, and moving me is not the answer" (p. 20).

Stalking has been carried out by men across racial, geographical, and economic lines. In speaking to its cause, Cook County, Illinois, state's attorney Jack O'Malley said in 1992 on a radio talk show in Chicago:

> There's an attitude problem out there . . . a mindset that some people have that they have an inherent right to control others. Someone wants to terminate a relationship—and the other party doesn't want to let go. It's human nature, but it's an attitude we've got to change. (quoted in Miller, p. 18)

O'Malley is correct. Somehow we have to do a better job of educating people that no one owns someone else. Somehow, people have got to learn that they will on occasion lose in love, but that they cannot turn to violence as a way of "fixing" their rejection. Violence solves nothing. The very first instance in which a man uses physical violence against a woman, she needs to consider ending the relationship then and there. That message has to become a part of young people's learning about key signs in the early part of a relationship.

Murder

I recently had two students in my interpersonal relations classes discuss with me, and then the whole class, how someone very close to them had been murdered by a lover. The first student, Vicki, had a daughter whose boyfriend lay in wait for her and then slashed her with a knife, making more than 60 stab wounds, and leaving her to die in her parents' home. He had physically abused her before. She was trying to gently end their relationship when he killed her. The second student, Kim, was a sister of a woman in her 20s whose husband of two years killed her. He beat his wife so badly that her skull was cracked open and over one hundred bruises were found on just one leg. He left her to die in a ravine. He too committed this murder in a fit of anger after she had threatened to leave him. He had not physically abused her before, but unknown to her, he had beaten his previous girlfriend.

These individuals told of what their loved one meant to them. They told of the great hopes their loved one had for life and of how the murders created anguish in the minds of family members and in their interpersonal relationships. They told of their own valiant efforts to find peace, meaning in the murders, and to commit themselves to helping others who face similar losses. They told of their grieving that cannot end and they wept.

It may be impossible for any person who has not personally experienced the loss of a loved one in this way to understand sufficiently the pain it inflicts on families. But we need to know that people murder their partners and that they do it where we live too—in every town in America. Each of us should try to hear and share the stories of the survivors—and as importantly witness their tears. In her presentation, Kim made this plea to other young women (and men) who find themselves in abusive relationships:

Do not endure a relationship in which it is necessary for you to wear blinders. Turning your head from or closing your eyes to a bad situation will not make it go away. . . . You are the only person who has the power to make the decision to end the hurt. After the decision is made, help is available.

In these stories, each of the men who killed their partner had a history of being violent and committed the crime when the women were attempting to leave them. These are not necessarily the sole causal factors in a pattern of violence that culminates in murder, but they often are part of the causal chain. Other factors that are repeatedly present when there is a pattern of physical violence in a close relationship will be discussed below.

A classic case in Boston illustrates why people sometimes decide to kill their partners. In 1989 Charles and Carol Stuart, who had been married a few years, were returning from a night out. Charles, a fur salesman, stopped his car on a city street and later claimed that while they were parked, a black man forced his way into the car, killing Carol and wounding Charles. This story became a raging media event for a few days as Stuart recuperated. City leaders vowed that they would find the killer and make the streets safe. But Stuart had invented the entire story. He shot his wife that night, and then wounded himself. After a few days of panic and budding racial conflict in Boston, Stuart drove to a bridge, got out of his car, and jumped to his death. The police had been getting close to discrediting his story. His brother, who knew that he had committed the murder, was beginning to break. Stuart stood to gain a large sum of money from his wife's life insurance policy; but beyond that, he was trying to cover up a series of affairs with women whom he had encountered through his fur business.

A race war in Boston was barely averted with the discovery of the truth behind Charles Stuart's tale. But his tale and the murder illustrate the extent to which people sometimes go to get rid of a spouse or lover who stands in their way—between them and fortune, other lovers, or a host of other desires.

A more common scenario involving the murder of a lover occurred in 1993 in Indiana. After being engaged to Mark Francis, 25, for a couple of years, Michelle Yelachich, 20, of Hebron, Indiana, decided that she wanted to break off the engagement. It seems that Francis periodically beat and threatened her, just as he had beaten and threatened his other girlfriends. Only a few days after the engagement had been called off by Yelachich, Francis armed himself with his brother's 9mm Beretta handgun, walked into the Yelachich home, and shot both Yelachich's parents before chasing Yelachich to her bedroom and shooting her once in the head. Then he shot himself. All four died from their gunshot wounds.

Francis apparently often flew out of control when matters became shaky in his love life. His history of violence with his lovers was known to the local community. Other women who had been involved with Francis, and who had pressed charges against him for physically abusing them, were fortunate enough to escape Yelachich's fate. It also turns out that Yelachich and Francis had gone through a previous breakup a year before their deaths. But after Francis had attempted to take his life at the Yelachich home, Michelle, presumably out of sympathy, had agreed to get back together with him.

Why did Francis threaten suicide in this earlier situation? He may have assumed that trying to take his own life would show Yelachich how much he loved her and could not do without her. This step is part of the general syndrome of violence or threatened violence. It is drastic but sometimes effective. Francis had not developed the communicative skills and maturity to express his hurt and his continued affection for Yelachich, and to bid her best wishes. He could not tolerate the rejection or the idea that Yelachich had a will of her own and a relationship goal different from his.

Murder by females of their lovers also occurs fairly regularly. The predictive indicators of earlier anger and violence, however, do not necessarily occur when the female is the perpetrator. As an example, in the late 1980s a woman—a prominent San Diego socialite—stalked and shot to death her ex-husband—a well-known physician—and new wife as they slept. The murderer was convicted and sentenced to jail. The prelude to the murders apparently involved infidelity on the part of the ex-husband and a divorce proceeding involving bitter disputes over the division of property. Commentators on the events leading to these murders suggested that it was a classic tale of a wife "helping her husband to the top of the financial and social heap—only to be dumped for a younger woman" (*USA Today* article, September 25, 1991, by Carol Castaneda).

Women who have been abused regularly over a period of time and who have not found relief through the courts have, in increasing numbers, resorted to violence against their husbands/lovers. In the 1990s there have been many publicized cases of incarcerated women convicted of this type of murder seeking and sometimes obtaining pardons for their crime.

The number of young women murdering people close to them has increased considerably in the 1990s. A spate of well-publicized incidents have occurred (June 25, 1992, Associated Press release, "Girls accused of murder in flurry of new cases," printed in the *Iowa City Press-Citizen.*)

- In Madison, Indiana, four girls ages 16 and 17 were convicted of torturing and burning alive a 12-year-old girl with whom they had been friends.

- In Houston, Texas, a 15-year-old "hitgirl" recruited by a 13-year-old boy to murder his grandmother was sentenced in May 1992 to more than 22 years in prison. The grandmother survived two gunshot wounds.

- A Beaverton, Oregon, 16-year-old was charged in April 1992 with plotting with her boyfriend to kill her mother to get money to rent an apartment. The mother was severely beaten and died.

Why did these young women turn to violence against close others? In some cases, they are retaliating against people whom they think have hurt them. In other situations, such as the one involving the Indiana girls who burned to death their "friend," the destructive behavior appears to be similar to that exhibited by males who use violence against their competitors or enemies. A July 1992 *Chicago Tribune* analysis of this murder by Ron Grossman suggested that it may have occurred as a result of a love triangle among the 12-year-old girl and two of her killers.

These reports may be taken to suggest that, at present, women are increasingly turning to violence as a way of resolving relationship issues. The 1990s may become a marker decade for the substantial increase in women's violent acts and murder against their close others. The movie "Thelma and Louise" depicted a great degree of violence by two women against men, most of whom had harmed or harassed them in one way or another.

Physical Aggression

Physical aggression short of murder is a part of many close relationships. It has been estimated that about 10 percent of close relationships involve severe physical violence, at one time or another, usually with the male as the perpetrator (Herbert, Silver, & Ellard, 1991). Sixty to 70 percent of close relationships involve minor violence, such as one person slapping the other with intent to do harm.

Despite frequent breakups, women often return to the men who have beaten them. Why? Weber (1993) tells an instructive story of one women who had been physically abused by her husband. It shows the fear of being alone experienced by some young women with children:

I once talked about job interview skills with a group of high-school dropouts. One young woman, about 17 and mother of a 3-year-old boy, acted nonchalant, almost bragging, about a bruise on her face she said her latest boyfriend had put there when he was "pushing me around." I asked her if she wanted him to beat her like that, and she said, "No." So why did she stay with him, put up with it? "Because if I fight him, he'll just leave me!" she protested, as if this were obviously horrible. Would that be so awful? "Hell, yes, not having someone, being alone, hell, I'd rather die." I looked at her. "Well," I said, "you'll probably get your wish." (p. 30)

Herbert et al. (1991) conducted a study of 44 women who had been beaten, had left their partners, and then returned. Their major finding was that these women somehow reinterpret their situations and decide the abusive behavior is not that destructive and that the relationship is, on balance, positive and constructive for them. Another prominent explanation for why women continue to endure violence is what has been referred to as characterological self-blame (Andrews & Brewin, 1990), which leads to low self-esteem, depression, and feelings of helplessness. Janoff-Bulman (1979) introduced the idea of characterological self-blame to refer to victims' tendency to explain their victimization by focusing on their own personal deficiencies, rather than focusing on how others or the situation led to their victimization. All of these factors lead to the woman being—or feeling—entrapped and perceiving that she has no options but to endure and hope that her partner will reform his ways. But he seldom does (Gelles & Straus, 1988).

Marshall and Vitanza (1994) have provided one of the most compelling reviews and analyses of myths regarding physical abuse in close relationships. One myth is that violence occurs only in certain types of close relationships. But the evidence indicates that it occurs in all types of close relationships, across age, socioeconomic status, and education. Amazingly, one of the most common types of abuse involves physical aggression directed toward females who are pregnant by their attackers. Another myth is that only macho males inflict violence on their partners. It is true that many do, and male aggression toward females is usually more severe than female aggression toward males. As Marshall and Vitanza point out, however, in national sample data from 1985 collected by Straus and Gelles (1986) 12 percent of the people surveyed reported at least one act of violence perpetrated against a husband by a wife.

A third myth involves the presumed connection between alcohol and violence. Marshall and Vitanza discussed some of their own data showing wife battering to occur in alcohol-free homes and pointed to other work showing that about 45 percent of males convicted of battering had not used alcohol in association with the abuse they inflicted. Marshall and Vitanza do acknowledge, however, that alcohol often is associated with interpersonal violence—but say it is not necessarily the cause of such violence.

A final myth—the idea that violence occurs in cycles—was advanced by Walker (1984). According to this idea, there is a gradual escalation of tension and then the wife withdraws to avoid angering her partner, who unleashes a barrage of physical and verbal aggression. Then "loving contrition" occurs in which the abuser asks the victim for her forgiveness. At some later point, movement toward a violent episode recurs. Marshall and Vitanza pointed to contradictory evidence from their own work showing that for many couples, violence was unpredictable and that no interim period of kindness or forgiveness occurred.

As Marshall and Vitanza suggested, even in battering relationships, no man or woman is violent or even hostile all of the time. When a man is not violent, his partner may feel relief due to the absence of his aggression. She may even become attached to him in part because he has significant positive qualities that cause her to dismiss early signs of his violent nature.

It is widely assumed that men who abuse have seen abuse in their primary family, or that they themselves were once the target of severe abuse. So far, though, we can only speculate about the dynamics involved. To better understand them, we would need to track males' behavior from their family of origin (and their parents' behavior toward one another and their children) to their adult relationships.

Some people have an inordinate desire for power and control in their relationships (Gelles & Straus, 1988). They physically threaten and sometimes actually attack their partners and family members as a means of establishing power and control over them. They especially want to control their partner's sexual behavior, and violence often occurs when a partner shows sexual interest in someone else. In some cases, violent males were socialized in a macho subculture that emphasizes power and might as a statement of self-worth.

Jealousy also plays a role in some instances of relationship violence. In a review of theory and research on jealousy, White and Mullen (1989) noted that jealousy is strongly related to feelings of inadequacy in a relationship. Further, the more people feel dependent on their partner, the more jealousy will be aroused by any indication that he or she is interested in other people. Intense jealousy that cannot be controlled forms a foundation for possible violence. Jealous lovers who become enraged and violent can terrorize their partners and cause them to indeed become more interested in alternative relationships.

Social psychologist James Dabbs (e.g., Dabbs, 1992) has presented impressive correlational evidence about the elevated testosterone levels of males who are highly competitive in their work (e.g., trial lawyers) and of other males—who presumably do not have an acceptable outlet—who are violent and frequently in trouble with the law. Testosterone is a gonadal hormone that has muscle-building and masculinizing effects. More generally, Dabbs has argued that testosterone underlies men's dominance and desire for control. Regardless of hormone level, people can learn to be responsible in their behavior toward others. We have to be careful not to let hormone level be used as an excuse for destructive conduct.

Date or Acquaintance Rape

Date or acquaintance rape has become a major topic of discussion on college campuses and beyond during the 1990s. This phenomenon refers to forced sexual relations, usually by a man, when a couple is dating or visiting. Mary Koss and associates (1987) reported evidence on verbal sexual coercion (which they included in the category of date rape) for a nationwide sample of college students. They found that 44 percent of the women surveyed reported engaging in unwanted sexual intercourse because they felt overwhelmed by a man's continual arguments and pressure; 10 percent of the men reported obtaining sexual intercourse with unwilling women using this strategy. Furthermore, 11 percent of the women and 13 percent of the men reported engaging in unwanted sexual intercourse because their partners made them feel guilty or inadequate or questioned their sexuality.

Katie Roiphe (1993), a graduate student at Princeton, has challenged the figures being used to indicate the prevalence of date rape on college campuses and the rape crisis movement in general. Roiphe argues that Koss and colleagues included in their figures for college women who had suffered date rape women who did not believe that they had been raped. She suggests that college campuses are much safer than radical feminists claim and that by exaggerating the extent to which rape occurs on campuses, they are making victimization a source of status and unduly promoting fear on campuses. Koss rejoined by suggesting that many women do not know the legal definition of rape, and, in any case, the results of her survey clearly indicated that many women felt coerced into having sex (*NOW*, NBC television report on date rape, September 29, 1993).

It is difficult to exaggerate the pain and trauma many young women have experienced in the aftermath of coerced sex by acquaintances. What men who coerce women to have sex may not realize is that in the brief time in which they satisfy their need for sexual intercourse, they can adversely affect the woman's life for years or even a lifetime. The date rape movement, as Roiphe calls it, has made us all more aware of these effects.

Date rape often happens at or after parties at which heavy drinking has been taking place. Perpetrators sometimes claim that they couldn't control themselves because of the amount they had drunk. Victims, too, sometimes indicate that they would have been more wary if they had consumed less. But consuming alcohol seems to contribute less to rapes than other processes involved, including: the male's desire to control his partner; his desire for conquest and to brag to his buddies; and his underlying dehumanization of the victim and anger toward her or what she may represent. If such hatred is not involved, it is difficult to understand how anyone could force another into an act that might traumatize the victim for many years.

Charlene Muehlenhard and colleagues (1991) noted that the concept of date rape has now been extended to include marital rape. The percentage of married women who have been forced to have sex by their husband also is quite large; there is also a small percentage of married men who apparently have experienced forced sex by their wives. The principal way of coercing sex within marriage is to threaten to end the relationship if one's partner does not give in. Muehlenhard also reviewed surveys indicating that coerced sex occurs in homosexual relationships. In a study of 36 female and 34 male homosexual relationships, Waterman, Dawson, and Bologna (1989) found that 31 percent of the women and 12 percent of the men reported being forced by their partners to have sex.

Muehlenhard et al. described a number of factors that play a role in forced sex, including women's need to maintain a relationship for economic reasons; alcohol and drug intoxication; the sexual double standard; gender differences in perceptions of sexual interest (see Abbey's [1982] work showing that men interpret women's friendly actions as involving sexual connotations more often than do the women taking the actions); and stereotypes about masculinity and femininity (for instance, to be masculine is to be dominant and in control).

Lance Shotland (1989) theorized that quite a few instances of date rape result from a personality trait in some men that involves misogyny, or hatred of women. These essentially antisocial men look to dating for opportunities to rape women because it is difficult to establish that a rape occurred when a dating relationship exists. So these men are cunning as well as antisocial in their behavior.

A promising development is the formation of groups of men on college campuses who are dedicated to changing the script of sexual coercion in dating. One such organization, started at Duke University in 1992, was called Men Acting for Change. One of the founders, Jason Schultz, began his effort after one of his female friends was raped. He said, "I just saw on campus the way the rape education had been handled really alienated men." He was referring to professors' lecturing young men as if by definition they are guilty. His group tries to get men and women to come together to have discussions and debates about the dynamics of violence and sexuality. Men often point to women's seductiveness as one of the reasons that kissing and other flirting goes too far. Discussions such as those occurring at Duke may help the sexes better understand each other and also help people to be clearer when telling others what they want or do not want to do.

But this kind of enlightenment may be rare, as shown by the infamous activities of the Spur Posse in Lakewood, California. This group was composed of male high school athletes age 18 or over who had created a competition among themselves. Members were awarded points every time they had sexual relations with a woman. Members focused on the same women for sex on multiple occasions—the so-called "easy" lay women—and in some cases, the women were in their early teens.

The scheme led to national publicity in the spring of 1993 when the local police arrested four of the posse and charged them with rape. The charges were later dropped, and members of the posse then began to travel the national talk show circuit, bragging about their exploits. They argued that the women were entranced with them because of their good looks, athleticism, and general popularity. They suggested that sex with them represented a pinnacle experience for these women. They also contended that the women wanted to have sex with them essentially for the same reason—so they could brag to their friends.

When the women involved were interviewed, however, they claimed that the men had led them on—with the possibility of establishing a close relationship—in order to have sex with them and score points. They said that despite the fact that they willingly allowed the men to fondle them, they had not consented to the men's requests for sex. The local district attorney said that while the men's behavior was reprehensible, it did not meet the conditions for statutory rape. She implied that the evidence indicated the women's conduct in the sexual activities was such that the males' activities could not be deemed criminal. A psychiatrist commenting on the posse's activities said that the men were exhibiting pathological narcissism in their exploitation of others, and that the women who participated may have done so in order to be accepted and to enhance their chronically low levels of self-esteem. Whatever ultimately comes of this story, it stands as an extremely troubling commentary on the socialization of many men.

Incest

There is no darker aspect of close relationships than familial sexual abuse, or incest. Incest violates a person's basic sense of trust and security. It violates a person's sense of meaning in life. Incest robs a person of youthful vitality and causes an early "maturing" both of mind and body. Incest affects one's whole life, perhaps as no other event or sequence of events can.

Most often, incest is perpetrated by men, usually fathers, grandfathers, stepfathers, or brothers. However, mothers, grandmothers, and sisters have also committed incest. The victim is more likely to be female. Although data for the incestuous abuse of men are scant, my colleagues and I (Orbuch, Harvey, Davis, and Merbach, in press) recently completed a study involving a survey of a small sample of men who had experienced incest. Their recovery had been less successful than that of a similar group of female incest survivors. The males' reports suggested that the burden of going public and seeking help may be greater for men than women. Most service agencies are accustomed to dealing with women incest survivors. In this culture, in which men are expected to be strong and resilient, the male incest survivor often feels a great loss of esteem and vulnerability.

One of the most powerful first person accounts of incest ever written is Elly Danica's (1988) book *Don't*. Danica, then in her 40s, described how she was sexually and physically abused by her father from very early in her life well into her 20s. In this excerpt she spoke of the terror of the long ordeal she had experienced:

How do you live only night? Easy. Twenty-five years of darkness. Not easy. Hate as a companion. Nobody believes me at 18. Twenty. Twenty-three. At 25. Useless. Again. I vow to leave town with my hate. I vow to look for sunshine. I see a shrink.

Another shrink. Another. Finally a woman. Compassion. Now hate has sewn my lips down, stitched them to my teeth. I can no longer speak. Twenty-seven. Twenty-nine. Paralysis of the will. . . . Always useless. To everybody. Even to myself. Useless. (p. 12)

Danica's sense of isolation and despair at having no protection from her father earlier in her life are revealed in the following lines:

I yearn for someone to save me. Yearn for pity. There is no help. My grandmother is a continent, an ocean, away. I try to tell my teacher at school. She says: "You are subject to your father in all things. He is your lord as Jesus is your lord. He would do no harm or wrong. He is right in all things. If you are punished or hurt it is for your own good. If he is too rough it is because he loves you. Pray to Jesus for comfort. . . ."

There is no comfort so I pray for martyrdom. At least if I were dead . . . it would be over. (p. 15)

This passage illustrates what we (e.g., Harvey, Orbuch, Chwalisz, & Garwood, 1991) have found repeatedly in survey work with incest survivors. They often feel isolated and lack confidants with whom they can share their most horrible secrets and find support. If they go to one parent regarding another parent's abuse of them, the other parent sometimes says, "It did not happen. You are imagining it." If they go to a parent regarding a grandparent's or a sibling's abuse, they may receive an admonition to keep quiet, lest the family name and reputation be ruined in the community. Usually incest victims are quite young (sometimes even infants) when the incest starts. The wall of resistance and hostility they confront when they try to reveal what is happening represents a second blow against their feeling of trust and safety. They may simply withdraw because they sense there is no one to whom they can turn.

To recover early from incest, one needs to confide and get strong support from others. Incest survivors who were able to gain the support of emphatic and helpful others soon after the incest occurred —whether from authorities, family, or friends—report that their close relationships later in life are enhanced.

Danica was finally able to get her message out, and powerfully. She said at the end of her book:

> I have finally kept the promises I made to myself when I was very young. Some day I would write this story and when I did then and only then would I be able to like and respect myself. And I have kept both promises.
>
> I wake one day to find the "victim" self gone (though it is neither as simple nor as easy as that). I find instead a woman with her eyes and her heart open, strong, hopeful, and more determined than ever before. (p. 98)

There is a pattern to incest that begins when the victim is quite young. In a common scenario, the father begins early to groom the daughter to accept his affection. He crosses boundaries that remain intact in normal father-daughter relations and confuses role identity for the child. The father convinces his daughter to trust him, until eventually she becomes dependent upon him. At the same time, the father may try to alienate the daughter from her mother and her friends, thereby giving her the sense that she is isolated with him. Early on, she probably intuits that his advances are not right. Later, as she approaches puberty, she more clearly recognizes his advances as violations of her self and wrong, possibly horrifying or disgusting. All along, the father has prepared the daughter for more adult sexual activity. He bribes her with gifts and feigned support and tells her how important she is to him. He instigates the practice of watching one another dress and of being nude in each other's presence. As she begins to feel that the behavior is wrong, the father may threaten her with withdrawal of his love and support if she tells anyone. In this manner, the astute incest perpetrator may essentially imprison his victim within insuperable psychological walls. All the while, her feelings are being numbed. She may learn to accept his sexual advances by dissociation. She may "go away" in her mind during sex acts, or may put herself in a trance so that she will not feel the physical and psychological pain.

If discovered, the perpetrator of incest is usually defensive. Of course, he may contend that the story was all made up. Or, if he admits to having engaged in the sexual activity, he may argue that the daughter was a "slut" who seduced him. He also may suggest that he only fell "victim" to his daughter's advances because of his poor sexual relationship with his wife.

The male perpetrator may seem quite normal to the outside world. Psychologically, however, he is often an isolated person who tends to be rigid, paranoid, immature, and lacking in self-esteem. He places all responsibility for problems and mishaps on the outside world.

What about the effects of incest on the survivor? She has major trust problems in intimate relations, especially if she does not "come out" and seek help—whether from a professional, a support group, or a close friend. A person who keeps this dark secret for many years will probably have a variety of psychological problems such as depression and suicide fantasies, and physical maladies such as eating disorders and drug addiction. She might also experience periodic flashbacks of the sexual acts with her father or other relative (reminiscent of those experienced by people with post-traumatic stress disorder), especially at times when she is trying to be intimate with her spouse or lover.

Even if they marry, survivors often report feeling little closeness, empty, lonely, and paranoid. (Jennifer Danielson compiled this material from various sources [see especially Patton, 1992].)

Can we believe people who, after many years, begin to recall instances of sexual abuse early in their lives? Led by celebrities, such as Rosanne Barr and Oprah Winfrey, many people have publicly reported that they were the victims of incest early in their lives. They have done so, they say, both to take another step toward personal recovery and to help others who have kept similar types of secrets and who have suffered in the process. Well-known books advocate such reporting in order to come to grips with one's past. For example, in 1991 journalist Harriet Webster published *Family Secrets,* a book that persuasively argued that confessing dark secrets is often a step toward healing (see Pennebaker's [1990] *Opening Up,* discussed in Chapter 9). Ellen Bass and Laura Davis's *The Courage to Heal* (1988) describes the symptoms of incest in later life and encourages people to remember the actual events. By recalling and talking about them, Bass and Davis claim, one can begin to heal.

The Courage to Heal, however, has been criticized because it provides too general a profile of the unaware adult who may have been an incest victim many years earlier. Critics such as psychologist Carol Tavris (writing in the *New York Times Book Review,* January 3, 1993) contend that the profile could apply to almost any adult. In her analysis, Tavris also discussed strong evidence showing that in recalling incest, although people think they are remembering facts, they are often actually making things up. Such is the power of "reconstructive memory" and the mind's imaginative ability. Several court cases in the 1990s involve criminal charges brought by adults who claim their parents or other relatives perpetrated incest against when they were young. The accuracy of memory is an important issue in these cases.

Pornography

Some scholars and commentators on relationships argue that highly graphic pornography in movies, videos, the written word, and photographs often demeans and degrades women. Further, they say, relationships are adversely affected when men become addicted to pornography because they come to view women only as sex objects and to deemphasize loving and caring communication (Donnerstein, Linz, & Penrod, 1987). This argument does not address the fact that women too make considerable use of pornography.

Feminist writer Andrea Dworkin has argued:

Men use sex to hurt us. . . . Pornographers use every attribute a woman has. They sexualize it, then they find a way to dehumanize it and they sell it. And they sell it to men who get off on it. (quoted in Mark Wukas, *Chicago Tribune,* March 21, 1993, Section 6, p. 1)

A further argument is that children and teens invariably find and examine pornographic materials. James Check, a psychologist at York University in Toronto, reported that 90 percent of a sample of 14-year-old boys and 60 percent of a sample of 14-year-old girls had seen pornography on video at least once; 33 percent of the boys and 2 percent of the girls indicated that they regularly watched pornographic videos. As important, Check indicated that 29 percent of the boys reported that pornography was the most useful source of sex information that they had available. He also found that 43 percent of the boys and 16 percent of the girls indicated it was "maybe O.K." to hold down a woman and force sexual intercourse if she had gotten him sexually aroused; only 35 percent of the boys said it definitely was not

O.K. to force intercourse under these circumstances, while 71 percent of the girls said it definitely was not O.K.

All adults have the right, protected by the First Amendment, to view pornography. Many strong feminists endorse this right and recognize that certain types of pornography may not have negative impacts on human behavior. Too often censorship is promoted by groups who have a strong political or religious position but little strong evidence on pornography's effects. No doubt many well-functioning couples use pornography to facilitate their sex lives. At the same time, pornography advocates must be aware of the questions about whether the material degrades women and whether the material will be seen by minors and have a deleterious influence on how they view women and sexuality. Parents of young children have a special responsibility in this area.

What about violent pornography? Just like violence on the television and in movies, it most likely does not enhance human relationships. Whether it causes or contributes to sex crimes or violence is unclear. Surely, though, as famous sex criminals such as Charles Bundy (who raped and killed many young women in Florida, Utah, and possibly other states in the 1970s and '80s) have argued in their defense, viewing violent pornography probably serves as a catalyst for action for those who are disposed to violence through other influences.

Much of this issue for the couple in a close relationship involves their individual and joint interpretation of pornographic material. If they do not believe that it demeans women and that it is positive for them—or that it simply does not matter much—they are not likely to be adversely affected.

Divorce

Destructive behavior is often associated with divorce and dissolution. Consider these recent, highly publicized situations:

1. Starting in January 1992, Woody Allen and Mia Farrow engaged in a bitter custody battle in which Farrow accused Allen of sexually abusing two of her children. Farrow made the accusation after finding photographs of her oldest adopted daughter, Soon-Yi Previn, showing her nude in Allen's bedroom. Allen was acquitted by a medical panel of the abuse charge pertaining to their seven-year-old daughter, Dylan, and later charges were dropped by the state of Connecticut. In a September, 1993, news conference, Allen contended that the bulk of evidence overwhelmingly exonerated him and that the state's attorney general knew that early in the investigation. He argued that the long, drawn-out investigation by the attorney general and Farrow's charges of incest were designed to ruin his reputation and end any relationship he had with his daughter Dylan. Allen also said that charging incest now is being regularly used as a "smear tactic" in custody cases to try to prevent one spouse from having a relationship with his or her child. Finally, Allen admitted having begun a love relationship with Soon-Yi Previn starting when she was 20—at a point when legally and psychologically she was an adult. That relationship continues, and both the daughter, now 22, and Allen, now 57, have said they are in love with one another.

2. In 1992 a lawyer confessed to bursting into a courtroom and gunning down a prosecutor and another lawyer in Fort Worth, Texas. He was angry because a jury had awarded his ex-wife custody of their son. The two persons shot, however, had no relation to the custody decision. This incident was not the first in which people have been killed in the courtroom in divorce cases in the 1990s. As attorneys dealing

with divorce have said, family law involves the most volatile and potentially violent situations.

3. In a divorce and custody case that *Texas Monthly* (October 1992) called "the meanest divorce in Texas," Charles and Carolyn Smith, both wealthy and from prominent Houston families, fought for a decade for custody of their two sons. In this period, the boys were kidnapped by both parents on multiple occasions, and continuous legal battles were waged. Writer Skip Hollandsworth called the warfare "a classic Greek tragedy, with all the characters eventually brought down by their own rage and need for revenge" (p. 138). As of October 1992 Charles Smith had custody of the sons —despite a Texas court's order that he turn them over to their mother—and had fled to Cuernavaca, Mexico, to start a new life with his boys and new wife there.

As was discussed in Chapter 8, during the divorcing period people often act irrationally. They are capable of any number of destructive acts toward their ex-partners, children, friends, and themselves. Their emotions often swing back and forth between severe depression and ecstasy. People often feel that they have no control over their lives and that all their work to achieve a relationship, family, and home is being wrenched apart. The movie *The War of the Roses* vividly depicts the deterioration of a marriage, a period of confusion and chaos, and then an ensuing battle over property that, eventually, led to the destruction of most of the property and the violent deaths of both partners.

The greatest loss in these situations, however, often is felt by the children. Many children become considerably poorer as a result of divorce. Beyond the poverty is the psychological damage. What they see their parents do may influence how they act later in their own relationships. The divorce alone may have been traumatic for the child; seeing parents wage war against each other over custody or property could certainly cause lasting psychic damage.

In the end, destructiveness in close relationships mirrors what we see on a larger level, in the world and in relations among nations and groups of people. To the extent that the molar problems languish and defy ready solution, so do more microscopic problems found in the close relationship, or in the minds of people engaged in closeness.

FIRST, AWAKEN ON YOUR OWN.

THEN SEE SOMEONE ELSE.

—Zen Master Keizan

Chapter 11

ENHANCING

CLOSE

RELATIONSHIPS

WE HAVE NO MORE RIGHT TO CONSUME HAPPINESS
WITHOUT PRODUCING IT, THAN TO CONSUME WEALTH
WITHOUT PRODUCING IT.

—George Bernard Shaw

■

SELF-DISCLOSURE, LETTING ANOTHER PERSON
KNOW WHAT YOU THINK, FEEL, OR WANT,
IS THE MOST DIRECT MEANS
(THOUGH NOT THE ONLY MEANS)
BY WHICH AN INDIVIDUAL CAN MAKE HIMSELF KNOWN
TO ANOTHER PERSON.

—Sidney Jourard, *The Transparent Self*

Every close relationship can be enhanced, even if the enhancement involves laying the foundation for a gentler ending. Many relationships, though, can be genuinely assisted by information found in professional literature and through counseling.

A great number of books and articles have been written by therapists and counselors to help couples improve their relationships. Some of these resources are based on research; however, most come from the popular "self-help" genre. As consumers, we need to be especially careful when we assess the value of these books and of their authors' suggestions—are their prescriptions backed up by solid research and sound logic? We need to weigh the usefulness and validity of all sources of information, including magazines, television, and even the book you are holding in your hands.

In fact, I have a question about relationship books in general; if the prescriptions of these books "work," then should not close relationships in our culture improve over time? It is difficult to answer such a broad type of inquiry. But given all of the violence and problems surrounding divorce and dissolution today, one might well become pessimistic and wonder if we as researchers, writers, teachers, and therapists are really doing much to improve the state of close relationships. A tacit assumption of this book has been that couples who try to educate themselves about close relationships—reading widely and carefully considering what scholars and others have to say—and who readily discuss their relationship issues will function much better as a result of their actions.

Improving One's Prospects for Dating Before we discuss how to enhance close relationships, let us focus on how to improve one's prospects when dating. Frances Haemmerlie and Robert Montgomery have created a way of helping college-aged men and women overcome their anxieties about meeting each other. They arranged for men and women who were anxious about such meetings to casually

PEANUTS *reprinted by permission of UPS, Inc.*

interact for 10 to 12 minutes with opposite-sex members of their research team. The research assistants who interacted with the anxious male or female did not know the real purpose of the interaction. They were instructed to conduct a light, positive conversation with the subject, not to discuss sex, and not to make or accept a date during the conversation. Each subject interacted with several opposite-sex research assistants during the same session, giving him or her about three-quarters of an hour of "light, positive" social interaction.

On several measures, Haemmerlie and Montgomery (see Montgomery & Haemmerlie [1986] for a summary) found that the socially anxious college students reported less anxiety and more success in their subsequent heterosexual encounters and that the effect still was in place six months later. They concluded "nothing succeeds like success, and the perception of that success, in an area where one has previously been unsuccessful" (p. 507).

More generally, Haemmerlie and Montgomery's approach shows the value of warm social interaction, particularly for people who may not usually experience such interaction with potential romantic partners. Following Daryl Bem's (1972) theory of self-perception, Haemmerlie and Montgomery argue that when socially anxious people see themselves inspiring warmth from others, they begin to gain confidence that others will want to associate with them. Their work implies that effort and persistence are critical to learning social skills and meeting others for closeness.

Preventing Relationship Problems

Only connect —E. M. Forster

How can we prevent major problems in our close relationships? How can we uncover the major factors couples will face after marriage, and help them deal with those issues early on? Increasingly, the issue of preventing serious problems in marriages and close relationships is being addressed by researchers and others concerned with the tremendous divorce rate in the western world. A prominent research and therapy program concerned with predicting marital success and preventing divorce is being conducted by psychologist Howard Markman at the University of Denver (e.g., Markman, Floyd, Stanley, & Storassi, 1988). Markman trains couples to carefully focus on their behavior and to regularly discuss their thinking on important matters, such as their expectations of marriage. Partners also learn what behaviors please and displease their mate and develop contractual agreements to make changes in their behavior.

Markmam et al. (1988) found that couples who undertook a premarital education course (consisting of five 3-hour group sessions, which focused on improving their communication and problem-solving skills) experienced greater marital satisfaction than couples in the control group who did not take the course. The positive effects of the course appeared to last well beyond the length of the course—at both one and a half and three years into their marriages these couples continued to express greater satisfaction with their marriages than couples in the control group.

In addition to improving the perceived quality of their marriages, taking the course also appears to have improved the duration of their marriages—at the three-year mark, only 5 percent of the couples who took the course had dissolved their relationships, as compared to 24 percent of the couples in the control group. These results are impressive and deserve replication and extension. We do not yet know if the positive effects of the course would keep relationships together after 10 or 20 years had passed.

Markman and his associates (e.g., Stanley & Markman, 1992) are also developing instruments to assess partners' dedication and commitment to their close relationships. And premarital education has used Sternberg's (1986) triangular theory of love, discussed in Chapter 5, which involved emphases on either intimacy, passion, or commitment—or combinations of the three, in assessing whether partners have the same love orientations and warning them when major discrepancies exist.

Started in Spain by a priest in the late 1950s (O'Leary & Smith, 1991), marriage encounter and enrichment programs are now common throughout the United States. They are most often conducted by therapists or religious leaders and normally take a weekend or a week. Their goal is to strengthen ongoing marriages, and they often focus on long-term marriages that are encountering difficulty. Most of the couples participating are not yet on the precipice of divorce. To date, there has been little careful assessment of the outcomes of most of these programs, although one often hears participants speak of how their marriages have benefited. There have been scholarly critiques of particular marriage encounter programs (e.g., Witteman & Fitzpatrick, 1986) that have pointed out the limited degree of training these programs provide in communication and other intimacy skills.

These programs involve little modeling of positive approaches to dilemmas. Rather, they involve telling couples to go home and practice or to try certain techniques when difficulties arise.

One marriage enrichment program that was carefully assessed and has received a positive evaluation was started by Guerney (1977). It is sometimes called "conjugal therapy" and takes about five hours per week for four weeks. A leader helps a small group of couples work on problematic areas of their marriages. The sharing of positive feelings toward one another is encouraged and communication exercises are emphasized, with the leader modeling sound techniques. O'Leary and Smith (1991) indicated that a number of studies have found Guerney's program to be helpful in increasing trust, intimacy, communication, and overall marital satisfaction. It has also been found to be superior to other credible programs.

Most couples would be well-advised to consider both premarital and ongoing marital counseling and enrichment, to help them work on their relationships before nagging problems become major dilemmas. These approaches are not meant to be therapy, as such, and they assume that the participants want to remain in their present relationships. Perhaps the most important advice for couples considering a program would be that they get references from past participants and from local mental health workers who have had experience with the program leaders.

Formal programs have also been developed to help children adjust to postdivorce situations. As documented by Grych and Fincham (1992), a few of these programs, offered by therapists and counselors, have shown some success. A less formal approach that is becoming increasingly popular with schools, social-service agencies, and religious institutions involves the formation of groups of children who then meet regularly for months, or years, to discuss their feelings with one another and with a group leader. When carefully implemented, these group dialogues can permit children to vent their hurt and pain, gain perspective from others' experiences, and learn practical ways to deal with their parents' continued hostility and squabbling.

Is Love Enough To Sustain a Close Relationship?

Probably not. That is the answer provided by the well-known scholar and therapist Aaron Beck in his 1988 self-help book *Love Is Not Enough*. According to Beck, even if we feel strong love for each other, we still need to learn a lot about how to make our relationships work. Beck uses the cognitive approach, which emphasizes our interpretations of events, to address relationship problems. His analysis also emphasizes the power of positive thinking. Beck believes that people *can* rationally analyze a problem, can effectively communicate and negotiate about the problem, and the can cooperatively work toward a resolution. This is true whether they are dealing with a partner's affair or a simple annoying habit. People learn, unlearn, and relearn by interacting with each other. In Beck's system, people need to learn appropriate ways of thinking and behaving in certain situations and to carefully interpret their partner's thoughts and behavior. For Beck, a successful close relationship involves cooperation, commitment, trust, loyalty, and fidelity.

Here are a few of Beck's (1988) major assumptions, taken verbatim:

1. Couples can overcome their difficulties if they recognize first that much of their disappointment, frustration, and anger stems not from a basic incompatibility but from unfortunate

misunderstandings that result from faulty communications and biased interpretations of each other's behavior.

2. Misunderstanding is often an *active* process that results when one spouse develops a distorted picture of the other. This distortion in turn leads to the spouse's misinterpreting what the other says or does and attributing undesirable motives to him or her. Partners simply are not in the habit of "checking out" their interpretations or focusing on the clarity of their communications.

3. Each partner should take full responsibility for improving the relationship. You need to realize that you do have choices—you can (and should) choose to use whatever knowledge and insights you can gather to make yourself and your partner happier.

4. Partners can help themselves, each other, and the relationship if they adopt a "no fault, no blame" attitude. This approach will allow them to focus on the real problems and solve them more readily.

5. Actions by your partner that you attribute to some malevolent trait, such as selfishness, hatefulness, or the need to control you, are often most accurately explained in terms of benign (although misguided) motives like self-protectiveness or attempts to prevent abandonment. (p. 12)

Rational analysis is the process of regularly assessing whether our interpretations are as accurate as possible and communicating about them with our partner. An example of how he would use this technique to reduce negative "automatic thoughts" in sexual interaction is presented below.

Automatic Thought	*Rational Response*
My breasts are too small.	It doesn't bother him. Why should it bother me?
I'm not enjoying this very much.	I often enjoy it a lot. I can't expect to enjoy it every time. (p. 364)

Beck's approach involves a logical, well-conceived technique. I have often used his 1988 book in my relationship courses, and students have found much useful advice in it. However, Beck does not clearly deal with people's emotions and how they might be able to integrate their thoughts and feelings when conflicts arise. It may be a strain for people to counter thoughts that have validity. In the above example, for instance, it may be a bit simplistic for the woman to "rationally respond" that her partner is not bothered by her small breasts. Maybe she experienced the automatic thought because there had been hints in his nonverbal behavior that breast size does matter to him.

Regardless of how diligently we try, we sometimes cannot do much reframing, or cognitive analysis, of our relationship problems. Suddenly discovering that your partner has had a long-term affair while he or she has claimed to be very happy in the relationship can be devastating. Such a traumatic event may not be open to rational analysis for some time. Rather, the aggrieved individual may experience shock, betrayal, anger, denial, depression, and a variety of other negative emotions for a lengthy period. For many people, this reaction may continue well after the relationship has been terminated.

Systems Approaches to Therapy

Systems therapists believe that relationship problems are located in the patterns of interactions between people. They do not locate the problem within the individual, as do more psychologically oriented therapists. They view the family as a system maintained by both the healthy and unhealthy behaviors of its members.

Many families exhibit dysfunctional patterns, and they have persisted in these patterns over generations. These unhealthy patterns may endure for years unless an event occurs to destabilize the family and its routines. Such an event might be the sudden death of a parent. The extended family may try to come together in their grieving, but may discover that they do not know how to interact effectively. Sometimes these traumas shake up the pattern of relations to the point that more effective problem solving and communication start to occur. On other occasions, however, the dysfunctional family divides at a major stress point and never comes back together.

In their approach to therapy, systems therapists often see all members of a family in the same session; sometimes they will not even accept clients for therapy unless all members of the immediate family participate. In these sessions they focus on problems and how members of the family communicate about the problems. They believe that family members sometimes form coalitions against one another (e.g., mother and daughter form a coalition in their view that the husband squanders their resources). In therapy, the therapist may help family members understand how these coalitions may be working to impede effective communication. By doing this, the therapist may destabilize the family, thus forcing them to become more open about problems and effective in communication. I have seen family therapists demonstrate destabilizing, and it is a compelling approach when a family has stonewalled communication about its problems for years.

Unfortunately, it is difficult to get all members of an immediate family to participate in therapy. Invariably, members who do not participate play key roles in the family system. This can make family therapy less effective. Sometimes, also, family approaches are criticized for not giving enough attention to individual family members' thoughts and feelings. But I do not believe that criticism holds for the more flexible types of family therapy. See Salvadore Minuchin (e.g., his 1974 book *Families and Family Therapy*) for some of the most influential work in this area.

"Self-Help" Works

These days one hears myriad voices telling people how to improve, or save, their relationships. The following is just a few of the recommendations I have gleaned from "self-help" books and newspapers and magazine articles. To me, these are some of the best and most tenable suggestions available.

Rewrite Love Stories This idea coheres with the argument about the value of account making and confiding put forward by Harvey, Weber, and Orbuch in *Interpersonal Accounts* (1990, see discussion in Chapter 9). Psychotherapists Patricia Hudson and Willian O'Hanlon, who are married to each other, wrote a book titled *Rewriting Love Stories*. In this book, they said:

> Stories are part of our ways of understanding the world and what happens in our lives. . . .
>
> We each use stories to explain what happens in our relationships and to guess the future. When there are problems or when people disagree, it often becomes a matter of "dueling stories." Whose story is right and whose is wrong? Neither. Both are explanations that cannot be proved either right or wrong.
>
> Stories aren't just neutral, however. When people get into difficulties, they usually develop stories that don't enhance their relationships. Perhaps out of frustration, anger, or hurt, they come up with stories that poison their relationships. "You just

want to control me." "You're just like your mother." "You care for your family more than you care for me." "You're selfish." And so on. (p. 16)

Helping people understand the power of stories in how they lead their lives is a major step in and of itself. Hudson and O'Hanlon go beyond this step in their work with couples by examining different kinds of stories in the lives of the clients, their own lives, and the lives of others with whom they have worked. They tell stories from their own relationship to inspire couples and give them ideas about how stories matter. The specific techniques used by these psychotherapists are similar to those Beck uses. For example, one person's story of a problem area may involve a major distortion of the partner. Hudson and O'Hanlon work with the person, evaluating how this interpretation may be affecting interaction with the partner.

One problem with *Rewriting Love Stories* is that Hudson and O'Hanlon's approach has been oversimplified. For instance, it does not address the question when does the storytelling and examining process have no value? Also, as is true for most self-help books, there is no attempt to connect their ideas with some of the powerful writings on similar topics—such as Robert Coles's (1989) *The Call of Stories* and Jerome Bruner's (1990) *Acts of Meaning.* Finally, it would have helped to point out the value of couples writing to one another. The use of letters (even brief notes) to express feelings and interpretations is greatly underemphasized in this age of high technology. It can be a valuable experience for a couple, especially if they do it regularly.

Share Photographs   A simple but potent technique to help people get to know one another better involves their looking through picture albums of their individual and joint lives. The idea would be for both partners to share albums. Astute observers can learn to develop insights from the photos about their partner's childhood and some of the influences in his or her development.

The value of sharing photograph albums for relationship enhancement was suggested in an October 1992 article in *New Woman* by psychoanalyst Robert Akeret. Akeret recommended that couples not only look through photographs, but that they also try to verbalize their feelings about the people displayed. He suggested that people look for clues to the relationships among people in the photographs. Are they touching? Making eye contact? What would they say if they could talk—what was on their minds at that point in time? Such commentaries, according to Akeret, will lead to more stories and more in-depth self-disclosure.

I think that this idea is a gem but that a couple needs to be careful not to read too much into photographs. The stories that a couple applies to the people in the photographs probably relate more to the couple's own present experiences and world view than they do to the "historical characters" on display.

Fight to Grow In *Recovering Couples* Carol Smith (1992) provided a useful set of specific points about how to argue in a constructive manner and, in so doing, communicate carefully and respectfully with your partner. The logic is similar to Beck's. When a major argument develops, for example, it would help if each member of the couple tried to state the other's point of view and be open to revising his or her interpretation of that view in light of feedback from the other. Smith also suggested that couples try to use a common vocabulary in their communication, especially regarding topics of conflict, make encouraging rather than disparaging comments, observe one another's nonverbal behaviors to see how they resonate with what is being said, and take turns talking without interruption from the other. She went on to say that in some situations, couples should consider writing up "good faith understandings" regarding how they will try to resolve problems or make their relationship healthier.

Smith fails to spell out conditions under which such thoughtful and considerate behavior will not work. Signs of intense emotions such as shouting probably signal that the parties should cease and desist until cooler heads can prevail. People simply have not learned to be thoughtful and logical in many interpersonal areas, and that particularly includes issues of the heart.

Couples' arguments and fights often have as their underlying theme the desire of the partners to change one another or how the other understands something believed to be important in the relationship. In a classic study, Harold Kelley and his colleagues (Orvis, Kelley, and Butler, 1976) provided evidence that couples try to change one another's understandings in conflict situations. For example, a wife may try to get her husband to recognize that he still is tied to his mother's apron strings by calling him a "momma's boy" in the middle of a fight. Ann Weber (1993) reported the following quip by a comedian that speaks to this concern about whether one's partner will change: "The real problem when they marry is that women keep thinking their husbands will change after marriage, and men keep thinking their wives won't change—and they're both wrong!"

Avoid Undermining a Partner's Ego

In *Love, Intimacy, and Sex,* sociologists Jack Douglas and Freda Atwell (1988) presented a scenario of how big arguments can undermine a partner's ego and lead to major damage in a close relationship. They said:

> The greatest *feeling of threat* comes from those arguments in which the lover feels that the loved one intends to attack his or her basic sense of self. This is experienced as betrayal, a betrayal of trust and of the intimate communing that is at the heart of being in love. It is often referred to by expressions such as, "He

really knows how to hit me where it hurts the most," and "She purposefully hits below the belt." (p. 236)

Douglas and Atwell went on to give an example of a "below the belt" punch. It was a remark made by a wife at a dinner table with her husband and several guests present. In an off-hand way, she said her husband "was not much into sex." This remark, seemingly made in jest, was a potent public humiliation of her husband. The authors called it a "kick in his 'ego-balls.'" The remark came in the context of escalation of conflict between the married partners and the husband's probable series of affairs. From the point at which the remark was made, there was no hope of resolving the conflict in the relationship. It was the *coup de grace.*

Douglas and Atwell described the type of relationship in which remarks like these occur as insecure and vulnerable. On the other hand, they argued that partners who are both reasonably secure about themselves and the relationship tend to dampen potential threats launched by accident or because of temporary insecurities. While other people suffer temporary insecurities on occasion, those who desire to continue their relationships need to avoid browbeating or publicly humiliating their partner, even if the partner has transgressed in a major way against the relationship. Douglas and Atwell concluded that only through a maturing of self and the relationship do people usually avoid the pitfalls of conflict that escalates into personal attack. They suggested that such maturity too often does not occur until people have reached mid-life and experienced the lessons of loss.

Don't Overemphasize Lust Douglas and Atwell (1988) also argued that people too often become involved on the basis of lust rather than love. Too often, people mythicize the value of strangers with whom they desire to have relationships—believing that they want closeness with these others when they have far too little information to know if in-depth closeness is possible. Rather, lust or desire for sexual fulfillment with this "stranger" is the principal guiding motivation. Douglas and Atwell noted that even the most beautiful body in the world is soon taken for granted when it becomes a part of everyday life. They claimed that this is one reason why the partners of people with beautiful bodies still may drift away in search of new sexual stimuli. They argued that lust is the first aspect of romantic love to peak and the first to begin cooling after a relationship has been established. If there is no underlying foundation of closeness, there is little likelihood that the relationship will continue.

For Douglas and Atwell, therefore, the building of a happy love relationship depends far more on intimate communing and on caring love than it does on the intensity of adoration and mutual lust. They suggested that joint experiences, diligent work at building a close relationship, and enduring hardships together were crucial components of meaningful, durable intimacy: "the sharing of common suffering is probably the most potent form of intimate communing. The expression of adoration love in response complements the communing partnership and also inspires adoration in the caring lover" (p. 230).

Make a Commitment Commitment is closely related to taking responsibility for one's own decisions regarding close relationships. It represents a vital aspect of the principles of self-empowerment that were discussed earlier. If you have concluded that you are in the "wrong" relationship for you, do not blame the decision to become involved on others or something about the environment—"you were recovering from the loss of a very special relationship and needed someone badly." You also are responsible at least for part of the work that will be necessary if you want the relationship to improve and become "right" for you. Do not wait on other to take the lead and redress the issues. Begin the dialogue yourself.

Steven Carter and Julia Sokol, writing in the September 1993 issue of *New Woman* magazine, suggest that commitment involves "being present" in *all* of your relationships. Facing issues explicitly and disclosing your major concerns to your partner are part of your commitment to the relationship. Carter and Sokol say, "By keeping parts of ourselves hidden from others, we are creating distance and putting limitations on our capacity to connect and experience intimacy" (p. 102).

Carter and Sokol also emphasize being responsible for the little steps in relating. If you say you are going to call, call. If you make a lunch date, keep it. If you promise to write or visit, do it. Scheduling problems occur, but take into account possible problems in planning your schedule and be diligent in implementing your schedule. How we organize our lives should mean a lot to a partner.

One final point that Carter and Sokol make is for people searching for a long-term relationship. Do not fall in love with "potential." Do not indulge in "if only" commitment fantasies, as in "If only I could get my partner's ambitions and work attitude to change, all would be well with our relationship!" Forget it. What you see over time is what you get. Don't delude yourself.

Forgive Your Partner Robin Casarjian has written a book entitled *Forgiveness* (1992) that makes a strong case for the value of forgiveness as an aid to healing distressed close relationships and troubled minds and hearts in general. She discussed the importance both of forgiving your partner for hurtful actions directed toward you and of asking for forgiveness when you have hurt your partner.

In her book, Casarjian went to great lengths to analyze the subtleties of forgiveness. She argued that it has these elements: an attitude, in which people are able to accept responsibility for their actions and perceptions; a process, in which people can search diligently to understand one another's points of view when disagreements occur; and a way of life, in which people can regularly examine their relationships and explicitly deal with perceived misdeeds. She argued that forgiveness teaches us that we can resolutely disagree with others without withdrawing our love.

Casarjian also discussed what forgiveness is not. She contended that it is not pretending that everything is fine when you feel it is not. Similarly, I have argued that most types of grief are best addressed by gentle confrontations and not by suppression. When a person feels that a partner has engaged in a very hurtful action, then a variety of negative emotions such as anger, hostility, resentment, desire for revenge, and ultimately grief may follow. The expression of this grief to the injuring partner may be an essential first step toward the partner's sincere regret and apology, and eventual healing and forgiveness on the part of the injured partner. Casarjian posited that forgiveness is not assuming an attitude of superiority or self-righteousness. Nor is it necessarily changing your own behavior, such as ending an estrangement with someone whom you believe has hurt you. It may not even involve a verbal statement such as "I forgive you." It may be a silent and private thought that one simply files away.

Casarjian mentioned that writing to another person is one vehicle to ask for forgiveness. As an illustration, she suggested that when an affair has occurred, the person involved might consider writing to one of the injured parties asking for forgiveness (for instance, the husband of the woman with whom you had a sexual relationship). She noted that such an act would help the wrongdoer move toward recovery, even if he or she never sends the letter. I have some pause about this tactic. I think that the individual should carefully consider whether further harm might result from any type of additional action—especially the sending of a letter to the aggrieved party.

Share Memories of Past Lovers This recommendation is more personal. It is useful for us to judiciously disclose the broad outlines of our past relationships to one another because these relationships affect how we feel and behave in our present relationship. It is important to be thoughtful and considerate when we discuss our past love life with a present lover, who will probably assume that this information is highly relevant to what he or she might expect in the future.

The private, unique aspects of past relationships should always be kept private. It is likely to be off-putting to your partner to blurt out everything about your romantic past the first time this type of disclosure is being shared. There may even be some past relationships that you should keep to yourself.

What should we disclose when the opportunity for such sharing arises? When there is an opportunity, we should discuss why we believe the relationships started; how much closeness was involved in the relationships at their zenith; how the relationships progressed over time; and why we think they ended. In describing and commenting on endings, it is important not to lay all the blame on the other person. Stress the positive and constructive elements of the past relationship. Although we may have been hurt, we also probably experienced love, warmth, hope, and many other positive emotions.

Though it may be impossible in many cases, there is something to be said for trying to continue friendships with past lovers. This is how a male writer put it in a September 1991 *Glamour* magazine article entitled "Breaking up, staying friends":

> I try particularly hard to remain friends, or at least privileged acquaintances, with my ex-fiancee and my other exes. No, I don't do it to keep options open for reconciliation. I do it because these women hold the keys to crucial parts of my identity, especially my sexuality. While I was with each, I gave pieces of myself I'd never before given anyone else. . . . Now, the only way left for me to experience the part of me I gave to her is

somehow to experience her. It's almost as if she is keeping a part of me; I take up a small room in her museum. To visit me, I visit her. . . . Treat ex-lovers with care. They may be your future pals. (p. 164)

The Self-Help Movement   The majority of readers of self-help books are women. In *Women and Self-Help Culture* Wendy Simonds (1992) analyzed why self-help activities have been subscribed to so often by women during the last decade or so. Her conclusions, which were based in part on interviews with a small group of women, are as follows: Self-help books allow some women to feel better about themselves, and others to take needed actions to improve their lives. Ultimately, however, these books provide only an illusory cure for what ails us collectively as a culture. The addiction rhetoric in them suggests that each victim's problems are unique and not part of the more general problems all people encounter, and that recovery is an ongoing process and the self can never be truly or totally recovered. Ironically, there is a high degree of addictiveness to self-help activities. Whether reading books or magazines or watching talk shows on television.

Simonds argued that women and men alike are becoming increasingly self-involved. The Horatio Alger spirit of the late 19th century (that emphasized people can do anything through dedication and hard work), she said, enjoys a rejuvenation in self-help books, which stress the relationship between personal exertion and personal success. This movement's emphasis on personal success is filled with paradox for women. Women's selfhood remains bound up with others—in caretaking and nurturing others' development. Thus, as women have felt betrayed by this focus in their identity, they have sought the liberating advice of self-help gurus, who have outlined ways in which they can be more in charge of their own destiny and less burdened by their cultural script.

Gender disparities underlie self-help authors' analyses of self-knowledge for women: Identity, for women, is especially difficult to define. Sometimes, according to self-help authors, we need a lot of changing; at other times we need self-acceptance. Acceptance in fact becomes a sort of paradoxical basis for accomplishing change. Identity becomes a messy compilation of past experiences that need to be sorted through and reprioritized. The changes advocated by self-help authors for women have changed very little since Friedan wrote *The Feminine Mystique* in 1963: women have been encouraged to place less value in involvements with others and to pay more attention to personal development. (p. 223)

Self-help books for women often depict men as wanting to be cared for, but having no need to care in return. Also, because reciprocity in caring is so difficult to attain, men are frequently cast as obstacles that women work around as they forge meaningful relationships. In the end, Simonds said, the women's self-help movement is about paradoxes that confront all people. She said: "Buying self-help, whatever form of media it takes, is about alienation and hope; about personal dissatisfaction and social inadequacy; about wanting to conform to achieve magical happiness and about wanting to create new arrangements" (p. 226).

Simonds seems to feel that the self-help movement is a mixed blessing for women. We may extrapolate that it is probably a mixed blessing for all people who participate in it. Some, but not all, self-help literature has no foundation in scholarship, research, or sound logic. But when carefully conceived, this literature may be valuable to people who do not have a lot of time or money to devote to more in-depth enhancement activities, such as taking classes and workshops and going for short-term therapy.

I would suggest that people read this literature with a healthy skepticism. For instance, they should consider the following questions: (1) Do the authors provide references that could be checked to evaluate their suggestions? (2) Do the authors try to sell other expensive products, such as their own videotapes and workshops, as part of their book? (Not a good sign.) (3) Do the authors make absolute statements as part of their arguments? There are no simple or unqualified truths concerning close relationships.

Predictions For Close Relationship Trends

In this final discussion, I would like to address more explicitly what I believe will be some major trends in close relationships over the next century.

Too many teenagers will continue to plunge into marriage. On the other hand, other people will stay single until even later in their lives than they do now. It will not be uncommon for people to stay single well into their 30s. Some divorced and widowed individuals will still try to remarry, while some others, including retirees, will live together with no intention of marrying.

There will be continued high rates of divorce, and these will probably spread to countries now experiencing lower rates. One cannot see on the horizon a set of forces that offsets people's increasing inclination to look to divorce to solve their problems.

There may be further reform of divorce laws. Glenda Riley (1991) suggested that the mechanism of divorce needs serious reform in this country. She argued that because of the many difficulties and trauma sometimes associated with divorce proceedings and child custody and support judgments, different courts should adjudicate divorce, child custody, child support, and division of assets. This would not be easy, because of the expense involved in separating these functions. I do believe, however, that careful, sensitive, and timely court judgments surrounding divorce must become the rule rather than the exception. It is essential that stereotypes regarding who is best qualified to be awarded custody be challenged and that children be better protected against parents using them in custody and support disputes. Although it also may be too expensive, the use of mediation prior to divorce proceedings is a positive step toward more humane ways of separating people's assets and helping them try to solve custody issues.

On matters of sexual orientation, today most gay teens do not feel safe enough to declare their sexual identity until college, when they are often met with disbelief and anger from their parents. I believe that our society will become more tolerant and open over time, allowing people in their late teens to "come out" earlier. This assumption is based in part on the strides gay and lesbian individuals are making in areas such as employment and running for public office in the 1990s. Increasingly, people are coming to realize that sexual orientation very likely has little to do with how one carries out his or her job. It is my experience that college students tend to be more tolerant of sexual orientation differences among their colleagues.

Even if there is no cure for AIDS, "casual sex" is likely to continue at a high rate in the general population, especially if the disease is not rampant among heterosexual persons. "Casual sex" is usually not so casual, and indeed it may help people learn about their own and others' sexuality. Of course, "casual sex" may be associated with more negative outcomes as well. For example, it may lead to a jaded, noncompassionate attitude about sex and sexual partners. People will have to continue to be careful in their choice of partners and to practice safe sex.

A number of other trends are likely to continue well into the twenty-first century. There will be many interracial and interreligious couples. Even more couples will commute many miles between job and home. Finding quality jobs in the same place will still be difficult for dual-career couples, who will continue to be more prevalent than "traditional" one-career couples. Couples in the middle years will simultaneously care for young and adult children and elderly parents in the same household. The "sandwich generation" may find that the squeeze on their resources is even greater, as their parents die at later ages and adult children continue to return home when their careers are uncertain or slow in development.

Similarly, more and more couples will decide that one or both parties should take leave from their careers and concentrate on child care activity. Child care will continue to be expensive and often of poor quality. Increasingly, public law and policy will support two-career marriages and the need to simultaneously implement effective work and parenting practices. As is true now, many couples will wait until well into their 30s to have children. U.S. Census data indicate that the proportion of women giving birth for the first time after age 35 increased 350 percent from 1980 to 1990. In coming years, more people in their 30s will feel prepared psychologically and financially to have families than was previously true. With advances in medical technology, the risks associated with the pregnancies of women in their 30s, and possibly older, will likely be less serious.

Many couples will continue to recognize the importance of each person's personal development within the context of the relationship and family. More egalitarian close relationships will exist than ever before. They will be based on regular dialogue about issues and challenging the way things have been done in the past. As is true today, many people will not be able to achieve this type of relating early in their relationship careers or in their present relationship. They will need experience, patience, and commitment to make a close relationship work. The number of couples who are involved in various types of "nontraditional" close relationships should continue to grow, as societal norms about relationships continue to be relaxed. The nature and concept of family already is in flux in this culture, and that trend too should continue. Couples and affiliated others will increasingly decide to form units and live together based on their psychological similarities.

Many of these predictions are based more on my own guesses and deductions from the available literature that has been reviewed in these chapters than they are on a strong foundation of research evidence. For further analysis of future trends in close relationships, see these recent textbooks on relationships: Sharon Brehm's (1992) *Intimate Relationships;* Elaine Hatfield and Richard Rapson's (1993) *Love, Sex, & Intimacy;* and the volume edited by Ann Weber and John Harvey (1994), *Perspectives on Close Relationships.*

Odyssey of the Heart is really about hope. Hope that we can improve ourselves, and in so doing, improve our relationships. By preventing some of the major problems in relationships, or even by preventing some relationships form going too far. Hope that injured relationships can be repaired. Hope that lost relationships can be found, at least in one's mind and memory, and given peace there. Hope that the "self-help" movement is, on balance, a positive step for a society that appears to have an insatiable desire to try to fix broken psyches and relationships. And finally, hope that my optimism about the state of close relationships is neither sugar-coated nor far-fetched, but rather well-reasoned and based on our individual readiness, as well as our readiness as a culture, to recognize the means by which we can improve our close relationships.

The unavoidable consequence of human social life is a realization of the essentially private and subjective nature of our experience of the world, coupled with a strong wish to break out of that

privacy and establish contact with another mind.
— Harold Kelley (*Personal Relationships,* 1979, Erlbaum)

A book must be the axe for the frozen sea within us.

—Franz Kafka

REFERENCES

Abbey, A. (1982). Sex differences in attributes for friendly behavior: Do males misperceive females' friendliness? *Journal of Personality and Social Psychology, 42,* 830-838.

Ahrons, C., & Rodgers, C., & Rodgers, R. H. (1987). *Divorced families.* New York: Norton.

Altman, I., & Taylor, D. (1973). *Social penetration.* New York: Holt, Rinehart & Winston.

Andrews, B., & Brewin, C. R. (1990). Attributions of blame for marital violence: A study of antecedents and consequences. *Journal of Marriage and the Family, 52,* 757-767.

Averill, J. R., & Boothroyd, P. (1977). On falling in love in conformance with the romantic ideal. *Motivation and Emotion, 1,* 235-247.

Bailey, B. L. (1988). *From front porch to back seat.* Baltimore: Johns Hopkins University Press.

Bass, E., & Davis, L. (1988). *The courage to heal: A guide for women survivors of child sexual abuse.* New York: Harper & Row.

Baumeister, R. F. (1991). *Meanings of life.* New York: Guilford.

Baumeister, R. F., & Wotman, S. R. (1992). *Breaking hearts: The two sides of unrequited love.* New York: Guilford.

Baxter, L. A. (1987). Cognition and communication in the relationship process. In R. Burnett, P. McGhee, & D. Clarke (Eds.), *Accounting for relationships: Explanation, representation and knowledge* (pp. 192-212). London: Methuen.

Baxter, L. A. (1994). A dialogic approach to relationship maintenance. In D. J. Canary & L. Stafford (Eds.), *Communication and relational maintenance* (233-254). New York: Academic Press.

Beach, S. R., & Tesser, A. (1988). Love in marriage: A cognitive account. In R. J. Sternberg & M. L. Barnes (Eds.), *The psychology of love* (pp. 330-355). New Haven, CT: Yale University Press.

Beck A. (1988). *Love is never enough: How couples can overcome misunderstandings, resolve conflicts, and solve relationship problems through cognitive therapy.* New York: Harper & Row.

Beck, A. T. (1967). *Depression: Clinical, experimental and theoretical aspects.* New York: Harper & Row.

Bellah, R. N., Madsen, R. Sullivan, W. M., Swidler, A., & Tipton, S. M. (1985). *Habits of the heart: Individualism and commitment in American life.* Berkeley: University of California Press.

Bem, D. J. (1972). Self-perception theory. In L. Berkowitz (Ed.), *Advances in Experimental Social Psychology (Vol. 6)* (pp. 1-62.) New York: Academic Press.

Bem. S. L. (1993). *The lenses of gender: Transforming the debate on sexual inequality.* New Haven: Yale University Press.

Bentz, V. (1989). *Becoming mature.* Hawthorne, NY: Aldine de Gruyter.

Berger, P. (1963). *Invitation to sociology.* Garden City, NY: Doubleday.

Bergquist, W., Greenberg, E., & Klaum, A. (1993) *In our fifties.* San Francisco: Jossey-Bass.

Bernard, J. (1982). *The future of marriage* (2nd ed.). New Haven: Yale University Press.

Bernikow, L. (1987). *Alone in America: The search for companionship.* Winchester, MA: Faber and Faber. (Reprint. Originally published: New York: Harper & Row, 1986.).

Berscheid, E., & Walster, E. (1978). *Interpersonal attraction* (2nd ed.). Needham, MA: Addison-Wesley.

Berscheid, E. (1988). Some comments on love's anatomy or, whatever happened to old-fashioned lust? in R. J. Sternberg and M. L. Barnes (Eds.), *The psychology of love* (pp. 359-374). New Haven: Yale University Press.

Berscheid, E., Snyder, M., & Omoto, A. M. (1989). The relationship closeness inventory. *Journal of Personality and Social Psychology, 57,* 792-807.

Billig, M., Condor, S., Edwards, D., Gane, M., Middleton, D., Radley, A. (1988). *Ideological dilemmas: A social psychology of everyday thinking.* London: Sage.

Blau, M. (1994). *Families apart.* New York: Putnam.

Blieszner, R., & Mancini, J. A. (1992). Developmental perspectives on relationship loss. In T. Orbuch (Ed.), *Close Relationship Loss: Theoretical Approaches* (pp. 142-154). New York: Springer-Verlag.

Blumstein, P., & Schwartz, P. (1983). *American couples.* New York: Pocket Books.

Bly, R. (1992). *Iron John: A book about men.* New York: Vintage Books.

Bowlby, J. (1969). *Loss: Sadness and depression.* New York: Basic Books.

Bradbury, T. N., & Fincham, F. D. (1992). Attributions and behavior in marital interaction. *Journal of Personality and Social Psychology, 4,* 613-628.

Brehm, S. S. (1992). *Intimate relationships* (2nd ed.). New York: McGraw-Hill.

Bringle, R. G. (1991). Psychosocial aspects of jealousy: A transactional model. In P. Salovey (Ed.), *The Psychology of Jealousy and Envy* (pp. 103-131). New York: Guilford.

Brown, R., & Kulik, J. (1977). Flashbulb memory. *Cognition, 5,* 73-99.

Browning, E. B. (1953) *Oxford dictionary of quotations* (2nd ed.). London: Oxford University Press.

Bruner, J. (1990). *Acts of meaning.* Cambridge: Harvard University Press.

Buss, D. M. (1994). *The evolution of desire.* New York: Basic Books.

Buss, D. M., & Barnes, M. F. (1986). Preferences in human mate selection. *Journal of Personality and Social Psychology, 50,* 559-570.

Buunk, B., & Van Driel, B. (1989). *Variant lifestyles and relationships.* Newbury Park, CA: Sage.

Buunk, B. P. (1991). Jealousy in close relationships: An exchange-theoretical perspective. In P. Salovey (Ed.), *The psychology of jealousy and envy* (pp. 147-177). New York: Guilford.

Byrne, D. (1971). *The attraction paradigm.* New York: Academic Press.

Byrne, D., & Murnen, S. K. (1988). Maintaining loving relationships. In R. J. Sternberg and M. L. Barnes (Eds.), *The psychology of love* (pp. 293-310). New Haven: Yale University Press.

Capuzzi. D. (1988). Adolescent suicide: Prevention and intervention. In J.Carlson & J. Lewis (Eds.), *Counseling the adolescent* (pp. 260-271). Denver: Love.

Carlsen, M. B. (1991). *Creative aging.* New York: Norton.

Carpenter, E. (1986). *Love's coming-of-age.* London: Metheun.

Carver, R. (1986). *Where I'm calling from: New and selected stories.* New York: Atlantic Monthly Press.

Casarjian, R. (1992). *Forgiveness: A bold choice for a peaceful heart.* New York: Bantam.

Cherlin, A. (1992). *Marriage, divorce and remarriage.* Cambridge: Harvard University Press.

Clark, M. S., & Mills, J. (1979). Interpersonal attraction in exchange and communal relationships. *Journal of Personality and Social Psychology, 37,* 12-24.

Coleman, J. C. (1984). *Intimate relationships, marriage, and family.* Indianapolis: Bobbs-Merrill.

Coles, R. (1989). *The call of stories: Teaching and the moral imagination.* Boston: Houghton Mifflin.

Coontz, S. (1992). *The way we never were: American families and the nostalgia trap.*

Cousins, N. (1993). *Head first.* New York: Penguin.

Cunningham, J. D., & Antill, J. K. (1981). Love in developing romantic relationships. In S. Duck & R. Gilmour (Eds.), *Personal relationships: Developing personal relationships* (Vol. 2) (pp. 27-51). New York: Academic Press.

Cupach, W. R., and Metts, S. (1991). Sexuality and communication in close relationships. In K. McKinney & S. Sprecher (Eds.), *Sexuality in close relationships* (pp. 93-110). Hillsdale, NJ: Erlbaum.

Dabbs, J. M. (1992). Testosterone measurements in social and clinical psychology. *Journal of Social and Clinical Psychology, 11* (3), 302-321.

Danica, E. (1988). *Don't: A woman's word.* San Francisco: Cleis Press.

Darley, J. M., & Fazio, R. H. (1980). Expectancy confirmation process in the social interaction sequence. *American Psychologist, 35,* 867-81.

Densmore, D., Giler, J. Z., & Neumeyer, K. (1992). *Re-defining Mr. Right: A career woman's guide to choosing mate.* Oakland, CA: New Harbinger.

Dindia, K., & Canary, D. J. (1993). Definitions and theoretical perspectives on maintaining relationships. In K. Dindia & D. J. Canary (Eds.), Relational maintenance [special issue]. *Journal of Social and Personal Relationships, 10* (2), 163-173.

Dion, K. L., & Dion, K. K. (1976). Love, liking, and trust in heterosexual relationships. *Personality and Social Psychology Bulletin, 2,* 191-206.

Donnerstein, E., Linz, D., & Penrod, S. (1987). *The question of pornography.* New York: Free Press.

Douglas, J. D., & Atwell, F. C. (1988). *Love, intimacy, and sex.* Newbury Park, CA: Sage.

Duck, S., Rutt, D. J., Hurst, M. H., & Strejc, H. (1991). Some evident truths about conversation in everyday relationships: All communications are not created equal. *Human Communication Research, 18,* 228-267.

Dutton, D. G., and Aron, A. P. (1974). Some evidence for heightened sexual attraction under conditions of high anxiety. *Journal of Personality and Social Psychology, 30,* 510-517.

Ehrenreich, B., Hess, E., & Jacobs, G. (1986). *Re-making love: The feminization of sex.* New York: Anchor/Doubleday.

Epstein, S. (1993). *You're smarter than you think you are.* New York: Simon & Schuster.

Erikson, E. (1950). *Childhood and society.* New York: W. W. Norton.

Erikson, E. (1963). *Childhood and society* (2nd ed.). New York: W. W. Norton.

Fehr, B. (1988). Prototype analysis of the concepts of love and commitment. *Journal of Personality and Social Psychology, 55,* 557-579.

Fehr, B., & Russell, J. A. (1991). The concept of love viewed from a prototype perspective. *Journal of Personality and Social Psychology, 60,* 425-438.

Fincham, F. D., & Bradbury, T. N. (1993). Marital satisfaction, depression, and attributions: A longitudinal analysis. *Journal of Personality andSocial Psychology, 64,* 442-452.

Fincham, F. D., & Bradbury, T. N. (1987). The impact of attributions in marriage: A longitudinal analysis. *Journal of Personality and Social Psychology, 53,* 510-517.

Fletcher, G. J. O., & Fincham, F. D. (Eds.) (1991). *Cognition in close relationships.* Hillsdale, NJ: Erlbaum.

Foa, U. G., & Foa, E. B. (1974). *Societal structures of the mind.* Springfield, IL: Charles C. Thomas.

Frankl, V. E. (1956). *Man's search for meaning.* New York: Washington Square.

Furstenberg, F. F., Jr., & Spanier, G. B. (1976). *Recycling the family.* Newbury Park: Sage.

Furstenberg, F. F., Jr., & Cherlin, A. (1991). *Divided families.* Newbury Park, CA: Sage.

Gately, D., & Schwebel, A. I. (1992). Favorable outcomes in children after parental divorce. In C. A. Everett (Ed.), *Divorce and the next generation* (pp. 57-78). New York: Haworth Press.

Gelles, R. J., & Straus, M. A. (1988). *Intimate violence.* New York: Simon & Schuster.

Gergen, K. (1991). *The saturated self: Dilemmas of identity in contemporary life.* New York: Basic Books.

Gerstel, N., & Gross, H. (1984). *Commuting marriage.* New York: The Guilford Press.

Giler, J.Z., & Neumeyer, K. (1992). *Redefining Mr. Right: A career woman's guide to choosing a mate.* Oakland, CA: New Harbinger & Marin.

Gilligan, C. (1982). *In a different voice: Psychological theory and women's development.* Cambridge, MA: Harvard University Press.

Goffman, E. (1959). *The presentation of self in everyday life.* Garden City, NY: Anchor-Doubleday.

Goldstein, R. (1990). *Fortysomething: Claiming the power and the passion of your midlife years.* Los Angeles: Taracher.

Goode, W. (1959). The theoretical importance of love. *American Sociological Review, 24,* 38.

Griffin-Shelley, E. (Ed.) (1993). *Outpatient treatment of sex and love addicts.* Westport, CT: Praeger.

Grych, J. H., & Fincham, F. D. (1992). Interventions for children of divorce: Toward greater integration of research and action. *Psychological Bulletin, 3,* 434-454.

Guerney, B., Jr. (1977). *Relationship enhancement: Skill training programs for therapy, problem prevention, and enrichment.* San Francisco: Jossey-Bass.

Guttman, J. (1993). *Divorce in psychosocial perspective: Theory and research.* Hillsdale, NJ: Erlbaum.

Hardin, P. (1993). *What are you doing with the rest of your life?* New York: New World Library.

Harvey, J. H. (1987). Attributions in close relationships: Research and theoretical developments. *Journal of Social and Clinical Psychology, 4,* 420-434.

Harvey, J. H. (in progress). The aftermath of long-term marriage.

Harvey, J. H., Flanary, R., & Morgan, M. (1986). Vivid memories of vivid loves gone by. *Journal of Social and Personal Relationships, 3,* 359-373.

Harvey, J. H., Orbuch, T. L., Chwalisz, K., & Garwood, G. (1991). Coping with sexual assault: The roles of account-making and confiding. *Journal of Traumatic Stress, 4,* 515-531.

Harvey, J. H., Orbuch, T. L., & Weber, A. L. (Eds.) (1992). *Attributions, accounts, and close relationships.* New York: Springer-Verlag.

Harvey, J. H., Orbuch, T. L., Weber, A. L., Merbach, N., & Alt, R. (1992). House of pain and hope: Accounts of loss. *Death Studies, 16,* 1-26.

Harvey, J. H., Weber, A. L., & Orbuch, T. L. (1990). *Interpersonal accounts: A social psychological perspective.* Oxford: Basil Blackwell.

Harvey, J. H., Wells, G. H., and Alvarez, M. D. (1978). Attribution in the context of conflict and separation in close relationships. In J. H. Harvey, W. Ickes, and R. F. Kidd (Eds.), *New Directions in Attribution Research* (Vol. 2) (pp. 235-259). Hillsdale, NJ: Erlbaum.

Hatfield, E., & Rapson, R. (1993). *Love, sex, and intimacy.* New York: Harper Collins.

Hatfield, E., & Sprecher, S. (1986). *Mirror, mirror: The importance of looks in everyday life.* New York: State University of New York Press.

Hazan, C., & Shaver, P. (1987). Romantic love conceptualized as an attachment process. *Journal of Personality and Social Psychology 52,* 511-524.

Heaton, T. B., & Albrecht, S. L. (1991). Stable unhappy marriages. *Journal of Marriage and the Family, 53,* 747-758.

Heider, F. (1958). *The psychology of interpersonal relations.* New York: Wiley.

Helmreich, W. B. (1992). *Against all odds: Holocaust survivors and the successful lives they made in America.* New York: Simon & Schuster.

Hendrick, C. (Ed.) (1989). *Close relationships.* Newbury Park, CA: Sage.

Hendrick, C., & Hendrick, S. (1986). A theory and method of love. *Journal of Personality and Social Psychology, 50,* 392-402.

Hendrick, S. S., & Hendrick, C. (1992b). *Romantic love.* Newbury Park: Sage.

Herbert, T. B., Silver, R. C., & Ellard, J. H. (1991). Coping with an abusive relationship: How and why do women stay? *Journal of Marriage and the Family, 53,* 311-325.

Herdt, G. (Ed.) (1992). *Gay culture in America: Essays from the field.* Boston: Beacon Press.

Hetherington, E. M., Cox, M., & Cox, R. (1982). Effects of divorce on parents and children. In M. Lamb (Ed.), *Nontraditional families* (pp. 233-288). Hillsdale, NJ: Erlbaum.

Heyn, D. (1992). *The erotic silence of the American wife.* New York: Turtle Bay Books.

Hill, C. T., Rubin, Z., & Peplau, L. A. (1976). Breakups before marriage: The end of 103 affairs. *Journal of Social Issues, 32,* 147-168.

Hinde, R. A. (1979). *Toward understanding relationships.* London: Academic Press, 1979.

Hite, S. (1987). *Women and love.* New York: Knopf.

Hochschild, A. (1989). *The second shift: Inside the two-job marriage.* New York: Viking.

Hojat, M. (1990). Can affectional ties be purchased? *Journal of Social Behavior and Personality, 5,* 493-502.

Hollis, J. (1993). *The middle passage: From misery to meaning in midlife.* Toronto: Inner City Books.

Holmes, J. G., and Rempel, J. K. (1989). Trust in close relationships. In C. Hendrick (Ed.), *Close Relationships: Review of Personality and Social Psychology* (Vol. 10) (pp. 315-359). Newbury Park: Sage.

Holtzworth-Munroe, A., & Jacobson, N. J. (1985). Causal attributions of married couples. *Journal of Personality and Social Psychology, 48,* 1399-1412.

Homans, G. C. (1961). *Social behavior: Its elementary forms.* New York: Harcourt, Brace & World.

Horowitz, M. J. (1986). *Stress response syndromes.* (2nd ed.). Northvale, NJ: Jason Aronson.

Hudson, L., & Jacot, B. (1991). *The way men think: Intellect, intimacy and the erotic imagination.* New Haven: Yale University Press.

Hudson, P. O., & O'Hanlon, W. H. (1991). *Rewriting love stories: Brief marital therapy.* New York: W. W. Norton.

Hulbert, H. D., & Schuster, D. T. (Eds.) (1993b). *Women's lives through time.* San Francisco: Jossey-Bass.

Hunt, M. (1966). *The world of the formerly married.* New York: McGraw-Hill.

Irish, D. P., Lundquist, K. F., & Nelsen, V. J. (Eds.) (1993). *Ethnic variations in dying, death, and grief: Diversity in universality.* Washington: DC: Taylor & Francis.

Janoff-Bulman, R. (1979). Characterological versus behavioral self-blame. *Journal of Personality and Social Psychology, 37,* 1789-1809.

Janoff-Bulman, R. (1992). *Shattered assumptions: Towards a new psychology of trauma.* New York: Free Press.

Jessor, R., Costa, F., Jessor, L., and Donovan, J. E. (1983). Time of first intercourse: A prospective study. *Journal of Personality and Social Psychology, 44* (3), 608-626.

Jones, E. E. (1990). *Interpersonal perception.* New York: W. H. Freeman.

Jones, W. H., & Burdette, M. P. (1994). Betrayal in close relationships. In A. L. Weber & J. H. Harvey (Eds.), *Perspectives on Close Relationships* (243-262). Boston: Allyn & Bacon.

Jourard, S. (1964). *The transparent self.* New York: Van Nostrand Reinhold.

Kelley, H. H. (1983). Love and commitment. In Kelley, H. H. et al., *Close Relationships* (pp. 265-314), New York: W. H. Freeman.

Kelley, H. H., & Thibaut, J. W. (1978). *Interpersonal relations: A theory of interdependence.* New York: Wiley-Interscience.

Kelley, H. H., Berscheid, E., Christensen, A., Harvey, J. H., Huston, T. L., Levinger, G., McClintock, E., Peplau, L. A., and Peterson, D. R. (1983). *Close relationships.* New York: W. H. Freeman.

Kenrick, D. T., & Trost, M. R. (1989). A reproductive exchange model of heterosexual relationships: Putting proximate economies in ultimate perspective. in C. Hendrick (Ed.), *Close Relationships: Vol. 10: Review of Personality and Social Psychology* (pp. 92-118). Newbury Park, CA: Sage.

Kessler, S. (1975). *The American way of divorce.* Nelson Hall: Chicago.

Kinsey, A. C., Pomeroy, W. B., Martin, C., & Gebhard, P. H. (1953). *Sexual behavior in the human female.* Philadelphia: W. B. Saunders.

Knapp, M. L. (1984). *Interpersonal communication and human relationships.* Newton, MA: Allyn & Bacon.

Koss, M. P., Gidycz, C. A., & Wisniewski, N. (1987). The scope of rape: Incidence and prevalence of sexual aggression and victimization among a national sample of college women. *Journal of Consulting and Counseling Psychology, 7,* 162-170.

Kotre, J., & Hall, E. (1990). *Seasons of life.* Boston: Little, Brown.

Kundera, M. (1984). *The unbearable lightness of being.* New York: Harper & Row.

Kurdek, L. A. (1991). Correlates of relationship satisfaction in cohabitating gay and lesbian couples. *Journal of Personality and Social Psychology,61,* 910-922.

Kurdek, L. A. (1992). Relationship stability and relationship satisfaction in cohabitating gay and lesbian couples. *Journal of Social and Personal Relationships, 9,* 125-142.

Kurdek, L. A., & Schmitt, J. P. (1987). Perceived emotional support from family and friends in members of homosexual, married, and heterosexual cohabitating couples. *Journal of Homosexuality, 14,* 57-68.

Laing, R. D. (1970). *Knots.* New York: Pantheon.

Lawson, A. (1988). *Adultery: An analysis of love and betrayal.* New York: Basic Books.

Leary, M. R. (1983). *Understanding social anxiety: Social, personality, and clinical perspectives.* Beverly Hills, CA: Sage.

Lee, J. A. (1976). *The colors of love.* Englewood Cliffs, NJ: Prentice Hall.

Levine, S. (1984). *Meetings at the edge: Dialogues with the grieving and the dying, the healing and the healed.* Garden City, NY: Anchor Press.

Levine, S. V. (1984). Radical departures. *Psychology Today, 18,* 20-27.

Levinger, G. (1983). Development and change. In Kelley, H. H., Berscheid, E., Christensen, A., Harvey, J. H., Huston, T. L., Levinger, G., McClintock, E., Peplau, L. A., and Peterson, D. R. (Eds.), *Close relationships.* (pp. 315-359). New York: W. H. Freeman.

Levinger, G. (1992). Close relationship loss as a set of inkblots. In T. L. Orbuch (Ed.), *Close relationship loss* (pp. 213-221). New York: Springer-Verlag.

Levinson, D. J. (1978). *The seasons of a man's life.* New York: Ballantine books.

Lewin, E., & Lyons, T. A. (1982). Everything in its place: The coexistence of lesbianism and motherhood. In W. Paul, J. D. Weinrich, J. C. Gonsiorek, & M. E. Hotvedt (Eds.), *Homosexuality: Social, psychological, and biological issues.* (pp. 249-273). Beverly Hills, CA: Sage.

Lewis, C. S. (1961). *A grief observed.* New York: Bantam Books.

Lusterman, D. D. (1992). "Infidelity and PTSD." Paper presented at meeting of the American Association for Marriage and Family Therapy.

Mainiero, L. (1989). *Love, power, & sex in the workplace.* New York: Rawson Associates.

Markman, H., Floyd, F., Stanley, S., & Storassi, R. (1988). Prevention of marital distress: A longitudinal investigation. *Journal of Consulting and Clinical Psychology, 56,* 210-217.

Marshall, L. L., & Vitanza, S. A. (1994). Physical abuse in close relationships: Myths and realities, In A. L. Weber & J. H. Harvey (Eds.), *Perspectives on close relationships* (263-284). Needham Heights, MA: Allyn & Bacon.

Marshall, M. (1984). *The cost of loving.* New York: Putnam.

McAdams, D. P. (1988). *Intimacy: The need to be close.* New York: Doubleday.

McClanahan, K. K. (1986, October). The relationship of attitude similarity and romantic attraction. *Dissertation Abstracts International, 47* (4), 1790B-1791B.

McGue, M., & Lykken, D. T. (1992). Genetic influence on risk of divorce. *Psychological science, 3* (6), 368-373.

McKinney, K., & Sprecher, S. (Eds.) (1991). *Sexuality in close relationships.* Hillsdale, NJ: Erlbaum.

McWhirter, D. P. Sanders, S. A., & Reinisch, J. M. (Eds.) (1990). *Homosexuality/heterosexuality: Concepts of sexual orientation.* New York: Oxford University Press.

Mills, J., & Clark, M. S. (1982). Exchange and communal relationships. In L. Wheeler (Ed.), *Review of Personality and Social Psychology* (Vol. 3) (pp. 121-144). Beverly Hills, CA: Sage.

Minuchin, S. (1974). *Families and family therapy.* Cambridge, MA: Harvard University Press.

Montgomery, B. M. (1986). "Playing at love: Contents and contexts of flirtatious communication." Paper presented at the International Conference on Personal Relationships, Tel Aviv.

Montgomery, A. L., & Haemmerlie, F. M. (1986). Self-perception theory and the reduction of heterosexual anxiety. *Journal of social and Clinical Psychology, 4,* 503-512.

Moore, R., & Gillette, D. (1992). *The warrior within: Accessing the knight in the male psyche.* New York: William Morrow.

Morrell, D. (1988). *Fireflies.* New York: E. P. Dutton.

Muehlenhard, C. L., Goggins, M. F., Jones, J. J., and Sattrfield, A. T. (1991). Sexual violence and coercion in close relationships. In K. McKinney & S. Sprecher (Eds.), *Sexuality in close relationships* (pp. 155-175). Hillsdale, NJ: Erlbaum.

Murstein, B. (1988). A taxonomy of love. In R. J. Sternberg & M. L. Barnes (Eds.), *The psychology of love* (pp. 13-37). New Haven, CT: Yale University Press.

Murstein, B. I. (1974). *Love, sex, and marriage.* New York: Springer.

Myerhoff, B. (1978). *Number our days.* New York: Touchstone.

Myers, D. G. (1992). *The pursuit of happiness.* New York: Morrow.

Neeld, E. H. (1990). *Seven choices: Taking the steps to new life after losing someone you love.* New York: Delta.

Newcomb, T. M. (1961). *The acquaintance process.* New York: Holt, Rinehard & Winston.

Nisbett, R. E., & Wilson, T. D. (1977). Telling more than we can know: Verbal reports on mental processes. *Psychological Review, 84,* 231-59.

Norwood, R. (1985) *Women who love too much: When you keep wishing and hoping he'll change.* New York: Pocket Books.

O'Connor, M., & Silverman, J. (1989). *Finding love: Creative strategies for finding your ideal mate.* New York: Crown.

Olds, S. W. (1985). *The eternal garden: Seasons of our sexuality.* New York: Times Books.

O'Leary, K. D., & Smith, D. A. (1991). Marital interaction. *Annual Review of Psychology, 52,* 191-212.

Orbuch, T. L. (1988). *Responses to and coping with nonmarital relationship terminations.* Unpublished doctoral dissertation, University of Wisconsin, Madison.

Orbuch, T. L., Harvey, J. H., Davis, S., and Merbach, N. (in press). *Journal of Family Violence.*

Orvis, B. R., Helley, H. H., and Butler, D. (1976). Attributional conflict in young couples. In J. H. Harvey, W. J. Ickes, and R. F. Kidd (Eds.), *New directions in attribution research* (Vol. 1) (pp. 353-386). Hillsdale, NJ: Erlbaum.

Osherson, S. (1992). *Wrestling with love.* New York: Fawcett.

Palmer, L. (1987). *Shrapnel in the heart.* New York: Random House.

Parkes, C. M. (1972). *Bereavement: Studies of grief in adult life.* New York: Tavistock.

Patton, M. Q. (1992). *Family sexual abuse.* Newbury Park, CA: Sage.

Peck, M. S. (1978). *The road less traveled.* New York: Simon & Schuster.

Peele, S. (1975). *Love and addiction.* New York: Taplinger.

Pennebaker, J. (1990). *Opening up.* New York: Morrow.

Perper, T. (1985). *Sex signals: The biology of love.* Philadelphia, ISI Press.

Popenoe, D. (1988). *Disturbing the nest: Family change and decline in modern societies.* New York: Aldine de Gruyter.

Popenoe, D. (1993). American family decline: 1960-1990: A review and appraisal. *Journal of Marriage and the Family, 55,* 527-555.

Pruitt, D. G. (1972). Methods for resolving differences of interest: A theoretical analysis. *Journal of Social Issues, 28,* 133-134.

Raphael, B. (1983). *The anatomy of bereavement.* New York: Basic Books.

Ray, D. (1968). *Sam's book.* Middletown, CT: Wesleyan University Press.

Reibstein, J. & Richards, M. (1993). *Sexual arrangements.* New York: Scribner's.

Reis, I. (1986). *Journey into sexuality.* Englewood Cliffs, NJ: Prentice Hall.

Rempel, J. K., Holmes, J. G., and Zanna, M. P. (1985). Trust in close relationships. *Journal of Personality and Social Psychology, 49,* 95-112.

Rhodes, R. (1992). *Making love: An erotic odyssey.* New York: Simon & Schuster.

Riley, G. (1991). *Divorce: An American tradition.* New York: Oxford University Press.

Risman, B. J., & Schwartz, P. (1989). *Gender in intimate relationships: A microstructural approach.* Belmont, CA: Wadsworth.

Rodin, J., & Langer, E. J. (1977). Long-term effects of a control-relevant intervention with institutionalized aged. *Journal of Personality and Social Psychology, 35,* 897-902.

Rohrbaugh, J. B. (1992). Lesbian families: Clinical issues and theoretical implications. *Professional Psychology: Research and Practice, 23,* 467-473.

Rokeach, M. (1960). *The open and closed mind.* New York: Basic Books.

Rosenblatt, P. C. (1983). *Bitter, bitter tears.* Minneapolis: University of Minnesota Press.

Ross, M., & Holmberg, D. (1992). Are wives' memories for events in relationships more vivid than their husbands' memories? *Journal of Social and Personal Relationships, 9,* 585-604.

Rubin, L. B. (1983). *Intimate strangers: Men and women together.* New York: Harper & Row.

Rubin, L. B. (1990). *Erotic wars: What happened to the sexual revolution.* New York: Farrar, Straus & Giroux.

Rubin, Z. (1973). *Liking and loving: An invitation to social psychology.* New York: Holt, Rinehart, & Winston.

Rusbult, C. E. (1980). Commitment and satisfaction in romantic associations: A test of the investment model. *Journal of Experimental Social Psychology, 16,* 172-186.

Rusbult, C. E. (1983). A longitudinal test of the investment model: The development (and deterioration) of satisfaction and commitment in heterosexual involvements. *Journal of Personality and Social Psychology, 45,* 101-117.

Scarr, S. (1984). *Mother care/other care.* New York: Basic Books.

Schachter, S. L. (1959). *The psychology of affiliation.* Stanford, CA: Stanford University Press.

Schaie, W. (1988). Ageism in psychological research. *American Psychologist, 43,* 179-183.

Seidenberg, R. (1970). *Marriage in life and literature.* New York: Philosophical Library.

Seidman, S. (1991). *Romantic longings: Love in America, 1830-1980.* New York: Routledge.

Seligman, M. E. P. (1991). *Learned optimism.* New York: Knopf.

Shain, M. (1989). *Courage my love.* New York: Bantam.

Shaver, P., & Hazan, C. (1988). A biased overview of the study of love. *Journal of Social and Personal Relationships, 5,* 473-501.

Shaver, P., & Hazan, C. (1994). Attachment. In A. L. Weber & J. H. Harvey (Eds.), *Perspectives on close relationships* (110-130). Needham Heights, MA: Allyn & Bacon.

Sheehy, G. (1976). *Passages.* New York: E. P. Dutton.

Sherrod, D. (1989). The influence of gender on same-sex friendships. In C. Hendrick (Ed.), *Close relationships* (Vol. 10) (pp. 164-186). Newbury Park: Sage.

Shotland, L. (1989). A model of the causes of date rape in developing and close relationships. In C. Hendrick (Ed.), *Close relationships* (Vol. 10), (pp. 247-270). Newbury Park, CA: Sage.

Simmel, G. (1950). *The sociology of Georg Simmel* (K. Wolff, Trans.). New York: Free Press.

Simonds, W. (1992). *Women and self-help culture: Reading between the lines.* New Brunswick, NJ: Rutgers University Press.

Smith, C. C. (1992). *Recovering couples: Building partnership the twelve-step way.* New York: Bantam.

Snyder, M. E., Tanke, E., & Berscheid, E. (1977). Social perception and interpersonal behavior: On the self-fulfilling nature of social stereotypes. *Journal of Personality and Social Psychology, 35,* 656-666.

Sorenson, K. A., Russell, S. M., Harkness, D. J., and Harvey, J. H. (1993).Account-making, confiding, and coping with the ending of a close relationship. *Journal of Social Behavior and Personality, 8,* 73-86.

Spanier, G. B., & Thompson, L. (1987). *Parting: The aftermath of separation and divorce.* Newbury Park, CA: Sage.

Stacy, J. (1990). *Brave new families.* New York: Basic Books.

Stanley, S. M., & Markman, H. J. (1992). Assessing commitment in personal relationships. *Journal of Marriage and the Family, 54,* 595-608.

Steinem, G. (1992). *Revolution from within: A book of self-esteem.* Boston: Little, Brown.

Sternberg, R. J. (1986). A triangular theory of love. *Psychological Review, 93,* 119-135.

Sternberg, R. J., & Barnes, M. L. (Eds.) (1988). *The psychology of love.* New Haven: Yale University Press.

Straus, M. A. (1979). Measuring intrafamily conflict and violence: The Conflict Tactics (CT) Scales. *Journal of Marriage and the Family, 41,* 75-86.

Straus, M. A., & Gelles, R. J. (1986). Societal change and change in family violence from 1975 to 1985 as revealed in two national surveys. *Journal of Marriage and the Family, 48,* 465-79.

Stroebe, W., & Stroebe, M. S. (1986). Beyond marriage: The impact of partner loss on health. In R. Gilmour & S. Duck (Eds.), *The emerging field of personal relationships* (pp. 203-310). Hillsdale, NJ: Erlbaum.

Sullivan, H. S. (1953). *Conceptions of modern psychiatry.* New York: W. W. Norton.

Symons, D. (1979). *The evolution of human sexuality.* New York: Oxford University Press.

Tannen, D. (1990). *You just don't understand: Women and men in conversation.* New York: William Morrow.

Tavris, C., & Wade, C. (1984). *The longest war* (2nd ed). San Diego: Harcourt, Brace, Jovanovich.

Tennov, D. (1979). *Love and limerance: The experience of being in love.* NewYork: Stein and Day.

Thornton, A. (1989). Changing attitudes toward family issues in the United States. *Journal of Marriage and the Family, 51,* 873-793.

Turow, S. (1987). *Presumed innocent.* New York: Farrar, Straus, & Giroux.

Ullman, J. (1986). *The singles almanac.* New York: World Almanac Publications.

Ullmann, L. (1976). *Changing.* New York: Bantam.

Vaughan, D. (1986). *Uncoupling: Turning points in intimate relationships.* New York: Oxford University Press.

Viorst, J. (1986). *Necessary losses.* New York: Fawcett.

Viscott, D. (1974). *How to live with another person.* New York: Pocket Books.

Walker, L. E. A. (1984). *The battered woman syndrome.* New York: Springer.

Wallerstein, J. S., & Kelly, J. B. (1980). *Surviving the break-up.* New York: Harper Torch.

Walsh A. (1991). *The science of love.* Buffalo, NY: Prometheus Books.

Walster, E., & Walster, G. W. (1978). *A new look at love: A revealing report on the most elusive of all emotions.* Reading, MA: Addison-Wesley.

Walster, E., Walster, G. W., & Berscheid, E. (1978). *Equity: Theory and research.* Boston: Allyn & Bacon.

Waterman, C. K., Dawson, L. J., and Bologna, M. J. (1989). Sexual coercion in gay male and lesbian relationships. *Journal of Sex Research, 28,* 118-124.

Weber, A. L. (1993). Unpublished review of J. H. Harvey's *Odyssey of the heart: Closeness, intimacy, and love* .

Weber, A. L., and Harvey, J. H. (Eds.) (1994). Perspectives on close relationships. Needham Heights, MA: Allyn & Bacon.

Webster, H. (1991). *Family secrets.* Addison-Wesley.

Wegner, D. (1989). *White bears & other unwanted thoughts: Suppression, obsession, and the psychology of mental control.* New York: Penguin Books.

Weiss, R. S. (1975). *Marital separation.* New York: Basic Books.

Welwood, J. (1990). *Journey of the heart: Intimate relationship and the path of love.* New York: Harper Collins.

Wendkos, S. (1985). *The eternal garden: Seasons of our sexuality.* New York: Bantam.

White, G. L., & Mullen, P. E. (1989). *Jealousy: Theory, research, and clinical strategies*. New York: Guilford.

Wieland, Bob. (1990) *One step at a time: The remarkable true story of Bob Wieland*. Grand Rapids, MI: Zondervan.

Wilson, E. (1975). *Sociobiology: The new synthesis*. Cambridge, MA: Belknap Press of Harvard University Press.

Witteman, H., & Fitzpatrick, M. A. (1986). Compliance-gaining in marital interaction: Power bases, power processes, and outcomes. *Communication Monographs, 53,* 130-143.

Wortman, C., and Silver, R. (1989). The myths of coping with loss. *Journal of Consulting and Clinical Psychology, 57,* 349-357.

Zelnik, M., & Shah, F. K. (1983). First intercourse among young Americans. *Family Planning Perspectives, 15,* 64-72.

Zilbergeld, B. (1993). *The new male sexuality*. New York: Bantam.

Zill, N., Morrison, D. R., & Coiro, M. J. (1993). Long-term effects of parental divorce on parent-child relationships, adjustment, and achievement in young adulthood. *Journal of Family Psychology, 7,* 91-103.

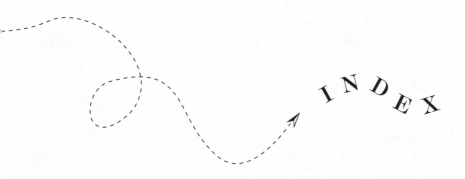